W9-BZB-290

INVESTMENT MEGATRENDS

DR. BOB FROEHLICH

WILEY

JOHN WILEY & SONS, INC.

Published by John Wiley & Sons, Inc., Hoboken, New Jersey.
Published simultaneously in Canada.

For general information on our other products and services or for technical support,
please contact our Customer Care Department within the United States at
(800) 762-2974, outside the United States at (317) 572-3993 or fax (317) 572-4002.

Wiley also publishes its books in a variety of electronic formats. Some content that
appears in print may not be available in electronic books. For more information about
Wiley products, visit our web site at www.wiley.com.

BobSpeak is a registered trademark owned by Dr. Bob Froehlich.

Library of Congress Cataloging-in-Publication Data:

Froehlich, Robert J.
  Investment megatrends / Bob Froehlich
    p. cm.
   ISBN-13: 978-0-471-76999-6 (cloth)
   ISBN-10: 0-471-76999-1 (cloth)
  1. Investments.   2. Demographic transition.   I. Title.
  HG4515.F74   2006
  332.6—dc22

                                        2005029942

Printed in the United States of America.

10   9   8   7   6   5   4   3   2   1

To the 5 "MegaWomen" who changed my life:

Betty (Rooney) Froehlich

My mother, who, until the day she died 11 years ago, was a constant source of encouragement, support, and love, convincing me to always reach for the stars.

Mary Ann (Froehlich) Mays

My sister, who put up with her little brother in those growing-up years and has now become my biggest hometown cheerleader and fan in Pittsburgh.

Marianne (Froehlich) Neidhart

My eldest daughter, who has shown me by her actions how far you will go in life if you are organized, think strategically, and work hard to be the best you can be.

Stephanie Froehlich

My youngest daughter, who has reminded me with her actions how far you will go in life if you are confident, enthusiastic, and have the "street smarts" to know what to question.

Cheryl (André) Froehlich

My lover and best friend, who throughout our relationship has evolved into my most trusted advisor, my confidant, my tireless supporter, my energizer, and my reason for living . . . and I almost forgot, my wife as well!

**Other Investment Books by
Dr. Bob Froehlich**

Where the Money Is
John Wiley & Sons, August 2001

The Three Bears Are Dead!
Forbes, April 1997

CONTENTS

ACKNOWLEDGMENTS

With this being my third book I have already acknowledged all of my friends, family, co-workers, industry colleagues, editors, and so on and so forth, in my first two books. In this book I decided to do something different. I am only acknowledging a very focused and limited group; my "para-authors."

I wish I could take credit for that catchy word, but I can't; it was my wife Cheryl who thought it up. You are probably familiar with the term paralegal. Paralegals are people who work real hard behind the scenes and seldom get thanked while the lawyers get all the credit. Well a para-author is the exact same concept. Para-authors are the people who work so hard behind the scenes while the author (me) gets all the credit.

Let me acknowledge my four para-authors. First, my daughter Stephanie (who works at NASDAQ) who was my number one research assistant for all of my company stock research as well as reading and revising the entire manuscript.

Next let me acknowledge my daughter Marianne (who works at the Securities & Exchange Commission) and her husband and my son-in-law Chris (who works at MB Financial), who both reviewed the manuscript page by page, providing advice, guidance, and support.

Finally, let me acknowledge my wife Cheryl (who works around the clock as a mother, wife, and is the glue that keeps our family together) who I am going to give the title of the Editor's Editor. In addition, she was my proofreader as well as asking the question "why?" or sometimes "why not?" This book would have never been possible without my four para-authors. Consider this acknowledgement your official "para-author byline" for Investment Megatrends:

Investment Megatrends

Author:

Dr. Bob Froehlich

Para-Authors:

Cheryl Froehlich

Stephanie Froehlich

Marianne Neidhart

Chris Neidhart

In addition, I have to thank my para-authors for being my sounding board, listening to all of my investment ideas and concepts all of the time. Their input, answers, suggestions, and sometimes "just that look" have helped me guide this book more than any of you will ever know. I do not have the words to adequately convey my gratitude to them.

DR. BOB FROEHLICH

Chicago, Illinois
December 2005

INTRODUCTION

My good friend and colleague, John Naisbitt, perhaps the greatest "futurist" of our time, first coined the term "megatrends" in the early 1980s. Megatrends are large social, economic, or political changes that are slow to form, however, once in place, their influence can last decades.

Demographics are a type of megatrend—they are slow to form, however, once in place, they will change the way people live, eat, work, play, and ultimately invest. Even though these trends are somewhat easy to spot, few, if any, investors focus enough on any demographic trend as they make their investment decisions.

During my investment career, I have had the opportunity to travel the globe meeting with financial advisors and business and political leaders around the world. I have been asked to give investment lectures on all six of the earth's inhabited continents: North America, South America, Europe, Australia, Africa, and Asia. As a result of my extensive worldwide travels, I have witnessed firsthand the evolving demographic changes taking place around the globe. These unique demographic trends can create investment opportunities if you understand the link between demographics and investments.

There are hundreds of demographic trends developing around the world. As a culmination of all of my travels and experiences, I have identified the four global demographic shifts that can make you rich over the next decade. While the numbers behind these global demographic shifts are important, they are about more than mere numbers. They are the stories of people and societies, the faces of children I have met from all walks of life, they are elders from different cultures with different values and traditions who have given me advice that somehow all come together to create the global demographic landscape. If you know where to look, this landscape is full of investment opportunities.

Chapter 1 begins by explaining and exploring the dramatic power and influence of demographic trends. It provides you with a new frame of reference spelling out exactly what to look for in demographics and, equally important, it tells you how to do it. This chapter becomes your road map pointing out the pitfalls and opportunities of demographic data, think of it as the who, what, when, where, and why of demographics.

Chapter 2 identifies the first of the four global shifts called "The Ponce de León Effect," focusing on the American baby boomer. This shift is named after the Spanish explorer Ponce de León who went in search of the fountain of youth. On April 2, 1513, he landed in St. Augustine, Florida, and took possession of the "New World" in the name of the king of Spain. He never found the fountain of youth but now almost 500 years later, the baby boomers have. The U.S. baby-boomer generation is more active and healthier than any previous generation in American history. Now with the mapping of DNA, we are able to unlock all of the medical and health mysteries that have baffled us for centuries. When you combine all of the advances of the biotech industry along with the advanced research that unlocking DNA provides us and then add 76 million baby boomers eager to buy whatever is developed to make them healthier, wealthier, and (presumably) wiser, it is easy to see why the Ponce de León Effect is one of the four great demographic shifts in the world today.

In Chapter 3, I explore the shift called "The Walls Keep Tumbling Down." It is focused on the new wave of Eastern European workers. When the Berlin Wall finally came crashing down, it was not simply a reunification of Western and Eastern Germany, but rather it set the stage for a dramatic shift in Europe as the remaining communist countries began the march from communism toward capitalism. Today the walls continue to tumble down. The creation of the European Monetary Union currently links 25 countries throughout Europe. There now is an unprecedented free flow of capital and, more important, a free flow of labor. This unleashing of low-cost labor in Eastern European countries is changing the labor landscape, not just in Europe, but it has implications all around the world as well.

Chapter 4 identifies global shift three as "The Rising Sun Is Clearly Setting" by focusing on the dramatic aging population of Japan. Nowhere around the globe is there a more pronounced boom of elders than in the land of the rising sun, Japan. It is the culmination of the aftershocks of World War II and what that shock did to slow birth rates combined with a stringent immigration policy, which together make these elder Japanese not only the most dominant demographic force in Japan, but one of the great demographic shifts in the entire world.

Chapter 5 focuses on the Chinese consumer generation with a shift called "Napoleon Was Right." Over 200 years ago, Napoleon astutely predicted when China awakes it will shake the world. He was right. China has awoken and it's shaking the world from its rafters. Over the next decade, Chinese consumers will have displaced U.S. consumers as the single most important driving force in the entire global economy. Currently, only four million Chinese consumers earn more than $10,000 per year. Over the next decade, that number will explode to over 150 million Chinese consumers earning over $10,000 per year. That will represent the largest consumption bubble of all time. Napoleon was right; this demographic shift is already changing the world.

Investment Megatrends concludes with Chapter 6, which shows you "How to Develop an Investment Megatrends Portfolio" for the next 10 years. It reexamines each of these four global demographic shifts and connects the dots to opportunities these shifts are creating in different sectors and regions of the world. It then identifies the five companies best positioned to benefit from each shift. This chapter will get you on your way to not just understanding the four greatest global demographic shifts in the world today, but how to use them to get rich as well.

Make sure you look at Appendix 1, "Demographic Web Sites." I have categorized the best demographic web sites by subject matter and I have even rated them for you so that you know which ones are best. Appendix 2 is a country-by-country ranking of all 25 members of the European Union based on key demographic indicators. This will serve as a nice reference snapshot. Also make sure you take a look at Appendix 3, which is a glossary and maybe one of the book's unique features called BobSpeak. Instead of your boring traditional glossary of investment and demographic terms, "BobSpeak" includes my opinion regarding the importance, the significance, and relevance of those terms. Think of it as the first opinionated glossary of investment and demographic terms.

And finally, don't forget to look at Appendix 4, "About R.I.S.E." (Redefining Investment Strategy Education). I am donating the financial proceeds of this book to R.I.S.E. R.I.S.E. has become the largest global student investment forum anywhere in the world and is held annually on the campus of the University of Dayton.

CHAPTER ONE

UNDERSTANDING THE POWER OF DEMOGRAPHIC TRENDS

It took us a long time to realize the power of demographic trends on Wall Street. We are in good company because throughout history, few—if any—civilizations have understood the potential power of such trends, even if they compiled demographic statistics.

The governments of ancient Egypt, Rome, and China all collected demographic data; their scope, however, was very limited. They counted their population so they would know how many people they could put in their military and how many people they could tax. Although in these respects, demographic surveys have been around since ancient times, the real foundation for demographics was set in the 1600s. It was then that governments moved beyond simply counting the living for tax and military purposes and began tracking how many people died, as well as compiling birth and marriage data.

THE FATHER OF DEMOGRAPHICS

In the early 1600s, priests in London were required by law to compile a list every week showing how many of their parishioners had died of the plague. These lists were called Bills of Mortality. The government used the lists to identify where outbreaks of the plague were occurring so they would know which areas to quarantine. The Bills of Mortality eventually expanded to list other causes of death as well. Later, data on births and weddings were added.

It was from the Bills of Mortality that the founder of demography arose. John Graunt was a simple London merchant who was fascinated by these lists. Even though he had no formal training, the more he analyzed the Bills of Mortality, the more questions he had. It became his life's work. In 1662, he wrote a book titled *Natural and Political Observations Made upon the Bills of Mortality*. His book raised issues about family size, health, and place of employment. It was this book that finally helped people recognize the potential in studying demographic trends. As interest began to grow, first in medical statistics tracking specific causes of death, statistical offices had to be created to gather and keep track of all this information. It wasn't until the 1800s that the concept of a national census finally caught on.

WHAT IS DEMOGRAPHICS?

What exactly did John Graunt discover? What is demographics? In its most basic form, demographics is the study of population change and the underlying structure of that population. Demographics is a basic and simple concept. A limited number of events can change populations, and each of these events can be counted and tracked. These events are commonly referred to as the *demographic equation*. The equation sets forth that a country's population size can only change because of three types of event: births, deaths, and migration.

From a technical perspective, demographic trends aren't listed as births, deaths, and migration. When statisticians track the individual births of an entire country, the nation's trend is known as fertility. Likewise, the results of tracking the individual deaths of an entire country is known as mortality. Thus, *fertility, mortality,* and *migration* make up the true demographic equation that drives all population changes.

FERTILITY

Fertility is simply the propensity of women in any given population to bear children. While to most casual observers, fertility (births) and mortality (deaths) both appear to be simple and straightforward, the analysis of fertility is much more complicated. First, people only die once and everyone dies, so mortality statistics are relatively easy to count. But fertility is much different. Women may have several children, or none at all. So with fertility, you are conducting an analysis of a repeated event. Second, death is typically determined by medical factors, and human factors only influence it to a limited degree. People do not usually choose to die, but their life may end due to an accident caused by someone else. That would be an example of a human factor, not a medical factor influencing mortality. But for the most part, medical factors, not human factors drive mortality. Just the opposite is true with fertility. Birth in most populations is subject to individual choice although governments may adopt laws that focus on and affect fertility. The simple way to think about it is that people get to choose to have a child; they generally don't get to choose to die.

There are two ways of measuring fertility, the single period approach and the lifetime approach.

SINGLE PERIOD APPROACH

The single period approach to fertility is the most common method. You are simply looking at how many births occurred in any one year or single period, which is where the name *single period approach* comes from. This approach has become very popular for two reasons. First, it is easy. Most government statistical agencies produce data on the number of births, classified by the age of the mother, in any given year. Second, it is up to date; it is the most current data there is.

But there are problems using this single period approach. The biggest problem is that fertility varies greatly from year to year, which means that looking at only one year can provide a misleading picture of a country's long-term fertility projections.

The most classic example of this occurred in Japan in the 1960s. Between 1960 and 1965, fertility levels were basically the same, so using any of those years as a single period to estimate the forecast would have obtained about the same results. Then in 1966, there was a dramatic drop in fertility. If you used that year to forecast the future, you would have been misled into thinking fertility would be down. In 1967 and 1968, fertility shot back up dramatically higher than any previous time in the 1960s. If you had used 1967 or 1968 as your single period approach, you would have forecasted that in the future, fertility would be much higher than it actually was.

The reason for all this volatility . . . the fiery horse. In Japan, 1966 was the "Year of the Fiery Horse." The Year of the Fiery Horse comes every 60 years in Japan. Japanese superstition says that women born in this year are not suitable as wives and will suffer from ill fortune. As a result, most Japanese parents decided not to have children in 1966. And the dramatic uptick in 1967 and 1968 fertility levels means that births were not canceled in 1966, they were just postponed until after the Year of The Fiery Horse.

LIFETIME APPROACH

One way around the shortcomings with the single period approach is to use the lifetime approach, where you measure the number of births or fertility rate in a person's lifetime. Using this approach to measure Japanese fertility in the 1960s results in less distortion. The problem is that data collection takes much longer. Childbearing years typically span 35 years from 15 to 50. So you must collect

data for all those 35 years to have a full picture of how many children each person had between ages 15 and 50. Add to the lack of
timeliness that, over 35 years four or five people are likely to have
come and gone from the government statistical agency that tracks
this trend, and the potential for mistakes increases as well. Nothing
is as simple as it seems, even counting births.

MORTALITY—CRUDE DEATH RATE

Mortality rates will vary greatly based on different characteristics.
The most obvious is age. But mortality rates can also be influenced
by a person's occupation and also by a person's sex. To understand
mortality trends, we must do two things. First we have to identify
and measure mortality differences. Second, and even more important, we have to line up those differences to a particular characteristic. Think of it this way, if the mortality rates of two occupations
differ greatly, that doesn't necessarily mean that the death was influenced by the occupation. Maybe this occupation requires more
experienced people, and thus those people are older. So did the occupation contribute to their death or should we have focused on
their age characteristic as the real factor?

The simplest and most widely used measure of mortality is the
crude death rate. It is a simple calculation of the total number of
deaths in a given period (usually one year) divided by the total
population.

However, since death is relatively a rare event, the crude death
rate is always a very small number. Because of this, the crude death
rate is almost always expressed as the number of deaths per thousand of a country's population.

Let's say a country has a population of 25,000,000 people. And
last year, 220,000 people died. You would simply divide 220,000
(which represents the total number of deaths in that year) by
25,000,000 (which is the total population). When you calculate
that, the answer is .0088. Because that number is so small, making
for difficult comparisons, the next step is to multiply it by one
thousand. Once you calculate that (.0088 × 1000), you have an

answer of 8.8. If you round that to the nearest number, it would be 9. So in this example, the country's crude death rate would be 9 per thousand. Meaning that of every 1,000 people last year in this country, 9 died. Not only does this make it easy to understand, it makes it easy to compare on a country-by-country basis to get a quick snapshot of mortality.

MIGRATION

Migration is the third and final element of the demographic equation. Migration has evolved over time into the weak link of the three elements of the demographic equation. Statisticians spend more time, attention, analysis, research, and understanding on fertility and mortality, whereas migration always comes in a far distant third. The reason is simple: Migration is the hardest and most complicated of the three elements to measure and analyze. Migration usually involves more than one country's population. When people move from the country where they were born to a different country, that move affects the population of both countries. Also migration is not a one-way street. People are traveling in both directions at the same time.

As if that doesn't pose enough of a problem, migration is also complicated compared with fertility and mortality. People only die once. In addition, the number of births from any one woman is limited by time and affected by age. Not so with migration. The number of times people migrate in their lifetime is unlimited. As a result, you tend to find more and better quality information on fertility and mortality than you do on migration.

WHAT IS MIGRATION?

Simply put, migration is defined as a change in a person's permanent place of residence. Although this may seem basic and straightforward, it is not. To begin with, what do you do with people who have no permanent place of residence? Nomadic tribes, for example, are still prevalent in Asia—they live in makeshift tents and travel from field to field. How do you count them? Should you even count them?

Next, some people inhabit more than one permanent residence, depending on the season of the year. Do we count these moves?

Migration also comes in many sizes, shapes, and forms. Migration can involve a move of a few miles, a few hundred miles, or thousands of miles.

GLOBAL MIGRATION

In our global economy and market, the most important element to capture about migration may be the global nature of these moves. Thus, it is extremely important to distinguish between internal migration, which involves a move within the same country, and international migration, which involves a move from one country to another.

In tracking migration trends, people who leave but whose move keeps them within the same country are classified as *out-migrants*, whereas people who leave and whose move takes them to a different country are classified as *emigrants*.

Conversely, people who move into a population in the same country but in a different location are called *in-migrants*, while people who move into a country from an entirely different country are classified as *immigrants*.

Most measures of migration do not distinguish between immigration and in-migration or emigration and out-migration; thus these measures of migration can be misleading.

WHAT SHOULD YOU LOOK FOR?

With the foundation now being set for the demographic equation of fertility, mortality, and migration, it is time to interpret all this demographic data.

There are four basic rules to follow when looking at any demographic data:

1. *Focus on the extremes.* If any number is a real outlier, it deserves all your attention and you need to find out why it exists. Outliers occur for one of two reasons. Either there is a flaw or error in the data that caused the outlier or it was a unique circumstance that could give you real clues to future trends.

2. *Cluster the data.* You will always be able to group or cluster some of the data. Then, within that cluster, look for natural groupings. Are most people in this cluster from the same occupational category; or are they in a certain income level, be it high or low; or possibly do they all have poor health? Clustering allows you to begin to see beyond the numbers.

3. *Identify patterns.* Fertility, mortality, and migration all vary by age, occupation, and ethnicity. These patterns will help develop the groundwork for future trends.

4. *Draw comparisons.* This is the most important of the four rules. Draw comparisons, draw more comparisons, and when you are done, draw even more comparisons. The real underlying power of demographics is in drawing comparisons of the data with other places around the world. Then, you need to repeat the exact same procedure; only this time, compare your data to different time periods in the part of the world from which this information came. That way you can quickly see how this demographic trend has evolved and how that trend compares with the rest of the world.

GOVERNMENT USE

The use of demographic data to make informed decisions just might be the one area where governments are actually a step ahead of the business world.

Demographic data has always been one of the cornerstones of state and local government planning. It is a key element that government officials take into account when they are trying to prioritize which services to cut and which services to expand or establish. For local governments, demographic data determines where the police station should go, the fire station, the library, the playgrounds, and so on. It is also a critical factor in highway and transportation planning.

PLAYGROUND DEMOGRAPHICS

Having worked in local government and even spent time as a city manager for the town of Beavercreek, Ohio, I can tell you from firsthand experience that demographic decisions are a way of life in local government. The easiest example is in the location of a playground. Superficially, it sounds simple, but that is never the case. Someone on the City Council will usually say, "Let's locate the next playground so the poorer children in our city can use it most."

The first step is going to the Parks Department for the current location of all parks, to identify where new parks are needed. Next stop is the Planning Department to find out all the available land locations where it would be suitable to build a park. Demographics will help make the decision for us. The U.S. census data list by census tract the number of children, and their ages, in low-income families. You simply find the census tract with the greatest number of young children in low-income families and that is where the park needs to go—provided there isn't already one there and there is land to build one in this census tract.

What the city is attempting to do here is find a census tract that doesn't have a playground, but has the space for a playground and, most important, has the largest number of young children in low-income families. Demographics will determine the location.

SOCIAL SECURITY DEMOGRAPHICS

The federal government, as well as state and local governments, use demographic data. In many respects, one of the biggest, most complicated, and politically charged issues facing government is what to do about Social Security. And like it or not, Social Security is all about one simple thing: demographics. The funding of the Social Security System depends on the age distribution of the population because the age distribution of the population will determine the number of working persons and the number of elderly persons not working.

This age distribution is the product of past trends in fertility, mortality, and migration. The factors that make up our demographic equation will shape the age distribution of the population in the future. Fertility is the most important factor in determining the age distribution of a population; thus, it is a key issue driving the financial issues around Social Security. The overall decline in fertility rates over the past 100 years (with the lone exception of the baby-boom generation, 1946 to 1964) has been the driving force in producing our current age distribution, which has a relatively low proportion of younger people and a higher proportion of elderly people.

But it is not just fertility. The overall decline in mortality has turbocharged the effects in raising the number of elderly persons. The substantial decline in mortality within the 65-and-over age group has pushed up the number of elderly persons in the population.

To understand where we are demographically with Social Security, you have to understand where we came from. Social Security was established in 1935. All you have to do is look at life expectancy between 1935 and today. In 1935, life expectancy for men was 59 and for women, 63. Keep in mind that back then, as now, "normal" retirement age was 65. With men dying at 59 and women dying at 63, it is no wonder that Social Security had no financial problems—few people lived to 65 to collect any benefits. Not so today.

Life expectancy for men today is 75. That means most men will collect Social Security benefits for at least 10 years. Life expectancy for women is 81 years, which means most women will collect Social Security for at least 16 years. With the potential of expected future gains in life expectancy, the number of years to collect benefits will grow even higher (see Figure 1.1).

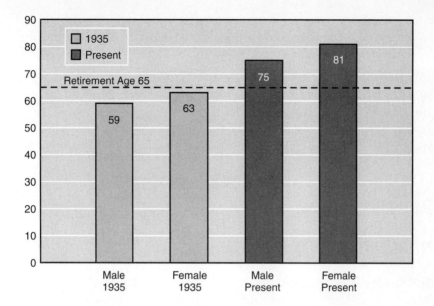

Figure 1.1 Life Expectancy and Social Security, 1935 and Present

PRIVATE SECTOR DEMOGRAPHICS

Like the local, state, and federal governments of the public sector, the private sector also is embracing demographics. Undoubtedly, its biggest use is in trying to understand and analyze consumer behavior. Demographic trends explain the meaning of consumption of a product in one location versus another. Thus, it is important to look at both the age distribution of both locations as well as any age-specific consumption data. The facts are simple: The consumption of most products will vary greatly depending on age. To understand why one store or location is consuming more than another store or location, you first need to understand the age distribution of both locations.

WHY NOT INVESTMENTS?

Did you ever wonder why demographic data is used in government and is used in business but is not typically used to drive investment decisions? We are missing the most important tool of all in investing—demographic trends. It is not the next economic release or earnings report that should drive our investment decisions, but rather demographics. Such trends have a longer-term impact and they are easier to predict. Demographics need to become an important tool for investors. The following examples show how the baby-boomer demographics in the United States have created investment opportunities.

DISCOUNT STORES

When discount stores first appeared in the United States in the early 1980s, they were volatile and only marginally successful investments. Now they are one of the hottest investment themes anywhere. And they are making money. Why the change? Are they doing a better job of marketing? No. Are they doing a better job with inventory control? No. Did they develop some secret strategic plan for success? No. The fact of the matter is that they aren't doing anything different today than they were in the 1980s. Why are they profitable all of a sudden?

Well, one major thing did change—demographics. When discount stores first appeared on the scene 15 to 20 years ago, baby boomers like me didn't shop discount stores. Now we shop at discount stores, as do a lot of other baby boomers. Fundamentally, this younger generation is no longer so young, nor is it any longer so free spending with its buying power. When this age group starts worrying about saving for their children's college tuition or paying off their mortgage, they usually end up at discount stores.

This accounts for only one of the two major demographic shifts that are driving the success of discount stores. The second has to do with senior citizens. When discount stores first appeared, senior citizens wanted no part of them, and why would they? They have worked hard their entire life, and now they get to shop in some warehouse with a cement floor, where everything is packed so high to the sky they cannot even read the labels? I don't think so, and neither did they. Something amazing has happened to those senior citizens of 15 years ago, who boycotted the discount stores. They are still alive today, and many of them didn't count on that. In addition to still being alive, many of them are still living on that same fixed income of 15 years ago. The number-one shopper in discount stores today is aged 65 and older. And why not? If the older generation is now living longer on its same fixed income, it makes sense that as part of the aging process, senior citizens are becoming more selective in their spending habits. They are becoming discount shoppers.

It is all about demographics. Even though the underlying theme and target of discount stores has not changed, the people who fit into the cost-conscious-buyer category are greatly expanding. Both of these demographic shifts (the baby boomers and senior citizens) are creating an expanding universe of potential customers for discount stores.

FOOD

The food sector is about to become one of the more exciting and dynamic sectors because of one simple fact—demographics. In the United States, the group of 18- to 24-year-olds now coming into adulthood is the first generation to be raised by "working moms." These 18- to 24-year-olds were raised with "meals on the run."

Think about how this generation goes grocery shopping. They stroll right past all the meat, baking ingredients, and other basic raw foods and head straight for the precooked ham, prebaked turkey, or the ready-to-go-salad bar deluxe. This generation knows that an oven can be used for something other than frozen pizzas—they are just not sure what. This is the microwave generation. The food sector must reach out to this group, who are much more proficient using microwaves than traditional ovens.

Fifty years ago, the average homemaker spent over 2.5 hours (150 minutes) preparing the family dinner. Today the average homemaker spends less than 20 minutes preparing the family dinner. If you don't think demographics can turn a sector on its head, consider this fact: Currently, for the first time in history, a majority of homemakers (over 50 percent) have never cooked a meal from basic ingredients. This demographic shift will change the food sector forever. Even though the food sector has been besieged by years of slow growth, look for consumer spending on ready-made food to accelerate in the next 10 years. This growth will be driven by demographics.

HEALTH CLUBS

Did you ever wonder why health clubs have been popping up everywhere? All of a sudden there are health clubs in hotels. Heck, there are even health clubs in most major office buildings today.

As a nation, did the United States all of a sudden decide that it needed health clubs everywhere, or did demographics play the key role? First, when you get older, your metabolism slows down. And when your metabolism slows down, something that you used to eat without it ever showing is suddenly appearing on your waistline. Second, when you were younger, you always seemed to have more time on your hands to exercise and to keep fit. As you grow older, the demand on your time becomes even greater, and thus the opportunity to find time to exercise is less and less frequent.

Think about it: The boomers in their 50s are all of a sudden putting on those extra pounds and taking on the shape that they thought only affected their parents. And these boomers are so busy, stretched between business and personal commitments, that there is no time left for them to exercise and stay fit.

What jumps up to fill this demographic need? You guessed it, the health club. Now you can go to the club at 5 A.M. before you leave for work. Or you can go to the club in your office complex during lunch hours. Traveling? No problem, just swing by the hotel health club. If the hotel doesn't have one on-site, I'm willing to bet that they have made arrangements for their hotel guests to use the facilities at a nearby health club. It is not just about getting fit; it is about getting older.

DRUGS

I have no idea which drug company is going to discover the next wonder drug. Nor do I know which drug company will merge with which to create the new global leader. What I do know is that demographics are making the pharmaceutical sector a great place to invest. In the United Sates, from the time of birth until children celebrate their fifth birthday, parents give their children on average eight different prescription drugs a year. For the next 40 years, however, that trend line is on a downward slope and never breaks trend. And no one is exactly sure why. Are they simply healthier? Or did they just stop going to visit the doctor? Or do they no longer listen to their parents when it comes to health matters? Most likely, it is a combination of the three.

Something magical, however, happens at age 45: The trend reverses itself. For the rest of their lives, people tend to increase the amount of prescription drugs they use each year. This trend currently plateaus at age 75. The average 75-year-old in the United States currently uses 18 different prescription drugs a year. That trend helps to explain why, with only 5 percent of the world's population, the United States accounts for over 40 percent of the world's pharmaceutical sales.

SOURCES OF DEMOGRAPHIC DATA

As an investor, I hope that you now realize the importance of demographic trends and the impact they can have on investment results. Knowing their importance, however, is not enough. It is one thing to know the importance of demographic trends and what to look for, but you still have to know where to look. As an investor where can you find all this data?

CENSUS BUREAU

We might as well start with the biggest and the best—the U.S. Census Bureau. It is the largest producer of demographic data anywhere in the world. The Bureau of the Census conducts the Census of population and housing every 10 years. The census provides the population counts needed to apportion seats among the states in the U.S. House of Representatives. For the entire decade, this census data fills many needs. The federal government uses it to allocate funds under numerous federal grant programs. And as previously described, local governments can use census data to locate a new park, but because it is not very timely (every 10 years), it is best used when analyzing long-term trends.

NATIONAL CENTER FOR HEALTH STATISTICS

The National Center for Health Statistics is the leading source for national, state, and local data on births and deaths. It is also the primary source for marriage, divorce, and health data as well. It is important to note that the registration of vital events is a state government function, not a federal government function. Thus, these vital statistics are obtained through state-administered registration systems. Statistics on births, deaths, marriages, and divorces are published monthly with a lag of about nine months. Final statistics for a given year for births, deaths, marriages, and divorces are published with a lag of about a year and a half.

IMMIGRATION AND NATURALIZATION SERVICE

The Immigration and Naturalization Service (INS) is the federal agency responsible for compiling and publishing statistics on immigration into the United States and on naturalizations. The data is presented in its *Statistical Yearbook of the Immigration and Naturalization Service.* This yearbook provides statistics on international admissions classified by categories: immigrants, nonimmigrants (temporary), refugees, asylees, and parolees. It also has statistics on naturalizations and deportations. It does not, however, collect data on emigrants (the number of immigrants or residents departing).

SURF THE WEB

An excellent way to gather and analyze demographic data is though online sources on the Internet. Table 1.1 lists some of the best

Table 1.1 Demographic Web Sites by Category

Articles/Commentary

Advertising Age's American Demographics magazine	www.AdAge.com
Council of Professional Association on Federal Statistics	www.members.aol.com/copafs
Cyberatlas/ClickZ	www.clickz.com/stats
Rand Corporation	www.rand.com
U.S. Social Security Administration	www.ssa.gov
Population Index of Princeton University	http://popindex.princeton.edu

Children

Anne E. Casey Foundation	www.aecf.org
Federal Interagency Forum on Child and Family Statistics	www.childstats.gov
U.S. National Center for Educational Statistics	www.nces.ed.gov

Health

Population Council	www.popcouncil.org
Public Health Foundation	www.phf.org
U.S. Centers for Disease Control and Prevention	www.cdc.gov
U.S. Centers for Disease Control and Prevention—Wonder	http://wonder.cdc.gov
U.S. National Center for Health Statistics	www.cdc.gov.nchs
Urban Institute	www.urban.org

United States

CASI Marketing Systems	www.demographics.casi.com/free_menu.html
Easi Demographics	www.easidemographics.com

(continued)

Table 1.1 *Continued*

United States

Econ Data	www.econdata.net
Economic Information Systems	www.econ-line.com
FedStats	www.fedstats.gov
Geo Stat	http://fisher.lib.virginia.edu
Minnesota Population Research Institute	www.ipums.umn.edu
Premier Insights	www.premierinsights.com
U.S. Bureau of the Census—	www.census.gov
U.S. Bureau of the Census—American Factfinders	www.factfinder.census.gov
U.S. Bureau of the Census-Housing and Household Economics	www.census.gov/hhes
U.S. Bureau of the Census—Population Data	www.census.gov/population
U.S. Bureau of Labor Statistics	www.bls.gov
U.S. Internal Revenue Service	www.irs.gov

International

Population Reference Bureau	www.prb.org
Statistics Canada	www.statcan.CA
United Nations	www.un.org
University of Texas—Demographic Data Link	www.lib.utexas.edu/government
U.S. Bureau of the Census—International Data Base	www.census.gov/ipc/www/idbnew.html
U.S. Bureau of Economic Analysis	www.bea.doc.gov
U.S. Department of Homeland Security	www.uscis.gov/graphics/shared/statistics/index.htm
U.S. Central Intelligence Agency—World Factbook	www.cia.gov/cia/publications/factbook

demographic web sites on the Internet today. In Appendix 1, I give a brief commentary about each of these web sites as well as a rating on their usefulness.

AGE CHARACTERISTICS

When looking at statistics and data, whether on the Internet or on a paper copy, it is not enough to know what to look for in demographic trends and where to look for them. You also must grasp just why demographics are such a powerful investment tool. If you think of demographics and age characteristics as being one and the same, you will begin to see what I mean. Just think about the factors over which demographics and your age characteristics exert a major influence. First, your age characteristics are a key determinant of your consumption patterns. Not many 16-year-olds buy reading glasses. Likewise, not many 60-year-olds buy acne cream. And I've yet to see many 20-year-olds searching for just the right hair product to wash away the gray.

Second, your age characteristics greatly influence your level of savings and investing. Even though you may have great self-discipline and motivation to invest when you are younger, it is difficult because there are higher priorities such as raising your family or buying your first home. As you approach your 50s, however, you suddenly seem to save and to invest more. It is not because you are more motivated; it is because your age characteristics are now playing in your favor to help you save and invest. When you are 50, your children are grown and about to leave home and start life on their own. This frees up a great deal of cash. Also, that home that you have been paying a mortgage on for what seems like forever is just about paid off, which also frees up your cash flow. And finally, at age 50, your employer pays you the financial rewards that you thought you deserved at age 22. Your age characteristics just might be the most important factor you need to understand saving and investing.

Third, your age characteristics will determine both the size and the makeup of your household. Very few teenagers think of starting a family, whereas that is on the top of the list for most young adults in their twenties.

Fourth and finally, the age characteristics of a nation have a strong influence on government policy. When a nation is driven by younger age characteristics, it spends money on schools and recreational programs. Conversely, a nation that is driven by older age characteristics tends to spend its money on retirement and medical benefits.

If you are an investor and you know what people are going to buy, when they are going to save and invest, how many houses are going to be needed, and how many people will live in those houses, as well as what the government policies are going to be, why would you need to know anything else? In the following chapters, I explain the four most dramatic demographic shifts going on in the world today. After that, we will construct an Investment Megatrends portfolio based on these landmark demographic shifts, and together we will turn demographic trends into investment opportunities.

CHAPTER TWO

GLOBAL SHIFT 1: THE PONCE DE LEÓN EFFECT

THE AMERICAN BABY BOOMERS

Juan Ponce de León was a Spanish *conquistador* (Spanish term used to refer to soldiers, explorers, and adventurers). Ponce de León accompanied Christopher Columbus on his second voyage to the New World. He became the first governor of Puerto Rico. It was there that he first heard of the Fountain of Youth.

Over time, Ponce de León became dissatisfied with his material wealth, so he launched an expedition to find the Fountain of Youth. Instead, he discovered Florida, when on April 2, 1513, he reached land near what is now St. Augustine. He never found the Fountain of Youth but now almost 500 years later, the baby boomers have. The American Baby Boom Generation is more active and healthier than any previous generation in American history. But before studying these baby boomers, let's gain a broader perspective of the overall demographic picture.

DEMOGRAPHICS OF THE UNITED STATES

The overall U.S. population is now approaching 300,000,000. The U.S. Census Bureau groups or classifies these 300 million Americans into five groups:

1. *White (also called Caucasian):* This category comprises anyone whose racial origin is Europe or the Middle East.

2. *Black (also called African American):* This category is composed of anyone whose racial origin is one of the black ethnic groups of Africa.

3. *American Indian/Alaskan Native (also called Native American):* This category includes anyone whose racial origin is one of the ethnic groups of North, South, or Central America who maintains tribal affiliation.

4. *Asian (also called Asian American):* This category comprises anyone whose racial origin is any of the native peoples of East Asia, Southeast Asia, or the Far East.

5. *Native Hawaiian/Other Pacific Islander:* This category encompasses anyone whose origin is one of the peoples of Hawaii, Guam, Samoa, or other Pacific Islands.

Of these classifications, the majority of people in the United States are descendants of European immigrants who have arrived since the first colonies were established in what is now the United States. Within that broad classification, the top four countries represented are Germany, Ireland, England, and Italy.

Here is an interesting twist. Spain did not make the top four because few immigrants have come to the United States directly from Spain. However, Hispanics from Mexico, South America, and Central America are now the single largest minority group in the United States. This Hispanic category is based more on language than on race; the U.S. Census Bureau defines Hispanic as anyone from Spain or Spanish-speaking Latin America, so Hispanics may be of any race found in such countries as Mexico, Colombia, or Guatemala. This explains the increased use of the Spanish language in the United States.

The second largest group is composed of African Americans. The earliest Africans were servants and slaves, who arrived with the first generation of colonists.

The third significant minority population in the United States is Asian American. It may be the most diverse group because it includes China, Japan, India, Vietnam, Korea, and the Philippines.

KEY DEMOGRAPHIC INDICATORS

Within those broad categories, the trends are evolving in several ways. The population growth rate in the United States is less than 1 percent (currently 0.9 percent). The U.S. birth rate is 14.14 births per 1,000 population; the death rate is 8.25 deaths per 1,000 population; and the net migration rate is 3.31 migrants per 1,000 population.

In the United States, 20.6 percent of its population is under the age of 15; 67 percent is between 15 and 65 years of age; and the remaining 12.4 percent is 65 years of age or older. To give you some perspective on how this age structure has shifted, in 1900 about 34 percent of the population was under 15; 62 percent was between 15 and 65; and only 4 percent was 65 years of age or older (see Figure 2.1).

Life expectancy in the United States for the entire population is 77.6 years. For the male population, life expectancy is 74.8 years; whereas for the female population, it is 81.0 years.

The infant mortality rate for the total population is 6.5 deaths per 1,000 live births. It is a little higher in the male population (7.17 deaths per 1,000 live births versus 5.8 deaths per every 1,000 live births for females). The infant mortality rate has become a

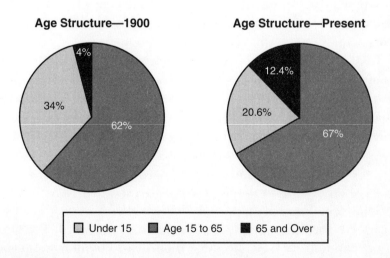

Figure 2.1 Shifting U.S. Age Structure: 1900 versus Present

highly watched demographic indicator. It is an effective way to measure the level of health care in a country because it is directly linked with the health status of infants, children, and pregnant women. In addition, it indicates access to medical care, living conditions, and public health practices.

Infant mortality is actually the death of infants in the first year of life. Infant mortality can be further broken down into neonatal death, referring to deaths in the first 27 days of life, and post-neonatal death, referring to deaths after 28 days of life.

Finally, literacy, which is defined as the number of citizens aged 15 or older who can read and write, is 97 percent in the United States, for both males and females.

THE BABY BOOMERS

In looking at the baby boomers, the most dominant force in U.S. demographics, we might as well start with the beginning. You can't have baby boomers without first having a baby boom—a period of increased birth rates within the same geographic boundaries. There have been numerous baby booms over time, and numerous theories about why they occur. The theories range from good harvests to victories in war to victories in sports, or even to a major blackout or power outage. About the only thing we agree on is that no one can agree on what causes a baby boom.

The baby boom in the United States was unusual in the length of time it lasted and the number of births. Anyone who was born between 1946 and 1964 is classified as a baby boomer. There are 76 million baby boomers in this period, of which I am one.

Unlike their parents, baby boomers had no firsthand experience or any childhood recollection of World War II. Many of these baby boomers either fought in the Vietnam War or organized and participated in antiwar demonstrations.

Relatively low college costs made college education widespread. For the most part, there was peace in the world. Travel was both cheap and easy. At the same time, mass communication was booming. Together, these factors were the foundation for the cultural and philosophical awakening of the Baby Boom Generation.

The 1960s were about drugs and political activism or even radicalism, which led to the short-lived hippie movement. By the 1970s, there was a revival of religious activity and fundamentalism that still influences Americans. By the 1980s, the baby boomers began to mellow and become part of the mainstream. In 1992, Bill Clinton became the first baby boomer to be elected president of the United States. He was, by the way, a draft resister of the Vietnam War. In 2001, George W. Bush, yet another baby boomer, was sworn in as president of the United States. In terms of political influence, there will probably be a baby boomer in the White House until 2020. A majority of the members of Congress will have been baby boomers until at least sometime after 2015. And a majority of the Supreme Court most likely will be held by baby boomers between 2010 and 2030. Thus, the potential political and public policy impact of baby boomers should not be underestimated.

From a business perspective, this generation has played a critical role in the development of both the technology and financial services industries. This time period, however, may go down in history as being best known for the rise of the American consumer. The Baby Boom Generation, in many respects, is the first consumer generation.

To get a clearer picture of these baby boomers, it is important to put into proper perspective exactly who came before them as well as who came after them in the demographic mosaic of the United States (see Table 2.1).

Table 2.1 U.S. Demographics through the Generations

Years Covered	Name Given
1883–1900	Lost Generation
1901–1924	GI Generation
1925–1945	Silent Generation
1946–1964	Baby Boom Generation
1965–1981	Generation "X"
1982–1997	Generation "Y"
1998–2025	Generation "Z"

FOCUSING ON THE DEMOGRAPHIC MOSAIC

The baby boomers' parents came from one of two generations: Older parents came from the *GI Generation,* and younger parents came from the *Silent Generation.* The baby boomers' grandparents (the parents of the GI and Silent Generations) are called the *Lost Generation.* Let's look at all three of these groups that preceded the baby boomers.

THE LOST GENERATION (1883 TO 1900)

The baby boomers' grandparents, often referred to as the Lost Generation, were born in the United States between 1883 and 1900. This generation, which entered adulthood during and shortly after World War I, acquired its name because these young people became disillusioned (or "lost") by the senseless slaughter and the savagery of that war. Americans of this generation felt inferior to Europeans. They would constantly complain that the work of American artists and authors lacked the culture, creativity, and breadth of European work. This constant feeling of being inferior to the European art and literary community led many American writers and artists of the day to spend large amounts of time traveling in Europe.

The term "Lost Generation" was coined by an American literary giant, Gertrude Stein (who was born in Pittsburgh, Pennsylvania). She used it to refer to a group of American literary notables who lived in Paris in the 1920s and 1930s. Among others, it included F. Scott Fitzgerald, Ernest Hemingway, and Stein herself.

Even with all these cultural misgivings, the Lost Generation is credited with the creation of American jazz.

The Lost Generation produced two U.S. presidents: Harry S. Truman and Dwight D. Eisenhower were born between 1883 and 1900. In addition, a majority of the members of Congress were from the Lost Generation for the decade between 1943 and 1953.

THE GI GENERATION (1901 TO 1924)

Many of the baby boomers' parents were from the GI Generation. This generation included anyone born between 1901 and 1924. Recently this generation has been fondly referred to as the "greatest generation," based on Tom Brokaw's book of the same name. In his book, however, he identifies the greatest generation as those who were born in the latter half of the 1901 to 1924 time frame.

The initials GI (government issue) refers to an enlisted person in any of the U.S. armed forces as well as a veteran of any U.S. armed forces, especially a person enlisted in, or a veteran of, the army.

The GI Generation had a lot of firsts at both ends of the spectrum. At one end, they became America's first Girl Scouts and Boy Scouts. And 50 years later, they became the first generation of Americans to be labeled senior citizens.

This generation can best be captured by its "can do" attitude. They overcame communists and Nazis; they took on poverty by building model cities. It was truly a generation that felt that it could accomplish anything it set out to do. Perhaps its most lasting legacy is that it invented, perfected, used, and began to stockpile the atomic bomb—a weapon so deadly and so massive in scope that many historians say it changed the world forever.

There were seven GI Generation presidents: Lyndon B. Johnson was born in 1908, and Ronald Reagan was born in 1911; two years later in 1913, both Richard Nixon and Gerald Ford were born. In 1917, John F. Kennedy was born. And in the last year of the GI Generation, 1924, both Jimmy Carter and George H. W. Bush were born. The GI Generation had a majority in Congress from 1959 to 1975, and there was a majority on the Supreme Court from 1967 to 1991.

THE SILENT GENERATION (1925 TO 1945)

As a baby boomer, if your parents weren't from the GI Generation, they were born in the Silent Generation, which included anyone born between 1925 and 1945. It was called the Silent Generation because it was stuck between the "I can do anything" GI Generation (or greatest generation) and the "it's all about me" Baby Boom Generation. Between those two forces, it was hard for anyone else to get in a word.

This generation seemed to have been born in the wrong place at the wrong time and was cautious, indifferent, and silent. They came into the world too late to become World War II war heroes and too early to be free-spirited baby boomers, protesting war. Instead, they became an early-marrying crowd of risk-adverse technicians. Conformity was the order of the day, and it was also how to get ahead in the business world.

They were the first generation to witness the fragmentation of the family fiber, an explosion of cultural diversity, and the birth of the United States as the most litigious nation in the world.

The Silent Generation did not produce a single U.S. president. It does boast three first ladies (Jacqueline Bouvier Kennedy, Eleanor Rosalynn Smith Carter, and Barbara Pierce Bush). It had a majority in the Supreme Court for one year, 1993. No wonder this generation was so silent.

Now let's focus on the generations that have followed and will follow the Baby Boom Generation. The children of the Baby Boom Generation are either from Generation X or Generation Y. And the grandchildren of the baby boomers will be Generation Z.

GENERATION X (1965 TO 1981)

The first of the baby boomers' children were called Generation X. This generation comprises anyone born in the United States between 1965 and 1981. At first, this generation was called the Baby Buster Generation, because there were so few of them compared with the Baby Boom Generation.

The origin of the term Generation X goes back to Great Britain in 1964. A British writer named Jane Deverson was asked by a major magazine editor to conduct a series of interviews with teenagers. After extensive interviews with a wide range of youths, she assembled somewhat unnerving findings. Her study revealed that most teenagers didn't respect their parents, didn't believe in God, and slept together before they married. As if that wasn't bad enough, they also disliked the Queen (Queen Elizabeth II). These findings were so shocking for the times that the magazine wouldn't publish the article. Deverson didn't want to see all her research go to waste, so she teamed up with a writer in the United States named Charles Hamblett to write a book about her study. He called it *Generation X*. The name has stuck with this generation since then.

Generation Xers have had to survive a childhood of divorce, space shuttle explosions, political corruption, inflation and recession, the Islamic Revolution in Iran, and devil-child movies. For the first time in modern history, divorce became commonplace and affected families of all social and economic backgrounds. As young adults, this group had to maneuver through a sexual barricade of AIDS and the new dating scene. While divorce rates soared, this generation looked to alternatives to traditional marriage that ranged from remaining single to "just living together" to same-sex couples.

Technology started to boom with the creation and spread of the Internet. The Internet rendered face-to-face communications unnecessary. For the first time in history, people could have near infinite knowledge at their hands every minute of every day. Technology jobs were the hot commodity.

Regarding employment, this generation would rather be a free agent than show extended loyalty to any corporation. From a labor perspective, Generation Xers were often criticized as slackers, but it cannot be debated that these slackers initiated the new spirit of entrepreneurialism in the United States that set the foundation for the dot-com and technology booms.

GENERATION Y (1982 TO 1997)

The children born to baby boomers after 1981 are called Generation Y. It comprises anyone born in the United States between 1982 and 1997. The Y Generation was the first to grow up with the Internet in its developed form, including instant messaging and music downloads. It came into awareness in a world where landline phones were becoming a thing of the past.

This generation is tolerant toward people from other nations and other cultures. This generation became the first to date people outside their own race or ethnic group in significant numbers. The

Y Generation tends to have a wide range of racial and ethnic diversity among their friends.

They tend to be confused about exactly what the "war on terror" is and exactly who is fighting whom. While they are aware of the world around them, they like to remain separate. The September 11, 2001, terrorist attacks have affected, shaped, and changed the world they are growing up in.

Many in this generation are visionaries. They are ambivalent toward authority and see it as something to work around rather than work against, so they are not hostile. Some have used their expertise to work hard, while others have not used what their parents have given them and have already begun to fail.

The Y Generation tends to have tremendous financial know-how. They are highly educated, savvy consumers. They are conscious of money and its impact on life. This generation has no interest in working at a Wal-Mart or a McDonald's. Instead, they have a taste for grandeur and greatness, sweeping projects, and expensive ideas.

This generation grew up and is still growing up during the world's great digital revolution. They have few, if any, memories or understanding of the Cold War. Many of this generation came of age during President Clinton's second term and the Monica Lewinsky scandal.

Maybe the single biggest impact on this generation was the dot-com boom, which created a desire for instant success among this group. And after all, why not? All around them, they heard about and saw young and intelligent people becoming billionaires overnight.

"Gen Y" cannot imagine life without DVD players, cell phones, iPods, digital cable, TiVo, and digital cameras.

The Y Generation has also commonly been referred to as the "why" generation as well, for obvious reasons.

GENERATION Z (1998 TO 2025)

Generation Z represents the grandchildren of the Baby Boom Generation. It comprises anyone born in the United States between 1998 and 2025. No one in this generation will have a first-hand memory of the terrorist attacks of September 11, 2001. Yet a lot of what happened because of 9/11, such as the Patriot Act and the War on Terror, will affect their lives. Generation Z was and still is being born into a time of great job insecurity and constant international crisis. The parents of many of these children are floundering in their jobs due to cost-cutting, downsizing, layoffs, and outsourcing, which in turn is creating a new call for energy conservation and hybrid vehicles.

Many in this generation will have to fend for themselves in high school and throughout life. They will struggle between being a team player versus a leader. They will be more confused and less assertive than prior generations as they question exactly what their role is.

GENERATION GAP

It is important to view the Baby Boom Generation in the context of the generations surrounding it because sometimes the real story lies in the gap between generations.

The so-called generation gap refers to any time there is a vast difference in cultural standards and values between a younger generation and their elders. This gap develops when younger and older people do not understand each other because of their different experiences, behaviors, values, habits, and opinions.

Although such gaps have existed throughout history, the term *generation gap* first gained widespread acceptance in the 1960s as a way to describe the cultural differences between the baby boomers and their parents. During the Baby Boom Generation, the two generations seemed to be at opposite ends of the spectrum, whereas past generation gaps had been marked by only slight differences. The baby boomers had dramatically different views from their parents on everything from fashion and music to politics. This situation became bigger than life because of the Baby Boom Generation's unprecedented size. Being the largest generation ever, gave the boomers a sense of great power and influence. Sheer numbers set the foundation for them to rebel against social values and traditions to a previously unthought-of degree.

Think about these dramatic differences for a minute. The baby boomers were all about rock 'n' roll and soul music, which their parents detested. On the fashion front, long hair on young men (yes it's true, at one time my hair was almost down to my shoulders) was a way to shock elders and make the point that this generation was not going to accept the values and norms that their parents and society had established. And finally, the biggest generation gap may have been on the political front. The Baby Boom Generation engaged in large-scale protests against the Vietnam War on virtually every college campus. Meanwhile, all that their parents could remember was the unquestioned support the entire nation had for World War II. Indeed, this Baby Boom Generation may have had the largest generation gap in all of recorded time.

AGING OF THE BABY BOOMERS

Now, with the proper context, let's refocus on this Baby Boom Generation, which has created the single most influential demographic trend in the history of the United States. As the boomers age, they are ready to write their most dramatic chapter yet: They will dominate the social, business, and political fiber of the United States for the next quarter of a century.

Many doubters believe that the impact of the baby boomers will be insignificant, but the numbers tell a different story. There are 76 million baby boomers in the United States out of a population of nearly 300 million. Looked at another way, over one-fourth of all living Americans are baby boomers. When one-fourth of a country's population can be categorized or classified into any one group, that group will influence everything it touches and change it forever. The baby boomers have redefined every stage of their lives. When a few hundred people share an idea, it is interesting; when a few thousand people share an idea, it may even amount to a trend; when a few million people share an idea, it is a movement. However, when 76 million people share an idea, it is a revolution.

To understand what this revolution is going to mean, we should look backward first. Whether we give the baby boomers credit for the changes, their needs and desires at every single stage of their lives have become the dominant concerns of American business and political leaders. Let's quickly look at what these baby boomers have done on a decade-by-decade basis since they first arrived in the 1950s.

THE BABY-FOCUSED 1950s

In the 1950s when the first baby boomers were born, something happened that had never before occurred in the United States. A diaper industry was born. Not only did the arrival of the boomers create a new sector, but it became a profitable sector as well. With 76 million infants, a diaper industry makes all the sense in the world.

That was just the beginning of the influence of all these children on society. As these babies began to walk, parents had to put shoes on them. The baby shoe sector began an explosive growth rate that it had never seen before, nor has it seen since.

When these toddlers took their first steps, the event had to be recorded for posterity. Thanks also to some technological advancements, the photo sector took off as well: 76 million first steps, 76 million first days at school, 76 million first lost teeth, and so on, had to be photographically captured. It is no wonder that cameras were popping up everywhere. In fact, the turning point for the camera industry was this explosive growth spurt in the 1950s.

Along with diapers, shoes, and cameras, 76 million children needed to be nourished, and so the canned baby food industry expanded with rapid growth as this sector struggled to keep up with the changing demands of different flavors and varieties that these babies demanded. Continuing on this food theme, by the late 1950s the newest food invention was sugarcoated cereals. Why do you think the young baby boomers were so hyper and energetic? They were the first generation to be carbohydrate charged every morning with a vast variety of sweetened cereals. When young viewers watched the Saturday morning cartoons on the black-and-white television set in the mid- to late-1950s, almost every commercial was for some brand of sugarcoated cereal.

The final sea change in the 1950s was the explosion in pediatric medicine. When you have 76 million children with a cold and a runny nose, creating a medical practice exclusively for children is a no-brainer.

THE CHILD- AND TEEN-FOCUSED DECADE OF THE 1960s

After being fed, clothed, and cared for, these children now needed to be educated. In the 1960s, elementary school buildings sprang up throughout the United States making for the biggest elementary school building binge ever. It is unlikely that society will ever see one like it again, short of a similar baby boom. After all, how many times in a country's history is it likely to be confronted with having to find enough classrooms for 76 million students? Also, children love to be entertained. With that in mind, the 1960s saw a new wave of toys that not only dominated but also overwhelmed the marketplace. It started out with hula hoops, which—with 76 million children wanting one—quickly became a craze. Following the hula hoop, there came the Barbie doll and skateboards. Each new entertainment and toy became more successful than the one preceding it.

As the baby boomers grew into their teen years, a fast-food industry evolved to serve their cravings. From the 1960s on, almost every street corner sprouted another fast-food restaurant. This food sector explosion had everything to do with 76 million teenagers wanting to eat french fries and wanting them served fast! The baby boomers made millionaires out of the founders of McDonald's and Kentucky Fried Chicken.

THE YOUNG ADULT-FOCUSED 1970s

As the 76 million baby boomers moved into their young adult years, they started to settle down, get married, and raise a family.

Their number one priority became buying a house. The real estate explosion the country witnessed in the 1970s was all about the baby boomers. It had absolutely nothing to do with the economy in the 1970s. And no special financing innovation or one-time incentive to close real estate deals fueled this explosive growth. Real estate agents were there to benefit from this housing boom, but they certainly didn't cause it. The real estate explosion in the 1970s had everything to do with baby boomers wanting to buy a home and wanting to buy it now! It didn't happen all at once either. Because this generation spanned 19 years, the demand for housing lasted a lot longer than most other baby boomer trends to date. With 76 million people wanting to buy a home, real estate prices had nowhere to go but up. Want proof that the baby boomers caused the real estate explosion of the 1970s? In that decade, the value of real estate increased in every state in the United States.

THE ADULT-FOCUSED 1980s

Now that these baby boomers had their homes and started to raise their families, they shifted their attention to getting ahead in the business world. They were suddenly changing from the hippies of the 1960s into the yuppies of the 1980s.

The 76 million baby boomers now focused on advancing in their careers. Seemingly out of nowhere came financial news networks like CNBC and CNN. Why? Well, because 76 million people were trying to figure out how to get ahead in the business world. The *Wall Street Journal* entered a period of record growth and hit all-time subscription highs. *Forbes* and *Fortune* magazines also hit all-time subscription highs during this decade.

Another trend evolved in the 1980s: Many of these baby boomer families were two-income families. For the first time in a majority of families, both the husband and wife worked outside the home. Popping up to fill this newfound need were child-care centers and day-care centers. It was the baby boomers' focusing on their two-income careers that created the day-care sector.

THE MATURE ADULT-FOCUSED 1990s

As the baby boomers approached the magical half-century mark, they got serious and started to focus on retirement. When people worry about retirement, they are really worrying about having enough money for retirement, and so they begin to focus on investments and the markets. The great bull market of the 1990s was only partly driven by low inflation and low interest rates spawned out of the new global economy. The great bull market of the 1990s was the result of a simple fact: Seventy-six million baby boomers who were worrying about their retirement realized that the only way they could accumulate enough money was to be in the stock market.

And boy, were they in the stock market in a big way in the 1990s. Look at what the Dow Jones Industrial Average accomplished in the 1990s. In 1991, it crossed 3,000. Two years later in 1995, it crossed both 4,000 and 5,000. In 1996, it crossed 6,000. The very next year, 1997, it crossed both 7,000 and 8,000. In 1998, it crossed 9,000 and as the decade closed in 1999, it crossed the seemingly insurmountable landmark of 10,000 on the Dow.

But the baby boomers are nowhere near being done yet. They haven't stopped driving the stock market to all-time highs—they have just started.

Beginning January 1, 1996, every minute of every day for the next 10 years, seven more baby boomers would turn 50 years of age.

As people hit that magical half-century mark, they get even more worried about retirement and put even more money into the stock market. These over-50 baby boomers have more money than ever before in their lifetime to plow into the stock market because demographics are now playing in their favor: They are in their peak earnings years, their children have moved out (which helps reduce costs), and their homes are now paid for.

First of all, the kids are gone. When parents reach the age of 50, their children tend to be almost grown up and ready to move out of the house and be on their own, although this "empty nest" saga can be a tremendous emotional strain (my wife and I simply can't imagine our two girls finally being gone from the house), the financial strain is reduced. Raising children is a costly endeavor. When they finally grow up and are on their own, it frees up a significant source of cash flow that now can make its way to the stock market.

Second, by the time people reach 50, the family home is usually paid for or the mortgage is close to being paid off. For many years, this mortgage payment was the greatest expense in the budget every month. Now, finally, it is gone. Picking up the void once again is—you guessed it—the stock market.

Third and finally, at age 50, something magical happens. Workers are at their peak earning years because employers are finally paying them what those workers thought they were worth at age 22. It only took an additional 28 years for management to realize how much talent those people have brought to the table.

Baby boomers are probably going to be the most active 50-year-olds who ever lived. One thing that they are absolutely intent on is feeling youthful and not looking anything like their parents. Did you ever think of this: Perhaps the four-wheel drive sports utility vehicle (SUV) craze became so popular because baby boomers were apprehensive about driving the same station wagons their parents drove!

THE SENIOR CITIZEN-FOCUSED
DECADES OF THE NEW MILLENNIUM

Now that these baby boomers are becoming card-carrying senior citizens, they will be unlike any previous group of senior citizens. First, this group is not going to stand for gray hair and wrinkles. Instead of "working" in the traditional workplace, these senior citizens will focus on working at playing. And finally, they are going to be around a whole lot longer than previous demographic waves of senior citizens. Thus, unlike earlier senior citizen groups, not only will these baby boomer seniors focus on spending, they will focus on saving and investing as well. A confluence of three trends will distinguish this baby boomer generation as they become senior citizens.

THE TRAVEL AND ENTERTAINMENT TREND

One thing is for certain: This group of baby boomer senior citizens will turn the travel and entertainment sector upside down. They have wanted to be entertained throughout their lives. Now, along with entertainment, they will travel more than ever before.

Three factors will likely cause a boom in travel. First is the mobility of families today. Baby boomers' parents seldom settled far from their birthplace. Family reunions and visits to kin were relatively easy—all they had to do was drive across town and they could probably see everyone. That is not the case anymore. Baby boomers taught their children to be independent and to follow their dreams, no matter where they led them. Thus, the United States now has a group of senior citizens whose children and grandchildren are spread out all across the country, and sometimes around the globe. It is a whole lot easier for the retired grandparents to travel to see the family than it is for the family to come to them. This very well could be the first generation of "grannies on the go." Unlike their parents, who expected all family visits to occur back at their house, these seniors will be happy to hit the road making the tour at all family and extended-family stops.

Second, the globalization of the world's economies has opened up new avenues to explore around the world. As capitalism and tourism are embraced, these seniors will want to see it all and experience it all in their lifetime. Instead of the travel-torn, weary-eyed grandparent getting off the Greyhound bus after a long trip, these seniors will be likely flying a new airline "Grandparents 'R' Us," exclusively catering to senior citizens.

Third, these baby boomer seniors are affluent, and thus they have disposable income both for travel and for entertainment. If ever there was a generation that could pay to have a vacation weekend "on the moon," this generation is it. After all, they grew up living the dream that President John F. Kennedy planted in their mind about space travel. This generation will not stand for letting any other generation beat it to trips in outer space.

The most fascinating aspect of the baby boomers may be their desire for entertainment. Perhaps after earning so much money, they want to enjoy life as well.

Why would baby boomers pay hundreds of dollars for a room at the Ritz-Carlton or a Four Seasons hotel when they could sleep at a Holiday Inn for under $100? They are willing to pay the price because they see their choice as more than just a place to sleep; they view the entire event as entertainment—from the time the doorman greets them, to the bellman who takes their bags, to the clerk who takes them to their room, to the butler who fills the ice bucket, to the maid who places chocolates on the pillows at night, to the concierge who stands ready to get guests whatever they need.

Is the coffee at Starbucks really that much better, or do people just like being entertained and are willing to pay for it? It can be fun watching other coffee drinkers struggle with all the choices they have to make before they can get a simple morning drink. Maybe even more important, however, is that the baby boomers know they can customize their drink exactly the way they want it.

Once consumers have everything they need, it is no longer simply about buying something; now it is about "if you will provide me with some entertainment; I will buy your product at any price."

To count the baby boomers as their customers, businesses must transform every product and every service into an entertainment experience.

THE HEALTH AND FITNESS TREND

One thing that money cannot buy is good health. Make no mistake about it, baby boomers did not lead a healthy life so that they could sit around playing checkers when they retire. They intend to continue to be extremely active and the only way that can happen is to keep up their health focus.

This is not a passing fad. Baby boomer senior citizens will force every senior citizen center to have state-of-the-art workout equipment and health club facilities. They also know that what they eat is key to staying healthy. These baby boomer seniors will continue to eat right and eat healthy, changing the focus of the food sector forever.

THE FINANCIAL ADVICE TREND

Historically when people reached the age of 65, they were not too worried about investing and saving; they were more worried about making sure that their last will and testament was in order, but not anymore. When these boomers reach the young age of 65 that means that their life expectancy is now 86. In other words, they have 21 more years to live so they had better continue to save and invest. The only problem is that these seniors want to travel and be entertained and not worry about every nuance of the market. Enter the stockbroker turned financial advisor. This dinosaur is back from the possible extinction list and will be one of the best possible sectors in the coming decades. When you are busy ruling the world, you convince yourself that the future will always look like the past. The dinosaurs never saw it coming! Stockbrokers, however, are not dinosaurs. They did see it coming, and they evolved from a transaction-oriented career to value-added financial advice. The baby boomer seniors will have more financial and market information at their fingertips than any generation ever. The only problem is that they don't have the time to process it. Look for these senior citizens to turn their financial well-being over to a financial advisor. As a result, the brokerage industry will witness an unbelievable growth spurt. In addition, this baby boom senior citizen generation is the first generation in the history of the United States that will accumulate more wealth than the generation that follows it. The sheer size of the Baby Boom Generation means there will be more people with more money to transfer. That is why the next generation will actually have less wealth. Looked at another way, "transfer of wealth" is more important to this generation than to any other generation in history. To transfer their wealth in the most efficient and effective way possible, they need the help of a financial advisor. The biggest legacy of the baby boomers may be that they will make the stockbroker turned financial advisor into one of the most important and respected sectors in the world . . . certainly a rightful place for professionals who are caring for the financial health of 76 million people.

Another reason for the financial advisor boom is the complexity in the baby boomers' lives, especially from a financial investment perspective. Every minute of every single day, somewhere, some market is open and something is happening that will affect their investments. They need someone to simplify a life that gets more and more complex.

Think about it: When these boomers grew up, the choice of coffee was pretty simple—do you want it black or do you use cream or sugar? Sanka was the only decaffeinated coffee that was available. And there was no sweetener substitute. Think of all the decisions baby boomer senior citizens have to make to order a cup of coffee at Starbucks today. Who knows, by the time they are through, they may have ordered a double decaf, grande latte, double skim mocha with raspberry syrup and whipped cream, with a touch of nutmeg and cinnamon.

Then the boomer goes to the greeting card store to pick up a card for a friend and finds a maze of options. Is the card for a "friend," an "old friend," a "good friend," "best friend," "like family friend," "used to be a friend/friend again friend?" Unable to reach a decision, the would-be purchaser leaves the store empty-handed—after all, it would be rude to choose a "good friend" card for someone who believed she was the sender's "best friend." These baby boomer senior citizens are tired of life's growing complexity. They want someone to order their coffee, pick up their greeting cards, and most important, take responsibility for their financial assets and financial well-being for the rest of their lives.

THE CHANGING LANDSCAPE

Thousands of the 76 million baby boomers celebrate a birthday every single day. This graying of America is the most dramatic demographic revolution of our time. While everyone has an opinion on how the aging of the baby boomers will affect the United States, we still have more questions than answers. One thing we know for sure is that these ramifications are unprecedented and will change

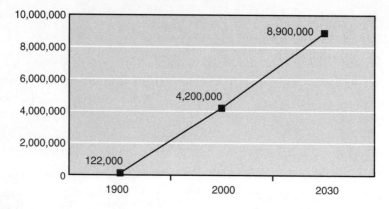

Figure 2.2   Senior Seniors Are Coming (Age 85 and Over)

politics, health care systems, stock markets, retirement systems, and even the labor markets.

The one thing that we can all agree on is basically how that changing landscape will look. In the year 2000, we had 35 times as many Americans over the age of 85 as there were in 1900 (see Figure 2.2). Also, in 2000 there were over 75,000 Americans at least 100 years of age. One hundred years earlier in 1900, there were only 3,500 of them. Meanwhile, as the baby boomers age, it is projected that by 2030, over 1 million of them will live beyond age 100, and a majority of them will be women (see Figure 2.3).

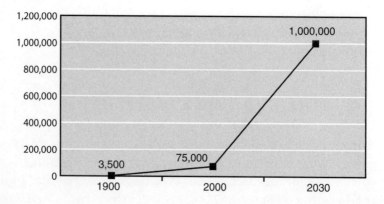

Figure 2.3   The Centurian Club (Age 100 and Over) Is Exploding

In addition, the baby boomers will begin to turn 60 in 2006, and 65 in 2011. In the coming decades, there will be a significant increase in the number of elder boomers and in their proportion to the total population. By 2030, the boomers' proportion will increase to 20 percent of the population up from a current level 13 percent, and the number of elderly will double. Put in different terms, from 2010 to 2030, the 65+ population is projected to spike by 75 percent to over 69 million people (see Figure 2.4). Then from 2030 to 2050, the growth rate is projected to grow about 14 percent with the number of elderly totaling about 79 million.

Also, the 85+ population is the fastest growing segment of the older population. The most rapid increases in the number of persons 85+ will take place between 2030 and 2050, when the baby boomer generation reaches these ages. By 2050, the 85+ group will rise from a current 1.4 percent to about 5 percent of the population. This group will show a significant increase in the number of centenarians.

Women will predominate among the elderly, especially among the oldest old. By 2050, it is projected that women 85+ will outnumber men 85+ by about 4 million, accounting for about 61 percent of the 85+ population. Most of the 85+ will be widows. The imbalance of the sexes and the low percentage of married women

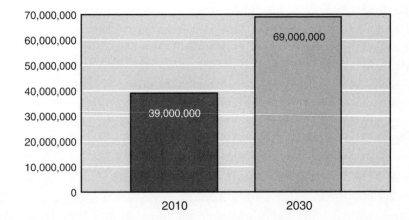

Figure 2.4   The Coming Senior Citizen Boom (Age 65 and Over)

have been associated with reduced income, greater poverty, poorer health, and greater risk of institutionalization of older women.

Finally, within the general elderly population, minority elderly populations are projected to increase substantially for the next three decades. While the white 65+ population is projected to increase by 95 percent between 1995 and 2030, older minorities will increase at a greater rate, including a 154.6 percent increase for African Americans, a 417.1 percent increase for people of Hispanic origin, and a 380.1 percent increase for people of other races (Asian, Pacific Islanders, American Indians). The rapid growth of these minority elder groups will greatly impact the demand for targeted supportive services.

NEXT INTERNET BOOM

Many baby boomers are tech-savvy. They grew up with black-and-white television and radios, but quickly adopted cell phones, VCRs, DVDs, microwave ovens, digital cameras, computers, cable TV, and satellite radio, not to mention the iPod. Could these boomers be ready to make their mark on the Internet as well by demanding a "wired" retirement? There is no doubt that these baby boomers will be far better connected than retirees today. Currently, only 20 percent of households with members over 50 have Internet access, half the rate of the population at large. The baby boomers meanwhile have the same Internet usage as the Generation Xers and Generation Ys that followed them. Also, baby boomers tend to be wealthier and better educated than generations before them, leading to higher Internet usage. This generation was forced to adopt technology at work, which spilled over into their home life. And if there are financial pressures on baby boomers as they near retirement because of questions and uncertainty about Social Security benefits, that would tend to keep those baby boomers working longer. Those extended years in the workplace would expose them to even more technology and computer usage, giving them an even greater comfort level with the Internet.

There are factors outside the baby boomers' control that will force them to be more Internet savvy as well. Most government agencies are moving more and more services and information online, as is the private sector with banks, brokerage firms, and retail shopping. When these baby boomers face age-related disability, their primary way to stay connected to their children, grandchildren, extended family, and friends may be through the Internet.

THE BABY BOOMER SANDWICH

The Baby Boom Generation has some unique aspects. One of them is what I refer to as the "baby boomer sandwich." Many baby boomer couples have one child in college and another child in high school. Meanwhile, both sets of their elderly parents now are in nursing homes. And suddenly it hits these baby boomers—they have to meet the financial needs of three generations: their parents, their own, and their children. This baby boomer sandwich poses the most serious challenge to the middle class. The upper class can absorb the costs because they can afford almost anything. They are, however, a very small group—currently only about 5 percent—of Americans. The poor have government programs as their financial safety net including Medicaid to pay for elderly parents' health care needs, and tuition loans and grants for college students. It is the middle class that must swallow a double-decker sandwich, if you will. Not only are they sandwiched between their elderly parents and their children, but they are also sandwiched between the upper and lower classes.

This could force some hard choices. Boomers might not be able to send their children to the college of their choice or put their parents in the nursing home they prefer. And most likely it means that they will not be able to retire when they want to.

The psychological impact of these forced choices is unprecedented. Will baby boomers tell their parents that they must enter a second-tier nursing home or tell their kids they can't go to the college of their dreams? And to make matters worse for these kids, they can't even get college loans or grants because their parents make too much money to qualify. And what about the baby boomers' own dreams when they realize that retirement may be put off forever? This leads to another unique aspect of the baby boomers: job hopping.

THE BABY BOOMER JOB HOP

The Baby Boomer Generation has seen its share of massive corporate layoffs, many fueled by major mergers and acquisitions. This generation was also the first to experience large numbers of divorces and the creation of second or blended families. Perhaps as a result of these two sea changes in their lives, the concept of long-term loyalty doesn't mean as much as it once did. Their parents grew up in a world where there was a long-term employment relationship. But in today's quickly moving global economy, there is no loyalty from corporations or their baby boomer employees.

In fact, baby boomers have held an average of nine jobs between the age of 18 and 36. While job hopping slows with the onset of late middle age, it still persists for this generation. Of baby boomers who started a job between age 33 and 36, 50 percent are not in that job three years later. And for that same group who started a job between age 33 and 36, over 75 percent are not in that job five years later. This is but another classic example of the generation gap. Once baby boomers' parents secured a job, they typically stayed with the company and retired from that same job because job security was a key measure of success at the time.

Not so with the baby boomers—they will change both jobs and careers to increase their pay, advance up the corporate ladder of success, or explore new opportunities.

Government policies have added fuel to this particular generation gap. The traditional defined benefit retirement plan is disappearing and is being replaced by the defined contribution 401(k) retirement plan. There are two differences. First, moving from defined benefit to defined contribution has shifted responsibility from the employer to the employee. If the burden for the retirement system is not on the employer, it really doesn't matter as much

if the employee job hops. The second difference is that these defined contribution retirement plans are portable, meaning that
employees can take them along anywhere they want to go.

BOOMER-SPEND

As we bring this chapter on baby boomers to a close, let's tie back
to one of our demographic sources: the U.S. Government's Bureau
of Labor Statistics (www.bls.gov). This web site will tell you what the
baby boomers are buying. The Bureau of Labor Statistics breaks
out consumer groups by decade, so if you go to the age 45 to 55
decade you are right in the heart of baby boomer land.

In Chapter 1, I explained that one doesn't just look at the demographic data but must draw comparisons as well. Let's do just
that by looking at what these baby boomers are buying compared
with the country as a whole.

Baby boomers spend more than the rest of the nation on food
away from home, which means they love to eat out. In addition,
baby boomers spend more on transportation (planes, trains,
cruises) than the rest of the nation; they also spend significantly
more than the rest of the nation on their vehicle purchases, which
means that they like expensive cars.

They also spend more on alcoholic beverages than the national
average, outspending every age group in the country other than
the category of adults 25 years and younger.

Demographic data also can be misleading. This doesn't necessarily mean that baby boomers drink more. My analysis suggests
that they are simply paying more. Instead of cheap lite beer, they
buy expensive premium imported beer. And if the whiskey is not at
least 30-year-old Scotch, don't even show it to them.

No matter how you cut it, these baby boomers are one of the
great consumer generations.

◆

CHAPTER THREE

GLOBAL SHIFT 2: THE WALLS KEEP TUMBLING DOWN

EASTERN EUROPEAN WORKERS

It is not often that entire continents get the opportunity to re-create themselves; however, that is exactly what is happening today on the continent of Europe. When nations are in transition, it becomes important to understand where they have come from, how they got here, and where they are going. To understand Europe, you not only must understand the sum of the parts, but must also be knowledgeable about the individual parts, or nations. What triggered this re-creation of Europe? History will record that the Berlin Wall fell on November 9, 1989, but to get a more complete picture of the changes, we need to look back to August 23, 1989. On that day, Hungary removed its border restrictions with Austria, and within a month, over 10,000 East Germans fled Communist Germany through Hungary. In two months, East Germans began mass protests against the government that continued to keep them behind the Wall, blocked from pursuing opportunities in Western Europe. Unemployment ran high, while the East German government was forced to reduce state benefits, food was becoming scarce, and the quality of living was in a downward death spiral. Meanwhile, jobs were plentiful in West Germany, and the quality of living seemed to improve each month. The protests were so overwhelming that the leader of the East German government resigned on October 18, 1989.

What happened next was a series of blunders (by the Communist government) that led to the fall of the Wall. The new government leader, Egon Krenz, decided that the only way to stop the massive protests in East Berlin was to let East Berliners apply for a visa to travel to West Germany.

THE BERLIN WALL FALLS

Now for the strange twist: East Berlin's Government Minister of Propaganda happened to be on vacation when it was decided to allow East Berliners to apply for visas. He was also unaware of the massive protests that had led to the decision. During a formal press conference on November 9, 1989, the Minister of Propaganda read a note that said East Berliners could cross the Wall to West Germany with proper permission. He was asked to whom this would apply and when would it take place. Because he had just come back from vacation and really didn't know, he replied that it would apply to anyone, beginning that day.

Within minutes, word spread and thousands of people went to the checkpoints to leave East Berlin for West Berlin. The guards were not sure what to do; the crowds grew by thousands upon thousands until the East German government was faced with two choices: Open the gates and let the Wall come tumbling down; or murder thousands upon thousands of the citizenry. They chose to open the gates. The Wall was history.

Less than a year after the Wall fell, East Germany and West Germany formally concluded their reunification on October 3, 1990.

In many respects, this set the foundation for the European Economic and Monetary Union (EMU).

THE EUROPEAN UNION

The actual foundation for the EMU dates back to 1951 when a coalition was formed called the European Coal and Steel Community. It included Belgium, the Netherlands, Luxembourg, France, Italy, and West Germany. This organization evolved over the years, changing its name first to the European Economic Community. By 1958, it became known as the European Community (EC).

Fifteen years later, in 1973, the original group of six countries began to expand by adding Denmark, Ireland, and the United Kingdom.

But it was the fall of the Berlin Wall in 1989 and the reunification of Germany in 1990 that set the stage for diplomatic relationships between Western, Central, and Eastern Europe. In 1992, the Treaty of Maastricht established the completion of the EMU as a formal objective and determined membership criteria on economic matters such as inflation, interest rates, and budget deficits. By that time, three more countries had joined the European Community: Greece, Spain, and Portugal. These 12 countries became the original members of the EMU (see Table 3.1).

In 1995, Austria, Finland, and Sweden joined the European Union, bringing the total number of member countries to 15. In 2004, the last walls left in Europe finally fell. On May 1, 2004, the EMU saw its membership roll swell with the admission of 10 more countries: Cyprus, the Czech Republic, Estonia, Hungary, Latvia, Lithuania, Malta, Poland, Slovakia, and Slovenia. The EMU now stood 25 countries strong, and for the first time in the modern era, Central and Eastern Europe could begin to act with one economic voice.

DEMOGRAPHICS OF THE EUROPEAN UNION

The overall population of the 25 member countries in the European Union is over 450 million, whereas the population of the United States is slightly under 300 million. The annual growth rate of the EU population, however, is only 0.2 percent compared with 0.9 percent in the United States—four times greater

In the European Union, 16 percent of its population is under 15 years of age (substantially less than in the United States, which

Table 3.1 European Union through
the Years

Country	Year Joined
Belgium	1951
Netherlands	1951
Luxembourg	1951
France	1951
Italy	1951
Germany (West)	1951
Denmark	1973
Ireland	1973
United Kingdom	1973
Greece	1992
Spain	1992
Portugal	1992
Austria	1995
Finland	1995
Sweden	1995
Cyprus	2004
Czech Republic	2004
Estonia	2004
Hungary	2004
Latvia	2004
Lithuania	2004
Malta	2004
Poland	2004
Slovakia	2004
Slovenia	2004

shows 20 percent of the population under 15 years); 67 percent of
the EU population is between the ages of 15 and 65 years (match-
ing the United States); finally, 15 percent of the European Union's
population is aged 65 years or older in sharp contrast to the United
States, where only 12 percent of the population is over 65. With
more people over 65 and less people under 15 than in the United
States, Europe's population is aging ahead of this country (see
Figure 3.1).

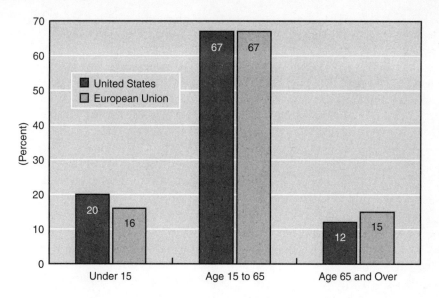

Figure 3.1 Current Age Structure: European Union versus the United States

The European Union has a birthrate of 10.2 per 1,000 population compared with the United States at 14.14. It has a death rate of 10.0 per 1,000 population, compared with the United States at only 8.25. And finally, it has a net migration rate of 1.5 migrants per 1,000 population, less than half of the U.S. level of 3.31. Compared with the United States, the European Union has less people being born, more people dying, and less people migrating—not the brightest picture (see Figure 3.2).

Life expectancy for EU residents is 78.1 years which is a little better than the United States at 77.6 years. For the male population it is 74.9 years, which is just about the same for U.S. males at 74.8. Life expectancy for the female population of the European Union is 81.4 years, which is slightly better than U.S. females who have a life expectancy of 81.0 years.

DEMOGRAPHIC PROFILES

This demographic picture fails to reveal the whole story. To understand the dramatic impact that the European Union is creating

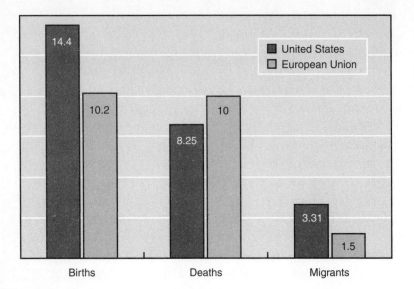

Figure 3.2 Current European Union versus United States: Births, Deaths, and Migrants per 1,000 Population

with the free flow of capital and labor, one must look at the individual demographics of all 25 member nations.

Instead of looking at these countries based on when they joined the European Union, we will analyze them based on their population since then; after all, this is a book about demographic trends.

GERMANY

Germany is actually the world's third largest economy, behind the United States and Japan. But it is the world's largest exporter, ahead of both the United States and China. Located in the heart of Europe, it is one of the world's leading industrialized countries. Because the German economy is so heavily export driven, it accounts for more than one-third of the country's entire economy. Germany has a diverse economic base by industry; it has a substantial presence in vehicles, steel, beverages, iron, coal, cement, electronics, chemicals, shipbuilding, and textiles. Germany had already privatized and restructured its railroad system and is now privatizing the airline, postal service, and telecommunication industries as well. It is bordered on the north by the North Sea, Denmark, and the Baltic Sea; on the south, by Austria and Switzerland; on the west, by France, Belgium, the Netherlands, and Luxembourg; and on the east, by Poland and the Czech Republic.

Germany has the largest population (82,431,390) of any of the 25 EU members. The population growth rate in Germany is flat at 0, which is under the overall EU population growth rate of 0.2 percent.

The age structure of Germany shows 14 percent of its population under 15 years of age, which is smaller than the EU average of 16 percent. Germany and the European Union both have 67 percent of the population classified between the ages of 15 and 65. Finally, 19 percent of the population is over 65 years of age as opposed to the European Union's average of only 15 percent.

Germany's birthrate of 8.33 births per 1,000 population is well below the EU average of 10.2. Its death rate of 10.55 per 1,000 population is only slightly ahead of the EU average of 10.0. Finally, the net migration rate is 2.18 migrants per 1,000 population, which is far ahead of the EU average of 1.5 migrants per 1,000 population.

Life expectancy in Germany is 78.66 years, which is better than the EU average of 78.1 years. The infant mortality rate is 4.16 deaths per 1,000 live births, which is lower than the EU average of 5.53 deaths per 1,000 live births. The literacy rate is 99 percent, which is also above the EU average of 98.51 percent (see Figure 3.3).

FRANCE

Although France has a diversified private sector comprising over 2.5 million companies, the French economy is greatly controlled and influenced by the government, which is the majority owner of the electricity, telecommunications, aircraft, and railway industries. France has become a manufacturing leader and is now the world's fifth largest exporter of manufactured goods behind the United States, Germany, Japan, and China. France is bordered to the North by the English Channel, Belgium, and Luxembourg; to the east by Germany, Switzerland, and Italy; its southern border is

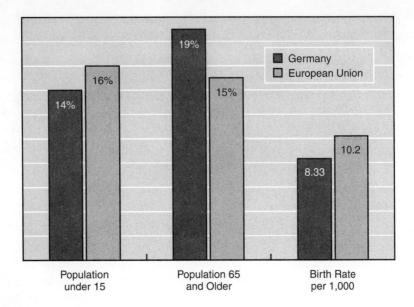

	Population under 15	Population 65 and Older	Birth Rate per 1,000

Figure 3.3 Germany versus European Union: Key Demographic Differences

comprised of the Mediterranean Sea and Spain; and on the west it is bordered by the Atlantic Ocean.

France has the second largest population of the 25 EU members with 60,656,178. Its population growth rate is 0.37 percent, which places it well above the EU growth rate of 0.2 percent.

In France, 19 percent of the population is below 15 years of age, which is much higher than the 16 percent EU average. In addition, a smaller percentage of its population is 15 to 65 years of age: 65.2 percent compared with 67 percent for the European Union. Finally, 16 percent of its population is over 65 years of age, which is slightly above the EU average of 15 percent.

France has a birthrate of 12.15 births per 1,000 population, which is much higher than the EU average of 10.2. It has a death rate of only 9.08 deaths per 1,000 population, which is well below the EU average of 10.0 per 1,000 population. Finally, its net migration rate is only 0.66 per 1,000 population, which is less than half of the EU rate of 1.5 per 1,000 population.

Life expectancy in France is 79.6 years, which is well above the EU average of 78.1 years. The infant mortality rate is 4.26 deaths per

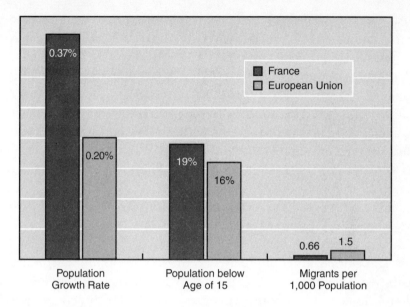

Figure 3.4   France versus European Union: Key Demographic Differences

1,000 live births, which is lower than the EU average of 5.53 deaths per 1,000 live births, and the literacy rate is 99 percent, which is slightly above the EU average of 98.51 percent (see Figure 3.4).

THE UNITED KINGDOM

The United Kingdom is a leading trading power and financial center. The service sector, especially banking and insurance, is the largest component of the United Kingdom's economy. Agriculture also plays a dominant role. The United Kingdom is highly mechanized and efficient among agricultural industries around the globe and produces over 60 percent of its food needs with less than 1 percent of its labor force.

The United Kingdom is often incorrectly referred to as Great Britain or Britain. Sometimes it is also incorrectly called England. The United Kingdom has one land border and that is with Ireland. The rest of the country is completely surrounded by bodies of water, the North Sea, the English Channel, the Celtic Sea, the Irish

Sea, and the Atlantic Ocean. The United Kingdom comprises four parts, and three of these four parts are located on the island of Great Britain: England, Wales, and Scotland. If you use the term England, technically you are only referring to one of the United Kingdom's four parts. Likewise, if you use the term Britain, or Great Britain, you are only referring to three of the United Kingdom's four parts.

That fourth part of the United Kingdom is Northern Ireland, located on the island of Ireland. This border between the United Kingdom's Northern Ireland and the Republic of Ireland is the United Kingdom's only international land border. However, technically, there is one other land border—under the English Channel where the Channel Tunnel connects the United Kingdom with France via train.

The United Kingdom boasts the third largest population in the European Union at 60,441,457—only a few thousand people less than France. It has a population growth rate of 0.28 percent, which is above the EU average growth rate.

The population under 15 years of age in the United Kingdom comes to 18 percent, which is much higher than the 16 percent average for the European Union. Meanwhile, 66 percent of its population is between the age of 15 and 65, slightly below the EU average of 67 percent. And finally, 16 percent of the population in the United Kingdom is over 65 years of age, which again is only slightly above the EU average of 15 percent.

The birthrate in the United Kingdom is 10.78 births per 1,000 population, a little above the EU birthrate of 10.2 per 1,000. It has a death rate of 10.18 deaths per 1,000 population, which is also slightly above the European Union death rate of 10.0 per 1.000 population. And finally, the net migration rate of 2.18 migrants per 1,000 population is well above the overall EU level of 1.5 migrants per 1,000.

Life expectancy in the United Kingdom is 78.38 years, which is in line with the European Union average of 78.1 years. The United Kingdom has an infant mortality rate of 5.16 deaths per 1,000 live births, which is slightly below the EU average of 5.53 deaths per 1,000 live births. The literacy rate of 99 percent is also above the EU average of 98.51 percent (see Figure 3.5).

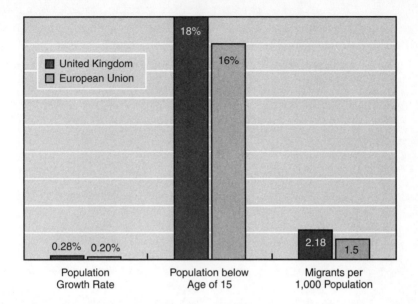

Figure 3.5 United Kingdom versus European Union: Key Demographic Differences

ITALY

Italy has a diversified industrial economic base and is unique because it has a great number of small and medium-sized businesses that serve as the backbone of the economy. Almost all the raw materials that this industrial economy needs must be imported, as well as 75 percent of the country's energy needs.

As a peninsula, Italy only has a border with land to the north, where it touches France, Switzerland, Austria, and Slovenia. The rest of Italy is surrounded by bodies of water: the Adriatic Sea, the Ionian Sea, the Tyrrhenian Sea, the Liguria Sea, and the Mediterranean Sea. Italy also has two main islands, Sicily and Sardinia.

Italy has the fourth largest population in the European Union at 58,103,033. Its population growth rate is nearly zero at 0.07 percent, well below the EU level of 0.20 percent. Only 14 percent of the population is under the age of 15 (compared with 16 percent for the entire European Union); 67 percent of Italy's population falls between 15 and 65 years of age, which is the same as the percentage for the

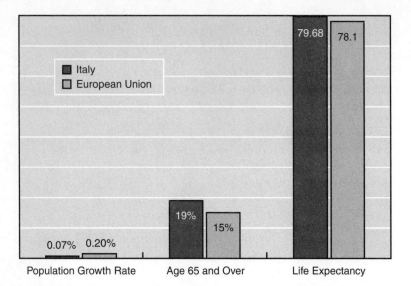

Figure 3.6 Italy versus European Union: Key Demographic Differences

European Union. And finally, 19 percent of its population is 65 years of age or older, which is well above the EU average of 15 percent.

The birthrate in Italy is 8.89 births per 1,000 population, which is well below the 10.2 EU level. Its death rate is 10.3 deaths per thousand, which places it ahead of the EU average of 10.0 per 1,000. Italy's net migration rate of 2.07 migrants per 1,000 population places it well above the EU level of 1.5 per thousand.

Life expectancy in Italy is 79.68 years, placing it well above the EU level of 78.1 years. It has an infant mortality rate of 5.94 deaths per 1,000 live births, which is above the EU average of 5.53 deaths per 1,000 live births. The literacy rate of 98.6 percent is right in line with the EU average of 98.51 percent (see Figure 3.6).

SPAIN

In many respects, Spain is an economic paradox. On the one hand, it has pushed hard for privatization and deregulation for a large part of its economy. On the other hand, it continues to focus on ways for the government to control and regulate the labor markets.

Maybe this paradox explains why Spain's economy seems never to quite catch up to the other major economies of Europe.

Spain is part of the Iberian Peninsula along with Portugal, one of its land borders. To the north, it borders France as well as the tiny principality of Andorra. The rest of Spain is surrounded by the Balearic Sea and the Mediterranean Sea to the east, the Bay of Biscay to the northwest, and the Atlantic Ocean to the west.

Spain has the fifth largest population in the European Union at 40,341,363. Its population growth rate is 0.15 percent, which places it behind the average for the European Union, which stands at 0.20 percent.

In Spain, 15 percent of the population is below the age of 15 (much less than the EU average of 16 percent) and 68 percent is between the age of 15 and 65 (slightly above the EU level of 67 percent). And finally, 18 percent of its population is 65 years of age and over, well above the EU average of 15 percent.

The birthrate in Spain is 10.1 births per 1,000 population, which is in line with the EU level of 10.2 per 1.000. It has a death rate of 9.63 deaths per 1,000 population, which puts it well under the European Union's death rate level of 10.0. Finally, it has a net migration rate of 0.99 migrants per 1,000 population, well below the EU figure of 1.5.

Life expectancy in Spain is 79.52 years, well above the EU level of 78.1 years. Spain's infant mortality rate is 4.42 deaths per 1,000 live births, well below the EU average of 5.53 deaths per 1,000 live births. It has a literacy rate of 97.9 percent, which is below the EU average of 98.51 percent (see Figure 3.7).

POLAND

Poland is located in Central Europe. It borders Germany to the west, the Czech Republic and Slovakia to the south, Ukraine and Belarus to the east and the Baltic Sea, Lithuania, and Russia to the north.

Poland has a very large agricultural sector made up of mostly private farms. It will become a leading producer of food in the European Union now that it is a member. Since Poland's return to

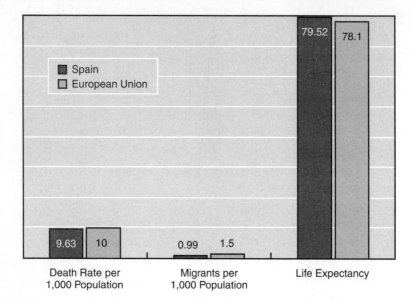

Figure 3.7   Spain versus European Union: Key Demographic Differences

democracy, it has orchestrated the privatization of small and medium-sized state owned companies, which are fueling the rapid development of its private sector. In addition, it has restructured and privatized major industries that used to be state controlled including telecommunications, energy, coal, steel, and transportation. Poland still has a fair share of economic problems, particularly in the health care and education areas.

Poland has the sixth largest population in the European Union at 38,635,144. It has a population growth rate of only 0.03 percent, which is well below the European Union level of 0.20 percent.

In age structure, 17 percent of Poland's population is below 15 years of age, which is higher than the EU average of 16 percent. A whopping 70 percent of its population is between the age of 15 and 65 years, well above the EU average of 67 percent. And finally, only 13 percent of its population is 65 years of age or older, which is way below the EU level of 15 percent.

The birthrate is 10.78 births per 1,000 population, placing it above the EU average birthrate of 10.2 per 1,000. Poland's death rate is 10.01 deaths per 1,000 population, in line with the EU level

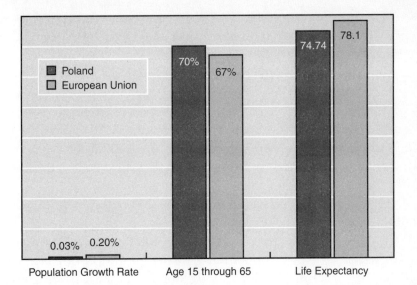

Figure 3.8 Poland versus European Union: Key
Demographic Differences

of 10.0. The net migration rate of −0.49 migrants per 1,000 population is obviously well below the EU net migration rate of 1.5.

Life expectancy in Poland is only 74.41 years, well off the EU average of 78.1 years. Infant mortality rate is 8.51 deaths per 1,000
live births, substantially above the EU average of 5.53. The literacy
rate is 99.8 percent, which is above the EU average of 98.51 percent
(see Figure 3.8).

THE NETHERLANDS

The Netherlands' economy is an industrial-based economy dominated by food, chemicals, and petroleum refining. In addition, its
extremely productive agricultural sector allows it to rank as the
world's third largest exporter of agricultural goods behind only the
United States and France.

The Netherlands is located in northwestern Europe and is bordered by the North Sea to the north and the west, by Germany to
the east, and Belgium to the south.

With a population of 16,407,451, the Netherlands has the seventh largest population in the European Union. Its population growth rate of 0.53 percent is more than double the growth rate of the European Union's 0.20 percent.

From an age structure perspective, 18 percent of its population is under the age of 15 (2 percent above the EU level of 16 percent); 68 percent is between 15 and 65 years (slightly above the EU level of 67 percent). Only 14 percent of the population is 65 years of age and over, which is below the 15 percent level of the European Union.

The Netherlands has a birthrate of 11.14 births per 1,000 population, well above the EU average of 10.2 births per 1,000. The death rate of 8.68 deaths per 1,000 is well below the EU average of 10.0 deaths per 1,000 population. The net migration rate is 2.8 migrants per 1,000 population, almost double the European Union's level of 1.5 migrants per 1,000 population.

In the Netherlands, life expectancy is 78.81 years, placing it above the average for the European Union, which is 78.1. The infant mortality rate is 5.04 deaths per 1,000 live births, which is below the EU average of 5.53 deaths per 1,000 live births. The literacy rate is 99 percent, which is above the EU average of 98.51 percent (see Figure 3.9).

GREECE

Greece's economy is still dominated by the state owned and controlled public sector, which accounts for more than half of its economy. Tourism plays a key role in the economy. Greece continues to be a global leader in the shipping industry. In terms of number of ships owned by any country, Greece ranks number one.

Greece is a peninsula in southeast Europe. Its only land boundaries are to the north where it touches Albania, Macedonia, Bulgaria, and Turkey. The Aegean Sea is its border to the east. The Mediterranean Sea provides the southern border and the Ionian Sea is the border to the west.

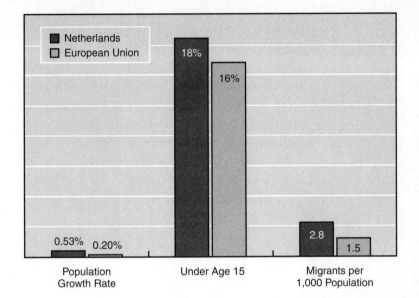

Figure 3.9   Netherlands versus European Union: Key Demographic Differences

Greece has the eighth largest population in the European Union at 10,668,354. Its population growth rate is 0.19 percent, slightly below the EU level of 0.20 percent.

Only 14 percent of its population is under the age of 15 years, putting it well below the EU rate of 16 percent. The age group of 15 to 65 accounts for 67 percent of Greece's total population, the same proportion as in the overall European Union. The over 65-years-of-age group accounts for 19 percent of the population, which is much higher than the 15 percent level in the overall European Union.

Greece has a birthrate of 9.72 births per 1,000 population, which places it below the 10.2 birthrate level for the European Union. It has a death rate of 10.15 deaths per 1,000 population, which is only slightly higher than the 10.0 death rate for the European Union per 1,000 population.

It has a net migration rate of 2.34 migrants per 1,000 population, well above the EU average of 1.5 migrants per 1,000.

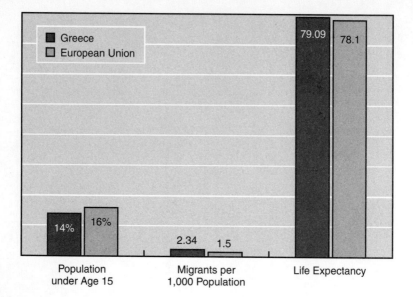

Figure 3.10 Greece versus European Union: Key Demographic Differences

Greece boasts a life expectancy rate of 79.09 years, which is much better than the EU level of 78.1 years. It has an infant mortality rate of 5.53 deaths per 1,000 live births, the same rate as the EU average. The literacy rate is 97.5 percent, which is below the EU average of 98.51 percent (see Figure 3.10).

PORTUGAL

Portugal's economy has witnessed the privatization and deregulation of many state-owned and state-controlled industries including the telecommunications and the financial services sector. A large portion of Portugal is still focused on agriculture. Abundant olive trees, vineyards, and wheat have given it a corner in the wine, olive oil, and cereal markets. Natural resources cover over one-third of the country, mainly in the form of pine trees, cork oak, and eucalyptus trees. In fact, Portugal produces over half of the world's cork. In addition to timber, it also has significant mining resources in uranium, tungsten, and tin.

Portugal is located in southwestern Europe and shares the Iberian Peninsula with Spain, which borders Portugal to the north and east. The Atlantic Ocean serves as its border to the south as well as the west.

With the ninth largest population in the European Union, Portugal is only a few thousand people behind Greece. Portugal's population is 10,566,212, and it has a population growth rate of 0.39 percent, just about double the EU rate of 0.20 percent.

In age structure, 17 percent of its population is below 15 years of age, which is 1 percent higher than the EU level; 66 percent of its population is between the ages of 15 and 65, which is slightly less than the European Union's 67 percent level. The proportion of its population 65 years of age or older is well above the EU average of 15 percent.

Portugal's birthrate of 10.82 births per 1,000 population is well above the EU level of 10.2 births per 1,000. It has a death rate of 10.43 per 1,000 population, which is also higher than the EU death rate of 10.0 per 1,000 population. It has a net migration rate of 3.49 migrants per 1,000 population, which is three times greater than the EU level of 1.5 migrants per 1,000.

Life expectancy in Portugal is only 77.53 years, which is less than the EU level of 78.1 years. It has an infant mortality rate of 5.05 deaths per 1,000 live births, which is below the European Union's average of 5.53 deaths per 1,000 live births. The literacy rate is 93.3 percent, well below the European Union's average of 98.51 percent (see Figure 3.11).

BELGIUM

Belgium remains one of Europe's most highly industrialized countries having led all of Europe into the industrial revolution in the early 1800s, particularly through the steel, chemical, and petroleum industries. In addition, Belgium developed a transportation infrastructure of ports and canals to go along with the surface transportation of highways and railroads that made it the jewel among industrialized European countries.

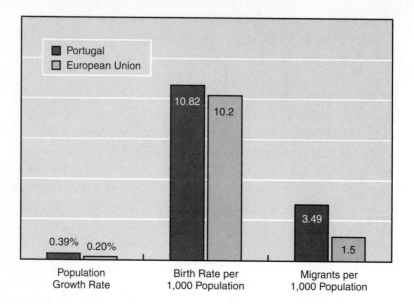

Figure 3.11 Portugal versus European Union: Key
Demographic Differences

The Belgian economy greatly depends on exports and imports. Belgium continues to be a major exporter of automobiles, food, iron, steel, textiles, plastics, petroleum, and other metals. It is a big importer of machinery and chemicals.

Belgium is located in Western Europe and is bordered by the Netherlands to the north, Germany and Luxembourg to the east, and France to the west; the North Sea forms its remaining north-west border.

Belgium rounds out the EU top 10 in population with 10,364,388 people, only a few thousand shy of Portugal. It has a growth rate of 0.15 percent, which is below the EU growth rate of 0.20 percent. Its age breakdown shows 17 percent of its population as being under 15 years of age (slightly higher than the EU average of 16 percent); 66 percent of its population is between the ages of 15 and 65, just slightly below the EU level of 67 percent for that age category. Finally, 17 percent of Belgium's population is 65 years of age or older, which is much higher than the European Union's average of 15 percent.

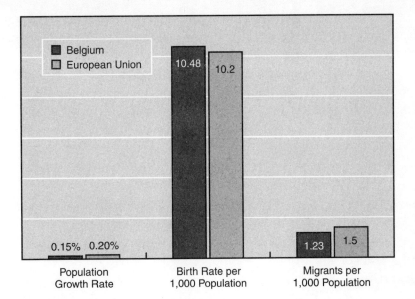

Figure 3.12 Belgium versus European Union: Key Demographic Differences

Belgium's birthrate is 10.48 births per 1,000, which places it above the EU level of 10.2. Its death rate of 10.22 deaths per 1,000 puts it above the EU level of 10.0. It has a migration rate of 1.23 migrants per 1,000 population, slightly below the 1.5 level for the European Union.

Life expectancy in Belgium is 78.62 years, which is better than the European Union's level of 78.1 years. It has an infant mortality rate of 4.68 deaths per 1,000 live births, which is below the EU average of 5.53. It has a literacy rate of 98 percent, which is slightly below the EU average of 98.51 percent (see Figure 3.12).

THE CZECH REPUBLIC

The Czech Republic's economy continues to progress now that it has moved from communism to capitalism. It continues to push forward with privatization of its telecommunications, energy, and banking industries.

The Czech Republic is a landlocked country in Central Europe. It is bordered on the north by Poland and on the east by Slovakia. Austria is at its southern border, and Germany is to the west.

It just missed making the top 10 in population, as it is only a few thousand people behind Belgium. The Czech Republic has 10,241,138 citizens. It has a negative population growth rate of −0.05 percent, well off the positive population growth rate of 0.20 percent for the overall European Union.

In the Czech Republic, 15 percent of the population is under the age of 15, which is slightly under the EU average of 16 percent. Seventy-one percent of its population is between 15 and 65 years of age, which is 4 percent higher than the EU average of 67 percent for that age category. And finally, only 14 percent of its population is 65 years of age and older compared with 15 percent for the European Union.

The Czech Republic has a birthrate of only 9.07 births per 1,000 population, which is much lower than the EU level of 10.2. It has a death rate of 10.54 deaths per 1,000 population, which puts it above the EU death rate of 10.0. The net migration rate of 0.97 migrants per 1,000 population is well below the EU net migration rate of 1.5.

In the Czech Republic, life expectancy is 76.02, well below the EU average of 78.1 years. Infant mortality is only 3.93 deaths per 1,000 live births, which is substantially below the EU average of 5.53. The literacy rate is 99.9 percent, well above the EU average of 98.51 percent (see Figure 3.13).

HUNGARY

Hungary has been privatizing once state-owned industries, and the private sector now accounts for over 75 percent of the economy. Both inflation and unemployment have improved dramatically, while health care reform and tax reform remain the two biggest issues.

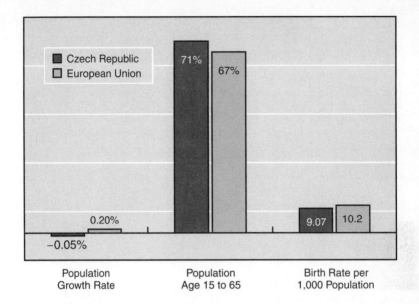

Figure 3.13   Czech Republic versus European Union: Key
Demographic Differences

Hungary, located in central Europe is another landlocked
country. It is bordered by Austria to the west; Slovakia and Ukraine
to the north; Romania to the east; and Serbia, Croatia, and Slovenia to the south.

It has the twelfth largest population (10,006,835) of the 25
members of the European Union. It has a negative population
growth rate of −0.26 percent, which is in stark contrast to the 0.20
population growth rate for the European Union.

In its age structure, 16 percent of its population is under 15
years, in line with the rest of the European Union. The age group
15 to 65 accounts for 69 percent of the population, 2 percent larger
than the EU level of 67 percent. Only 15 percent of Hungary's population is over the age of 65, which is the same as the EU average.

Hungary's birthrate is 9.76 births per 1,000 population, which
is lower than the EU birthrate of 10.2 per 1,000. Its death rate of
13.9 per 1,000 population, is substantially higher than the EU

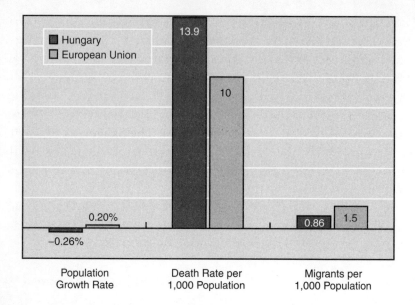

Figure 3.14 Hungary versus European Union: Key
Demographic Differences

death rate of 10.0. And last, it has a net migration rate of 0.86 migrants per 1,000 population, which is just about half of the EU average of 1.5.

In Hungary, life expectancy is only 72.4 years, which is in sharp contrast to the life expectancy level in the European Union of 78.1 years. Its infant mortality rate is 8.57 deaths per 1,000 live births, which is substantially higher than the EU average of 5.53 deaths per 1,000 live births. It has a literacy rate of 99.4 percent, which is above the EU average of 98.51 percent (see Figure 3.14).

SWEDEN

Sweden has pulled off the miracle of creating a social democratic system. It has a high-tech economy and some of the most extensive and exhaustive welfare benefits in the world. In addition to technology, the timber, hydropower, and iron ore industries create a resource base that fuels a strong foreign trade component.

Surprisingly, one-third of all Swedish stocks are owned by the Swedish government, the Swedish social security system, and the trade union pension funds. These trade unions make up one-third of the board of directors of every Swedish company with more than 100 employees.

Sweden is located in northern Europe. It is bordered by Norway on the west and Finland on the northeast. The Skagerrak Strait and the Kattegat Strait form the bodies of water that border it on the south and southwest. The Baltic Sea and the Gulf of Bothnia border it to the east.

Sweden has a population of 9,001,774, which ranks it as the thirteenth largest member of the European Union. Its population growth rate of 0.17 percent is slightly below the EU average growth rate of 0.20 percent.

In age structure, 17 percent of Sweden's population is under the age of 15, slightly higher than the EU level of 16 percent; 66 percent of its population falls between the ages of 15 and 65, slightly below the EU level of 67 percent; and 17 percent of its population is 65 years of age and older, 2 percent higher than the EU average of 15 percent.

Sweden has a birthrate of 10.36 births per 1,000 population, which places it above the EU average of 10.2 per 1,000. It has a death rate of 10.36 deaths per 1,000 population, which also places it above the EU death rate of 10.0. Its net migration rate of 1.67 migrants per 1,000 population is also higher than the European Union's net migration rate of 1.5.

In Sweden, life expectancy is 80.4 years, placing it well above the EU life expectancy of 78.1. It has an infant mortality rate of only 2.77 deaths per 1,000 live births, which is half the EU average of 5.53 deaths per 1,000 live births. It has a literacy rate of 99 percent, which is above the EU average of 98.51 percent (see Figure 3.15).

AUSTRIA

Austria has moved toward privatizing many of its state-owned industries. Even with this fundamental shift, labor unions remain very strong and vibrant in Austria. Its industrial base consists of

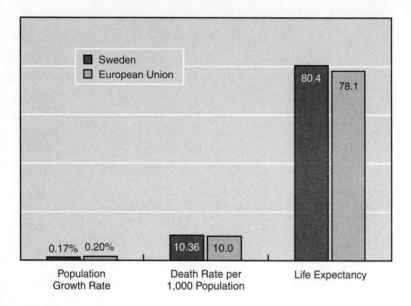

Figure 3.15 Sweden versus European Union: Key
Demographic Differences

iron, steel, and chemical plants. Its service sector is dominated by
tourism, especially in the winter months. A unique aspect of Austria is its economic relationship with Germany. Because Germany is
its biggest trading partner, Austria is extremely vulnerable to major
changes to the German economy.

Austria is located in central Europe and is landlocked. It borders Germany and the Czech Republic to the north and Slovakia
and Hungary to the east. Slovenia and Italy are its borders to the
south and Switzerland and Liechtenstein are to the west.

Austria, with a population of 8,184,691, ranks fourteenth in the
25-member European Union. It enjoys a population growth rate of
only 0.11 percent, almost half of the population growth rate for the
European Union.

From an age structure perspective, it is an exact mirror of the
European Union. Sixteen percent of its population is under 15
years of age, 67 percent is between the ages of 15 and 65, and 17
percent is 65 years of age or older, which is higher than the EU average of 15 percent.

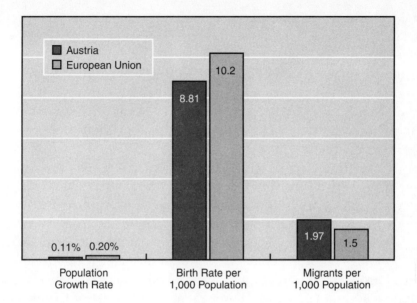

Figure 3.16   Austria versus European Union: Key
Demographic Differences

Austria's birthrate is only 8.81 births per 1,000 population,
which is well below the EU level of 10.2 per 1,000 population. It has
a death rate of 9.7 deaths per 1,000 population, which places it
slightly below the EU average of 10.0 deaths per 1,000 population.
Its net migration rate of 1.97 migrants per 1,000 population places
it well above the 1.5 migrant rate level for the European Union.

Life expectancy in Austria is 78.92, well above the EU average
life expectancy level of 78.1 years. Infant mortality is 4.66 deaths
per 1,000 live births, which is below the EU average of 5.53 deaths
per 1,000 live births. Austria's literacy rate is 98 percent, which is
slightly below the EU average of 98.51 percent (see Figure 3.16).

DENMARK

Denmark's economy is driven by a high-tech agriculture component and a vibrant small business community. Along with Sweden,
Denmark has extensive government welfare benefits. Foreign
trade is its lifeblood, especially in the area of food and energy.

Like Sweden, the Danish economy is highly unionized; 75 percent of the workforce belong to a union. These unions take a day-to-day role in managing the company's workplace and have a representative on the board of directors of most companies, but not all.

Denmark is a peninsula located in northern Europe. It borders the Baltic Sea to the east and the North Sea to the north and west and is attached to northern Germany, which provides Denmark its only land border to the south.

It has the fifteenth largest population (5,432,335) among the members in the European Union. In addition, it has a vibrant population growth of 0.34 percent, which puts it well above the EU average population growth rate of 0.20 percent.

In age structure, 19 percent of its population is 15 years of age and younger, a full 3 percent higher than that age group for the entire European Union; 66 percent of its population is between the ages of 15 and 65, slightly lower than the EU level of 67 percent. Only 15 percent of its population is 65 years of age or older, which matches the EU level.

Denmark's birthrate of 11.36 births per 1,000 population is well above the EU birthrate of 10.2 per 1,000 population. The death rate of 10.43 deaths per 1,000 population is much higher than the 10.0 death rate for the overall European Union. The net migration rate of 2.53 migrants per 1,000 population is substantially higher than the EU level of 1.5 migrants per 1,000 population. Denmark has a life expectancy of 77.62 years, slightly lower than the EU life expectancy level of 78.1 years. It boasts an infant mortality rate of 4.56 deaths per 1,000 live births, well below the EU average of 5.53. The literacy rate is an unbelievable 100 percent, obviously higher than the European Union's average of 98.51 percent (see Figure 3.17).

SLOVAKIA

Slovakia is slowly moving from a government controlled centrally planned economy to an open market economy. The banking sector is now completely privatized. Unemployment and inflation con-

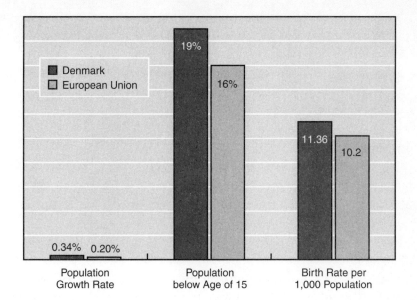

Figure 3.17 Denmark versus European Union: Key Demographic Differences

tinue to be the biggest issues. Slovakia is located in central Europe and is landlocked. It borders the Czech Republic in the northwest, Poland in the north, Ukraine in the east, Hungary in the south, and Austria in the southwest.

Slovakia's population of 5,431,363 is the sixteenth highest in the European Union. It has only 1,000 fewer citizens than Denmark. The population growth rate is 0.15 percent, which is below the EU growth rate level of 0.20 percent.

The population under the age of 15 comes to 17 percent, slightly higher than the 16 percent for the European Union; 71 percent of Slovakia's citizens are 15 to 65 years of age, well above the 67 percent EU level. A mere 12 percent of its population is over the age of 65, substantially lower than the EU average of 15 percent. The net migration rate for Slovakia is 0.3 migrants per 1,000 population, well below the EU level of 1.5.

In Slovakia, life expectancy is only 74.5 years, well below the EU life expectancy rate of 78.1 years. The infant mortality rate of 7.41 deaths per 1,000 live births is well above the EU average of

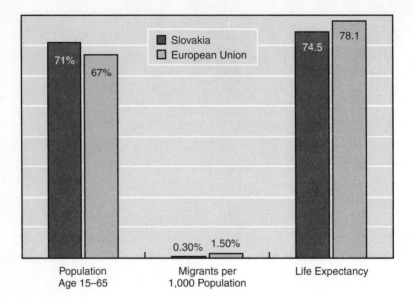

Figure 3.18   Slovakia versus European Union: Key
Demographic Differences

5.53 deaths per 1,000 live births. The literacy rate is 98 percent,
slightly below the European Union's average of 98.51 percent (see
Figure 3.18).

FINLAND

Finland has a highly industrialized economy. Its most important
economic sector is manufacturing, especially telecommunications,
wood, metals, engineering, and electronics.

Located in northeastern Europe, Finland is bordered by the
Baltic Sea to the southwest, the Gulf of Finland to the south, and
the Gulf of Bothnia to the west. Finland has land borders with Sweden to the west, Norway to the north, and Russia to the east.

Finland has the seventeenth largest population at 5,223,442. It
has a population growth rate of 0.16 percent, which is below the
EU average of 0.20 percent.

From an age structure perspective, 17 percent of its population is under 15 years of age, slightly higher than the 16 percent for the European Union; 67 percent of its population falls between the age of 15 and 65 years, the same proportion as for the overall European Union. Finally, 16 percent of its population is over 65 years of age, slightly more than the 15 percent average for the European Union.

Finland's birthrate of 10.5 births per 1,000 population is above the EU level of 10.2 births per 1,000 population. The death rate is 9.79 deaths per 1,000 population, which is below the EU level of 10.0 per 1,000 population. The net migration rate is 0.89 migrants per 1,000 population, well off the EU level of 1.5 .

Life expectancy in Finland is 78.35 years, slightly above the EU level of 78.1 years. It has an infant mortality rate of only 3.57 deaths per 1,000 live births, which is substantially lower than the EU average of 5.53. The literacy rate of 100 percent is considerably higher than the EU average of 98.51 percent (see Figure 3.19).

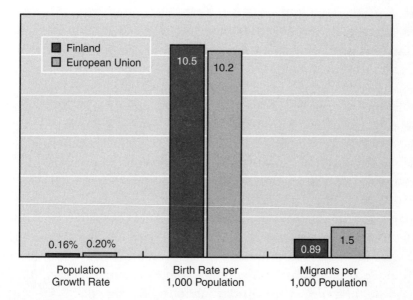

Figure 3.19   Finland versus European Union: Key Demographic Differences

IRELAND

Agriculture, once the most important component of Ireland's economy, is now dwarfed by industry, which accounts for almost half of the country's economy and close to 90 percent of its exports. In addition to its booming export trade, the economy of Ireland has also benefited from a rise in business and consumer spending.

A little known fact is that Ireland is the largest exporter of software-related goods and services in the world. Because it does not impose a tax on any royalties from copyrighted goods, a great deal of foreign software and foreign music is channeled through Ireland.

Ireland is located in Western Europe and covers about five-sixths of the Island of Ireland. The remaining one-sixth of the island of Ireland is known as Northern Ireland and remains a part of the United Kingdom; this is Ireland's only land border to the north. The rest of Ireland is bordered by the Atlantic Ocean to the west, the Celtic Sea to the south, and the Irish Sea to the east.

Ireland boasts the eighteenth largest population in the European Union with 4,015,676 people. It has a population growth rate of 1.16 percent, which is off the charts compared with the population growth rate for the European Union, which is only 0.20 percent.

An almost unbelievable 21 percent of its population is under the age of 15 years; this is 5 percent higher than the EU level of 16 percent. In Ireland, 68 percent of the population is between the ages of 15 and 65, a little above the 67 percent level for the overall European Union. Only 11 percent of Ireland's population is 65 years of age and older—an amazing 4 percent lower than the EU average of 15 percent.

As expected, the birthrate in Ireland is an eye-popping 14.47 per 1,000 population, compared with the EU level of 10.2 births per 1,000 population. The death rate is only 7.85 deaths per 1,000 population, which also puts it far below the EU death rate level of 10.0. The net migration rate of 4.93 migrants per 1,000 population is more than three times greater than the EU rate of 1.5.

Life expectancy in Ireland is 77.56 years, slightly less than the EU life expectancy level of 78.1 years. The infant mortality rate of

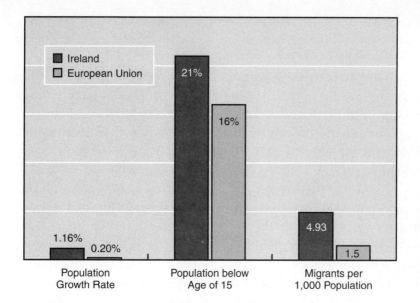

Figure 3.20   Ireland versus European Union: Key
Demographic Differences

5.39 deaths per 1,000 live births is only slightly below the EU average of 5.53 deaths per 1,000 live births. The literacy rate of 98 percent, again, is slightly below the EU average of 98.51 percent (see
Figure 3.20).

LITHUANIA

Lithuania has made great progress toward privatization and away
from state-owned and state-controlled businesses. The entire utility
industry and most of the transportation industry have become
completely privatized. Lithuania used to conduct a majority of its
trade with Russia, but now has diversified its trade among numerous European countries.

Lithuania is located in northeastern Europe. It borders Latvia
to the north and Belarus to the southeast. Poland forms its border
to the south as does Russia to the southwest. To the west lies the
Baltic Sea.

Lithuania, population 3,596,617, ranks nineteenth in the European Union. It has a negative population growth rate of –0.3 percent, putting it well below the EU growth rate of 0.20 percent.

In age structure, 16 percent of its population is under 15 years of age, the same as the EU rate of 16 percent; 69 percent of its population falls between the ages of 15 and 65 years, 2 percent higher than the EU level of 67 percent. Only 15 percent of its population is 65 years of age and older, the same average as for the European Union.

Lithuania's birthrate of 8.62 births per 1,000 population places it well below the EU level of 10.2 births per 1,000 population. The death rate of 10.92 deaths per 1,000 places it well above the death rate for the European Union, which is 10.0 deaths per 1,000 population. It has a negative net migration rate of –0.71 migrants per 1,000 population compared with the European Union's migration rate of 1.5 migrants per 1,000 population.

Life expectancy is only 73.97 years in Lithuania as compared with 78.1 years for the overall European Union. The infant mortality rate of 6.89 deaths per 1,000 live births is well above the EU average of 5.53 deaths per 1,000 live births. The literacy rate of 99.6 percent is also well above the EU average of 98.51 percent (see Figure 3.21).

LATVIA

Latvia continues to move away from state-owned and state-controlled business enterprises to an open economy. It is making great progress along the lines of privatization as most companies and all banks and real estate have been completely privatized. The government still owns sizable stakes in the utility industry.

Latvia has land borders with Estonia to the north and Russia and Belarus to the east. Lithuania's southern border and western coast border the Baltic Sea and the Gulf of Riga.

One of the smaller members of the European Union, Latvia has a population of 2,290,237 and ranks 20th. It has a large negative population growth rate of –0.69 percent, which stands in sharp

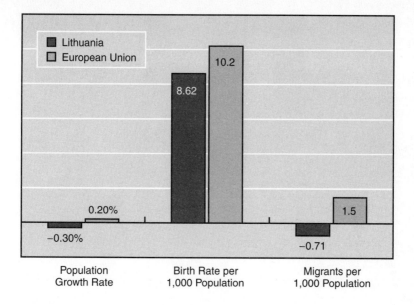

Figure 3.21 Lithuania versus European Union: Key
Demographic Differences

contrast to the 0.20 percent population growth rate for the entire
European Union.

Only 14 percent of its population is under the age of 15 compared with the average of 16 percent under the age of 15 for the entire European Union; 70 percent of its population falls between 15
and 65 years of age, 3 percent higher than the 67 percent level for
the European Union. Finally, 16 percent of Latvia's population is
65 or older, just above the EU average of 15 percent.

Latvia's birthrate is only 9.04 births per 1,000 population, well
off the EU level of 10.2 births per 1,000. It has a high death rate of
13.7 deaths per 1,000 population compared with the EU level of
10.0 deaths per 1,000 population. Its poor net migration rate is a
negative −2.24 migrants per 1,000 population, nowhere near the
EU level of 1.5 migrants per 1,000 population.

Life expectancy in Latvia is 71.05 years, well below the EU average of 78.1. Infant mortality rate is through the roof at 9.55 deaths
per 1,000 live births, almost double the European Union's average

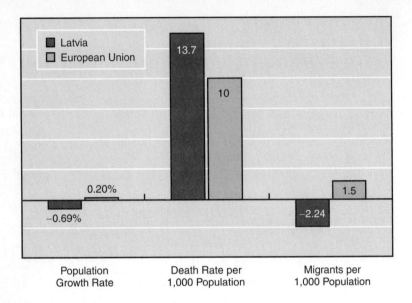

Figure 3.22 Latvia versus European Union: Key Demographic Differences

of 5.53 deaths per 1,000 live births. The literacy rate is 99.8 percent, which is above the EU average of 98.51 percent (see Figure 3.22).

SLOVENIA

Slovenia is showing great progress privatizing its telecommunications, banking, and utility sectors. It is also beginning to lift restrictions on foreign investment. The success of the Slovenian economy lies with an industrial base of aluminum, lead, zinc, wood, textiles, and chemicals.

Slovenia is located in central Europe. It is bordered on the south and the east by Croatia. Hungary provides the northeast border and Austria borders the rest of the north. The west is bordered by Italy and the Adriatic Sea.

Slovenia's population is 2,011,070, placing it at 21 among the 25 European Union members. It also has a negative population growth rate of −0.03 percent compared with the EU population growth rate of 0.20 percent.

Only 14 percent of its population is under the age of 15, well below the 16 percent average for the European Union. A whopping 71 percent of its population is between the ages of 15 and 65, which is 4 percent higher than for the European Union. Only 15 percent of its population is 65 years of age and older, which is the same as the EU level of 15 percent.

The birthrate in Slovenia is 8.95 per 1,000 population, well below the EU birthrate of 10.2 per 1,000. The death rate of 10.22 per 1,000 population is only slightly higher than the EU death rate of 10.0. Slovenia has a net migration rate of 1.0 migrants for every 1,000 population, which lags the EU average of 1.5.

Life expectancy in Slovenia is 76.14 years, well behind the EU life expectancy of 78.1 years. The infant mortality rate of 4.45 deaths per 1,000 live births is a good deal below the EU average of 5.53 deaths per 1,000 live births. The literacy rate of 99.7 percent is well above the EU average of 98.51 percent (see Figure 3.23).

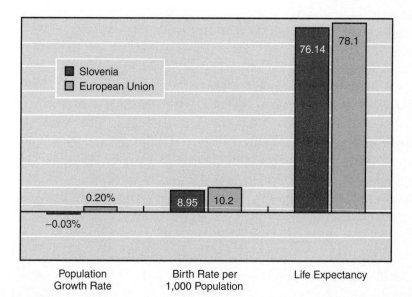

Figure 3.23   Slovenia versus European Union: Key Demographic Differences

ESTONIA

Estonia has also been successfully privatizing its economy, especially telecommunications, energy, and transportation. In addition, Estonia has a rapidly growing technology sector. With Russian oil transiting through Estonia's ports, this segment of the economy has turned around. A unique feature in Estonia is that in 1994 it became one of the first countries in the world to adopt a flat tax rate regardless of income levels.

Estonia is located in northeastern Europe. It borders the Baltic Sea to the west and the Gulf of Finland to the north. To the south and east it has land borders with Latvia and Russia, respectively.

Estonia, population 1,332,893, ranks 22 among the 25 European Union's members. It has a negative growth rate of −0.65 percent, well off the European Union's population growth rate of 0.20 percent.

Only 15 percent of Estonia's population is under 15 years of age, slightly less than the EU average of 16 percent; 68 percent of the population is between the ages of 15 and 65, slightly higher than the 67 percent for the European Union; 17 percent of its population is 65 years of age and over, 2 percent above the EU average.

The birthrate in Estonia is 9.91 births per 1,000 population, which places it a little below the 10.2 births per 1,000 population for the European Union. It has a high death rate of 13.21 deaths per 1,000 population compared with the European Union's level of 10.0 per 1,000 population. And, finally, it has a horrible net migration rate of −3.18 migrants per 1,000 population, at the other end of the spectrum from the EU migrant rate of 1.5 migrants per 1,000 population.

Life expectancy in Estonia is only 71.77 years, well below the life expectancy of the European Union, which is 78.1 years. It has an infant mortality rate of 7.87 deaths per 1,000 live births, which is substantially higher than the EU average of 5.53 deaths per 1,000 live births. The literacy rate of 99.8 percent is well above the EU average of 98.51 percent (see Figure 3.24).

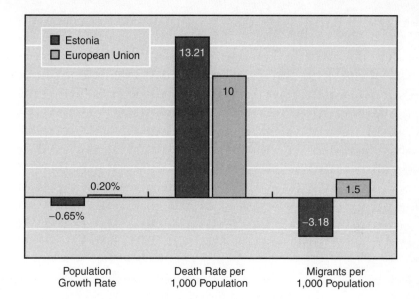

Figure 3.24   Estonia versus European Union: Key Demographic Differences

CYPRUS

The economy of Cyprus is driven by a confluence of three industries or sectors: agriculture, tourism, and government services. Water shortage remains the biggest problem and will continue to be until desalination plants are put in place.

Cyprus is an island nation in the Mediterranean Sea south of Turkey. It has only 780,133 citizens ranking 23 among the 25 members of the European Union. It does, however, have a robust population growth rate of 0.54 percent, which is more than double the EU growth rate of 0.20 percent.

An unbelievable 21 percent of its population is under the age of 15, a full 5 percent above the average for the European Union; 68 percent of its population is between ages 15 and 65, slightly above the EU level of 67 percent. Only 11 percent of its population is 65 years of age or older, dramatically less than the EU level of 15 percent.

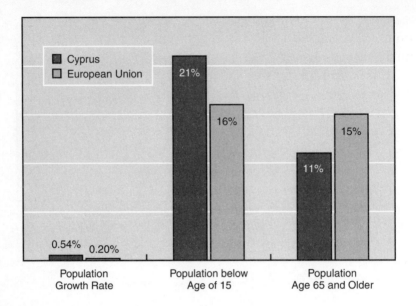

Figure 3.25 Cyprus versus European Union: Key Demographic Differences

Cyprus has a birthrate of 12.57 births per 1,000 population, well above the EU birthrate level of 10.2 births per 1,000 population. Its death rate is only 7.64 deaths per 1,000 population, far below the 10.0 death rate per 1,000 for the European Union. The net migration rate of 0.43 migrants per 1,000 population is well off the EU rate of 1.5 migrants per 1,000.

The life expectancy in Cyprus in 77.65 years, which is only a shade under the life expectancy of the European Union at 78.1 years. The infant mortality rate of 7.18 deaths per 1,000 live births is well above the EU average of 5.53 deaths per 1,000 live births and a literacy rate of 97.6 percent, which is well below the EU average of 98.51 percent (see Figure 3.25).

LUXEMBOURG

The industrial base of Luxembourg's economy is driven by steel, chemicals, and rubber. One of the fastest growing components in its economy is the banking and financial services sector. In addition, it has a small agricultural component based solely on small family-owned farms.

Luxembourg is located in Western Europe and is landlocked by France to the south, Germany to the east, and Belgium to the west.

As the second smallest of the 25-member European Union, it does not even have a half million people. Its rank is 24, with 468,571 citizens. It has quite a spectacular population growth rate of 1.25 percent—an astonishing six times greater than the EU average population growth rate of 0.20 percent.

Nineteen percent of Luxembourg's population is under the age of 15, well above the 16 percent level for the European Union, and 66 percent of its population falls between the ages of 15 and 65, only slightly under the EU average of 67 percent. Only 15 percent of its population is 65 years of age or older, the same as for the European Union.

Luxembourg has a solid birthrate of 12.06 births per 1,000 population, placing it well above the 10.2 birthrate for the European Union. The death rate is only 8.41 deaths per 1,000 population, well below the 10.0 death rate level for the European Union. Almost unbelievably, it has a net migration rate of 8.86 migrants per 1,000, which simply blows away the European Union's net migration number of 1.5 migrants per 1,000 population.

Life expectancy in Luxembourg is 78.74 years, which is a little better than the European Union's 78.1 years. The infant mortality rate of 4.81 deaths per 1,000 live births is below the European Union's average of 5.53. The literacy rate of 100 percent, is obviously above the EU average of 98.51 percent (see Figure 3.26).

MALTA

Malta's major resources are limestone and a favorable geographic location. The economy is almost totally dependant on foreign trade and is focused on freight shipping, manufacturing of electronics and textiles, and tourism. Malta produces less than 20 percent of its food needs, has no energy sources, and no fresh water supplies.

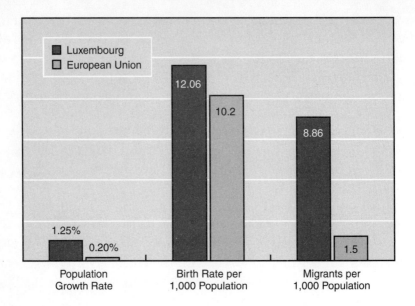

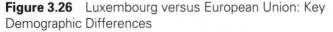

Figure 3.26 Luxembourg versus European Union: Key
Demographic Differences

Malta, an island nation in the Mediterranean Sea south of Italy, is the smallest member of the European Union. It ranks dead last in population with only 398,534 residents, but it has a robust population growth rate of 0.42 percent—double that of the European Union's 0.20 percent.

As far as age structure goes, 18 percent of its population is under the age of 15 (2 percent higher than the EU level), and 69 percent of its population falls between 15 and 65 years of age (2 percent greater than the EU average of 67 percent). Only 13 percent of its population is 65 years of age or older, which is below the EU level of 15 percent.

The birthrate in Malta is 10.17 births per 1,000 population, which is in line with the EU level of 10.2 births per 1,000 population. Its death rate of 8.0 deaths per 1,000 population places it well below the 10.0 death rate per 1,000 population for the European Union. It has a healthy net migration rate of 2.06 migrants per 1,000 population, placing it above the EU average of 1.5 migrants per 1,000 population.

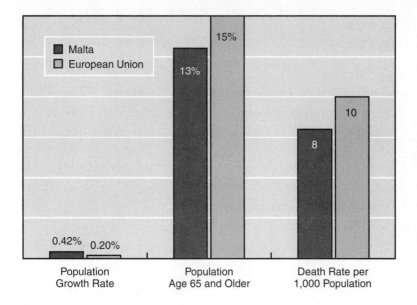

Figure 3.27 Malta versus European Union: Key Demographic Differences

Malta enjoys a life expectancy of 78.86 years, which is above the life expectancy average for the European Union. Its infant mortality is a very low 3.89 deaths per 1,000 live births, well below the EU average of 5.53 deaths per 1,000 live births. It has a literacy rate of only 92.8 percent, well below the EU average of 98.51 percent (see Figure 3.27).

REMEMBER THE FOUR RULES

With all these demographic facts and figures bouncing around (see Appendix 2 for a complete country-by-country ranking of individual demographic indicators), it is time to recall the four rules for looking at demographic data discussed in Chapter 1. I am going to use two of these rules: (1) Focus on the extremes—the outlier data points and (2) cluster the data. This will produce a great snapshot of some important demographic trends in the European Union.

POPULATION GROWTH RATE

The population growth rate for the European Union is 0.20 percent. To find the story, we must look at the outliers. The population growth rates for two countries stand tall among all others: Luxembourg, with the highest rate, at 1.25 percent; and Ireland, a close second, with a rate of 1.16 percent. The worst rate, a negative −0.69 percent, was in Latvia, closely followed by Estonia at −0.65 percent. In addition, there were four other countries with negative population growth rates that can be clustered together: the Czech Republic, Hungary, Lithuania, and Slovenia.

AGE STRUCTURE

The age structure of the European Union shows the following characteristics.

UNDER 15 YEARS OF AGE

For the 25-member European Union, 16 percent of the population is under the age of 15. Two countries stand out because 21 percent of their population is under the age of 15: Ireland and Cyprus. In addition, three other countries have 19 percent of their population under the age of 15: Denmark, France, and Luxembourg. At the other end of the spectrum, six countries logged in with the smallest percentage of their population (14 percent) under the age of 15: Germany, Greece, Italy, Latvia, Slovenia, and Spain.

AGES 15 TO 65

Sixty-seven percent of the population of the 25-member European Union falls into the 15-to-65 age category. The three countries with the highest percentage of their population in this category (71 percent) are the Czech Republic, Slovakia, and Slovenia. The country with the smallest percentage of its population in this age group is France (65 percent). Six other countries also are below the average at 66 percent: Belgium, Denmark, Luxembourg, Portugal, Sweden, and the United Kingdom.

Age 65 or Older

Fifteen percent of the citizens in the European Union's 25 member countries are 65 years of age or older. The three countries with the most people in this category (19 percent) are Germany, Greece, and Italy. Two countries shared the honor of having the fewest citizens in this age group—Cyprus and Ireland, with only 11 percent of their population being 65 years of age or older. Slovakia is right behind them with 12 percent of its population being 65 years of age or older.

BIRTHRATE

The average birthrate for the 25-member European Union is 10.2 births per 1,000 population. One country stood alone at the top—Ireland—with a birthrate of 14.47 per 1,000 population. Three other countries with high birthrates of at least 12 births per 1,000 are Cyprus, France, and Luxembourg. On the other side of the scale, five countries have a birthrate under 9 births per 1,000 population: Germany, Italy, Austria, Lithuania, and Slovenia.

DEATH RATE

The average death rate for the European Union is 10.0 deaths per 1,000 population. Three countries have death rates above 13.0 deaths per 1,000 population: Estonia, Hungary, and Latvia. At the other end of the spectrum, the fewest deaths were in Cyprus and

Ireland, which both boasted a death rate under 8.0 deaths per 1,000 population.

MIGRANT RATE

The net migrant rate for the European Union is 1.5 migrants per 1,000 population. No one comes close to Luxembourg on this one, where the rate of 8.86 migrants per 1,000 population is almost unthinkable. Also off the charts is Ireland, at 4.93 and Portugal at 3.49. If you wanted to know where everyone is heading in Europe, now you know. Conversely, the two countries with the worst migrant rates are Estonia, which was the lowest at −3.18 migrants per 1,000 population, followed by Latvia, with −2.24 migrants per 1,000 population.

LIFE EXPECTANCY

Life expectancy for the European Union is 78.1 years of age. So where do people live the longest and the shortest? Sweden is the only country with a life expectancy over 80 years of age. Four other countries have a life expectancy above 79.0 years: France, Greece, Italy, and Spain. On the flip side, where do you die the earliest? Two countries have life expectancy of only 71 years of age: Estonia and Latvia. Hungary is not far behind them with life expectancy at 72.

INFANT MORTALITY RATE

The infant mortality rate for the European Union is 5.53 deaths per 1,000 live births. Sweden has the lowest infant mortality of all at only 2.77 deaths per 1,000 live births. Three other countries have rates below 4.00 per 1,000: Czech Republic, Finland, and Malta. Conversely, three countries have infant mortality rates above 8.0 deaths per 1,000 live births: Latvia, Hungary, and Poland. Estonia is also very close with an infant mortality rate of 7.87 per 1,000.

LITERACY

Literacy is defined as the percentage of a population aged 15 and older that can read and write. The literacy rate for the European Union is 98.51 percent. Three countries share the highest literacy rate possible at 100 percent: Denmark, Finland, and Luxembourg. The only country with a literacy rate below 93 percent is Malta at 92.8 percent. Portugal, at 93.3 percent, is not that much better.

WHAT EXACTLY IS EASTERN EUROPE?

Now that we have a good understanding of the overall demographics of the European Union, let's focus on Eastern Europe and examine just what the unleashing of low-cost labor in Eastern European countries will do to the rest of Europe, and the rest of the world.

The traditional division of Europe used to be on a north-and-south basis. The countries bordering the Atlantic Ocean and the Baltic Sea composed the north and the southern Mediterranean Sea countries composed the south.

Not anymore. Now "Eastern Europe" refers to the countries that used to be under the control of the Soviet Union. The term *Iron Curtain* became widely used after World War II in reference to the ideological differences between the democratic countries of Western Europe and the communist countries of Eastern Europe. The Western European nations were thriving economically, whereas the Soviet-controlled Eastern European bloc continued to fall behind the rest of Europe. The communist-driven government policies of state control eventually caused their economies and standards of living to spiral downward.

DOUBLE IMPACT OF THE EUROPEAN UNION

The Iron Curtain is now gone and Eastern Europe and Western Europe have joined as one in the European Union. The first big impact of this union was the opening up of cheap labor in Eastern

Europe. The easiest way to make money in business is to always find ways to do things better, faster, and cheaper than you are doing it today. The way to do things better, faster, and cheaper in Europe is through Eastern Europe.

First Impact—Low Cost

When countries fall behind economically, there are ripple effects on health, welfare, and standards of living. These hardships do not turn around overnight, but with more income, things can get better. Think for a minute what the European Union means to the workers of Eastern Europe who, because of their poor standard of living, are the cheapest labor around. It is likely that more and more companies will begin to locate manufacturing operations in these countries to reap the financial benefit of low-cost workers. This, in turn, will help the overall economies of these Eastern European countries as well as help their own companies. National economic growth will beget corporate economic growth.

Many workers, however, will decide not to stay in Eastern Europe and will instead move to job opportunities in Western Europe.

Second Impact—More Flexible Labor Standards

It is the shift of Eastern European workers to Western Europe that will cause the second impact: more flexible labor standards. It is no secret to anyone that extreme antibusiness and antiprofit labor standards are major problems in industrialized Western Europe. Despite small concessions to management, the standards for work hours, vacations, layoffs, and terminations are still greatly tilted toward the employee and against the employer, which ultimately means against profits as well. This, too, will now change. As workers come from Eastern Europe to Western Europe, they will be less demanding and more willing to accept a job working more hours with less vacation and less pay. The workforce landscape is about to change dramatically.

In addition, these labor standards will become more flexible, not just because Eastern European workers are coming to Western Europe, but because Western European companies can now move their entire operations to other parts of the European Union, especially to the low-cost centers of Eastern Europe. Just the threat of all those jobs leaving France or Spain to go to Poland or Hungary will be enough to completely change the labor dynamics.

This can create a win-win situation. The Eastern European economies get stronger while Western European companies get more profitable, which in turn will drive the Western European economies as well.

This opening up of labor in Eastern Europe will finally bring about the structural reform needed in the labor laws, labor standards, and labor traditions of Western Europe.

THE GERMAN EXAMPLE

Germany, Europe's largest economy, illustrates how this immigration of new workers from Eastern Europe will happen.

The number of people entering the workforce for the very first time is now smaller than the number of people retiring in Germany. Looked at another way, the German workforce is now officially shrinking. Based on the current projection of new people seeking employment in Germany, and the absence of any new workers through immigration, the German workforce will fall by 40 percent by 2050.

Keep in mind that the growth in a country's workforce is one of the key drivers of a country's economic growth. If the workforce doesn't grow, neither will the economy.

Additionally, it is important to remember that a workforce is also a consumer force. If the growth in workforce slows, so too will the growth in consumption. Especially hard-hit will be sectors that rely solely on local consumers such as stores, restaurants, and pubs. When the owners face declining sales, they also face the risk of going out of business or filing for bankruptcy. But it gets even worse. Slower growth in an economy means less need for new capital investment in manufacturing and industrial companies. No new capital investment means that the average age of plants and equipment will rise and when that happens, these firms lose their global competitive edge.

The only way to stop this doomsday scenario is enlist immigrant workers from Eastern Europe.

Even if birthrates were to triple in Germany, it would take 20 years for these new birthrates to make their way into the workforce as adults. The only stopgap is to bring in an increasing number of Eastern European immigrants.

To convey some idea of the magnitude of this complex demographic puzzle, for Germany to maintain its current workforce and for new job entrants to remain at current levels, by 2050, 40 percent of its workforce will have to be immigrants. This migration figure is necessary merely to reach a breakeven point. Workforce growth would demand even higher migration levels.

This new convergence of demographic trends mixes countries with a growing workforce and low ratio of retirees with ones that have a shrinking workforce and a high ratio of retirees. The results can create unprecedented investment opportunities in Europe.

CONCLUSION

In 1946, shortly after the end of World War II, Winston Churchill first proposed what he called "a United States of Europe." His innovative idea was met with skepticism. Critics pointed out that Europe, unlike the United States, didn't have a single language and also unlike the United States, didn't even have a single currency, so how in the world could there ever be such a thing as the United States of Europe? Well, I am sure that Winston Churchill is smiling now that almost 60 years later, 25 European countries have joined together to create a monetary union by giving the authority of monetary policy to the European Central Bank and by launching a new currency called the *euro*. This re-creation of Europe has also changed the investment landscape. Some regions, countries, industries, and companies will fare better than others. But everywhere you look, there are new and exciting investment opportunities.

CHAPTER FOUR

GLOBAL SHIFT 3: THE RISING SUN IS CLEARLY SETTING

THE AGING JAPANESE POPULATION

Throughout history, Japan has been referred to as the "Land of the Rising Sun." Even the flag of Japan with its white background and large red disk in the center carries that message. The Japanese flag is called *Hinomaru,* which means "circle of the sun." Because Japan geographically lies to the east of China and the sun always rises in the east, from a Chinese perspective Japan is the land of the rising sun. The Japanese also call their country *Nippon* or *Nihon.* The two Chinese characters for Nippon can be translated as "origin of the sun" or "land of the rising sun."

Where Japan and its rising sun are concerned, history is about to take a turn. Instead of referring to Japan as the land of the rising sun, we will now need to refer to it as the land of the setting sun, at least from a demographic perspective.

CURRENT DEMOGRAPHICS

The overall population of Japan is 127,417,244, less than half of the population of the United States (currently nearing 300 million) and roughly one-fourth the population of the European Union,

which has 450 million residents. Japan has a population growth
rate of 0.05 percent. The European Union's growth rate of 0.20
percent is four times faster than Japan's, and the United States'
growth rate of 0.90 percent is almost 20 times faster.

The age groups in Japan are as follows: 14 percent of its population is under the age of 15, 2 percent less than the European
Union, which has 16 percent of its population under the age of 15;
and it is a whopping 6 percent less than the United States, where 20
percent of the population is under the age of 15. The age group between 15 and 65 accounts for 66 percent of Japan's population. Figure 4.1 shows that this percentage is in line with both the European
Union and the United States.

Finally, a seemingly amazing 20 percent of Japan's population
is 65 years of age or older. This is 3 percent higher than the European Union's level of 17 percent. Most investors think about and
talk about aging demographics in Europe being so bad; meanwhile, Japan's numbers are even worse, especially when you com-

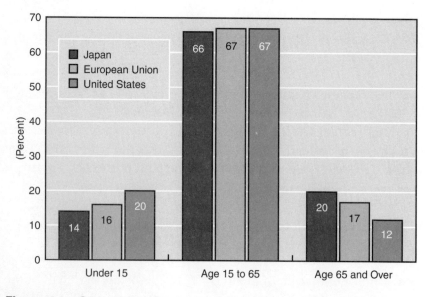

Figure 4.1   Current Age Structure: Japan, European Union, and
United States

pare them with the United States, where only 12 percent of the population is 65 years or older.

Japan has a birthrate of 9.47 births per 1,000 which is less than the European Union birthrate of 10.2 per 1,000 population, and drastically below the United States birthrate of 14.14 births per 1,000.

Japan's death rate is 8.95 deaths per 1,000 population, which is a good deal lower than the European Union's rate of 10.10 deaths per 1,000. It is only slightly higher than the United States death rate, which logs in at 8.25 deaths per 1,000 population.

One of the biggest stories, or should I say lack of story, is in the net migration rate. Japan's net migration rate is zero migrants per 1,000 population. That is correct, zero! In comparison, the European Union's migration rate is 1.5 migrants per 1,000 population, and the United States' net migration rate 3.31 per 1,000 population (see Figure 4.2).

If one story line is the net migration rate, then the other is life expectancy. Life expectancy in Japan is slightly over 81.15 years of

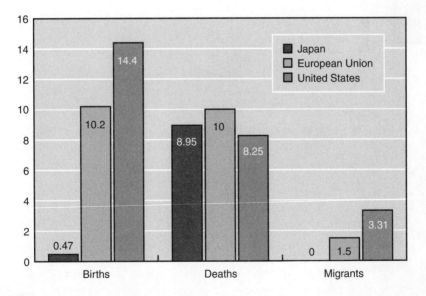

Figure 4.2   Current Births, Deaths, and Migrants per 1,000 Population: Japan, European Union, and United States

age. That is three years longer than the life expectancy in the European Union (78.1 years), and it is three and one-half years longer than the United States life expectancy (77.6 years). For the male population of Japan, life expectancy is 77.86 years. That number greatly outdistances both the European Union and the United States. Life expectancy for the male population in the European Union is 74.9 years, which is just about the same as it is for the United States' males, who log in at 74.8 years. The difference in life expectancy for females is even more dramatic. Japanese females can expect to live 84.61 years. That leaves both the European Union and the United States females in the dust, if you will. Females in the European Union have a life expectancy of 81.4 years, and life expectancy for U.S. females is only 81.0 years (see Figure 4.3).

Japan's infant mortality rate is 3.26 deaths per 1,000 live births. From the European Union's perspective, Japan would only trail one member, Sweden, which has an infant mortality rate of 2.77 deaths per 1,000 live births. But Japan's rate is better than the

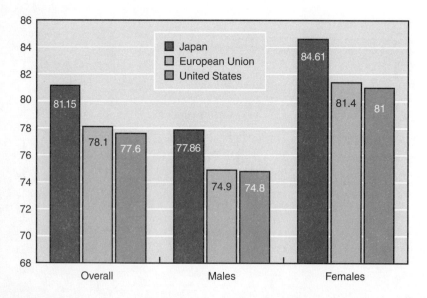

Figure 4.3 Current Life Expectancy: Japan, European Union, and United States

Czech Republic, Finland, and Malta, which are the only other members of the European Union to have an infant mortality rate under 4 deaths per 1,000 live births. The U.S. infant mortality rate is 6.5 deaths per 1,000 live births. Japan is clearly superior in this area.

The literacy rate in Japan is 99 percent which trails just a handful of European countries—Denmark, Finland, and Luxembourg all have perfect literacy rates of 100 percent. Japan is ahead of the United States, which has a literacy rate of 97 percent.

JAPAN IS AGING

As this demographic snapshot of Japan shows, Japan is aging. In many respects, if you are looking for a long life, look no further than Japan. The most recent life expectancy figures are staggering: Japan has the highest life expectancy anywhere in the world. On the flip side, the average number of children Japanese women will bear has reached an all-time low of one child. Because of these two trends, Japan has the most rapidly aging population of any leading industrial country.

As a result, Japan will soon drop out of the Top 10 Most Populous Nations. In 1950, Japan ranked fifth, following China, India, the United States, and Russia. Following Japan were Indonesia, Germany, Brazil, England, and Italy. One century later, we will witness a dramatic shift in the Top 10. By 2050, not only will Japan drop out, but so will Russia, Germany, England, and Italy. The new Top 10 Most Populous nations will look like this: India, China, United States, Pakistan, Indonesia, Nigeria, Brazil, Bangladesh, Ethiopia, and the Congo. The most shocking shift of all is that Japan is not in the Top 10!

The fallout from having the fastest aging population is a shrinking pool of workers to support the benefits received by senior citizens. Even in the best of market times, this demographic trend would be a problem. Because the Japanese equity markets in the past 15 years have experienced anything but the best of times, this trend is causing a real crisis in that nation.

HOW DID JAPAN GET HERE?

To fully understand where Japan is going, it is necessary to understand where Japan has been. The modern-day history of Japan began after World War II, which destroyed almost half of Japan's infrastructure including its industrial and manufacturing capacity. It was against the negative backdrop of this crippled economy that a positive new Japan emerged.

As Japan rushed to rebuild its factories after losing the war, it did so with the latest and greatest state-of-the-art equipment. In a very short time, because of modern technology, Japan was better positioned to compete than were the nations that had been victorious in the war but were still strapped with old machinery in their aging factories.

Japan made some key strategic decisions to invest heavily in the electric utility, steel, auto, and shipping sectors. It was these investments, along with the evolving electronics sector, that formed Japan's early economic base.

Japan fast became the envy of the world with its highly efficient and productive manufacturing base. Add to this a highly skilled and disciplined workforce with an extremely high savings rate, and it is easy to see how in a few decades Japan evolved from economic malaise to become one of the world's economic leaders.

IT JUST KEEPS GETTING OLDER

The real story of Japan today is not about its economy but about its demographics. The bottom line is that Japan is getting older and older. As we have seen from the data, Japan's aging population is hardly unique.

After Japan rebuilt itself after World War II, its older population held fairly steady. In fact, during the entire decade of the 1950s the Japanese population of 65 years or older (senior citizens) remained remarkably constant at 5 percent. The decades that followed, however, witnessed an explosion in this group. This age group doubled in size by the mid-1980s. As we began the new millennium, 17 percent of the Japanese population was 65 or older. By the year 2025, over a quarter of their population will be classified as senior citizens (age 65 or older). The most unique feature of this senior boom is in the speed of its occurrence. In the United States, it took 75 years for the 65-years-or-older group to double from 7 percent to 14 percent. In Japan, it took one-third of the time for the same expansion. Thus, not only will this shift make Japan the world's oldest society, but it will have taken place in a shorter span of time than in any other country anywhere in the world, ever before.

There was nothing magical about how or why this happened. The Japanese were having fewer children at the same time that life expectancy was dramatically improving. A confluence of three trends formed the foundation of fewer children and much smaller families. First, Japanese couples were getting married later. As later marriages boomed, couples had much less time on their biological clock to establish a family; and when those families were established, they were much smaller. Second, Japan is one of the world's most crowded places. When you have a relatively small island with a lot of people, it tends to dampen the desire to add more young ones to an already overcrowded environment. Third, and finally, woman began entering the working world outside the home. With women in the workforce, it changed the dynamics of raising a family and tended to influence those sitting on the fence trying to decide whether to have children, delay having children, or not have children at all.

At the same time that birthrates were dramatically dropping, life expectancy was at all-time highs. In fact, Japan has the highest life expectancy anywhere in the world today. Again, looking back to the years immediately after World War II, life expectancy in Japan for both males and females was 50 years of age. Today, life expectancy for males is approaching 80 years of age, and for females it is an amazing 85 years of age.

This aging population has a dramatic impact on the workforce. In the 1960s and 1970s, most Japanese companies had a mandatory retirement age of 55. In 1990, 20 percent of the Japanese workforce was made up of workers 55 or older. As we began the new millennium, that group accounted for over one quarter of the entire workforce in Japan. Think about this: In the years right after World War II, virtually no one over the age of 55 was working in Japanese companies. Now that age group accounts for over one quarter of the entire workforce.

You don't have to be an analyst or statistician to realize that this shift will put great pressures on any pension system. The even bigger pressure, however, could be on corporate profits, which will come under fire from rapidly rising personnel costs. These costs will continue to spike because, in a majority of Japanese companies, workers' compensation increases with age. Thus, an explosion in age in the workforce will also cause an explosion in salary and payroll costs for most Japanese companies.

It also causes a strain for these senior workers. In 1986, the Japanese government reformed the public pension plan by cutting the benefits and, more important, by moving the age at which benefits begin from 60 years of age to 65 years of age. The problem is a lack of jobs for this age group. There are only so many senior positions; and because of their knowledge and experience, most workers would be in these limited senior (not entry-level) positions. Also, it is financially desirable for Japanese companies to have younger workers because they are paid less and thus have a much smaller negative effect on a company's bottom line.

Any aging population presents unique problems for companies as well as for individuals trying to supplement inadequate public pension incomes.

THE POPULATION DENSITY FACTOR

Part of the aging phenomenon in Japan is due to the decline in birthrates, and part of that decline is due to how crowded it is in Japan. The technical term for the ratio of the population to land space is called *population density*—the number of people for every square mile of land. Looking at Japan and China, the economic engines of Asia, we can get a sense of just how crowded it is in Japan.

On the one hand, there are 308 Chinese for every square mile in China. On the other hand, there are 847 Japanese for every square mile in Japan, which makes it three times as crowded. To give you some perspective, the United States has but 70 residents for every square mile. The largest economy in Europe, Germany, has 608 people per square mile. (Japan, however, is not the most crowded country in Asia from a population density standpoint. South Korea has that dubious distinction with 1,119 residents per square mile.) What is important to understand about the population density issue is that its impact goes far beyond just birthrates and an aging population.

Population density can do strange things to demographic patterns. If the United States population density equaled that of Germany, it would place the total U.S. population at a little over 2.2 billion or almost twice as large as China's. On the flip side, if Germany had a population density as low as that of the United States, its total population would be barely 10 million people, roughly the size of Hungary, Belgium, or Portugal.

It was this population density that caused real estate values to skyrocket in Japan. Remember that inflation is caused by too much money chasing too few goods. Likewise, too many people chasing too few houses can cause real estate inflation. Owning a home in the central city became out of reach for most Japanese. And while demographic trends evolve and change over time, one trend that will remain constant in Japan is its geographic size. This characteristic will tend to keep population density figures extremely high, with a propensity to inflate real estate, even though some years and decades will not be as inflated as others.

Between the 1950s and the 1980s (a 30-year period), urban land prices increased only 15 percent. Then in the 1980s, in one decade, urban land prices doubled. For many families, housing in the central cities of these major urban areas became too expensive. More and more citizens had to live further away, which in turn lengthened the commute time, and two-hour daily commutes each way were not uncommon.

Another interesting perspective on population density is parkland. Even though Japan has a good deal of forest land, its natural acreage does not translate into city parks. In fact, Japan has much smaller and far fewer city parks than both the United States and the European Union.

WHAT IS AGING?

In terms of demographics, an entire population ages when the average age of a country's population gets older. This is a simple concept and is occurring in a lot more places than Japan.

It is the "why" part that is important. Several factors and issues tend to come together to influence why a country ages. First, population aging occurs when a country's fertility rate declines. The fertility rate of a population is the number of births per woman. The key number here is 2.1.

Anything below 2.1 children per woman is considered sub-replacement fertility: The 2.1 children per woman formula includes 2 children to replace the parents and one-tenth of a child to make up for early deaths of children and women.

Thus, when a country's fertility rate declines, the ratio of older people to younger people will rise.

The second factor that fuels an aging population is increasing life expectancy. Both Japan and parts of Western Europe are most affected by this aging population concept. Within the next 20 years, the largest demographic group will be those over the age of 65 and the country's average age will approach 50 years of age as well.

The United States, Canada, and Australia all have subreplacement fertility rates. However, they offset the low rates with high rates of immigration, which is why their populations are still growing.

THE IMPACT OF AGING

Aging cannot be looked at in isolation; it impacts the economy and government spending as well. From a purely economic perspective, older people are more inclined to save money than to spend it, which will lead to lower interest rates and little, if any, inflation.

Pension systems come under pressure in periods of population aging, with more people retiring and less people working to pay the retirees' benefits.

Health care, one of the biggest expenditures for most governments, comes under pressure as well. When a population ages dramatically, it forces a government to spend more and more on health care. Thus, governments have a double burden: Do they increase taxes to help pay for these health care costs (not a popular political move with an aging population living on a fixed income), or do they cut some of the government-provided health care benefits? Maybe they will have to take funding from other budget items such as education. Certainly an aging population with fewer young people does not need education spending at the same level as a younger population with more education needs.

Here is a final spending paradox: A majority of crimes are committed by people between the age of 15 and 25. Where the population is aging, with fewer people between the age of 15 to 25, crime rates fall. However, that doesn't necessarily translate to less spending on police matters. The reason is that safety and law and order are at the top of the list of most senior citizens' concerns. So governments may still be required to spend more on police even though the ratio of older people to young people should result in less crime and less spending on crime-related issues.

OLD-AGE DEPENDENCY

Maybe the best way to put this all into perspective is by looking at it through an old-age dependency focus. Japan's population currently enjoys the longest life expectancy anywhere in the world. The percentage of senior citizens, age 65 or over, in Japan's working population, is one of the highest in the entire world. When these factors are added together, it means that the age distribution of Japan's population must shift dramatically. By 2025, there will be one Japanese senior citizen for every two persons of working age, which will result in Japan having the highest old-age dependency ratio of any industrialized country in the world.

A country's population dependency ratio is used as an index to express the level of support. The old-age dependency ratio is calculated by dividing the aged population (65 or older) by the population of the working-age group (aged 15 to 65).

In the year 2000, the old-age dependency ratio for Japan was 26 percent. That meant 3.9 workers in Japan were supporting each senior citizen. That number was not that far out of whack with the rest of the industrialized world. The largest economy in Europe, Germany, had an old-age dependency ratio of 25 percent. And the largest economy in the world, the United States, had an old-age dependency ratio of 21 percent in 2000.

But the real story lies in where these old-age dependency ratios are going in the next 25 years. By the year 2025, the U.S. old-age dependency ratio will increase from its 20 percent level in 2000 to 33 percent. Germany's old-age dependency ratio will climb from its 25 percent level to 36 percent. But in Japan, the old-age dependency ratio is about to explode from 26 percent in 2000 to 47 percent in

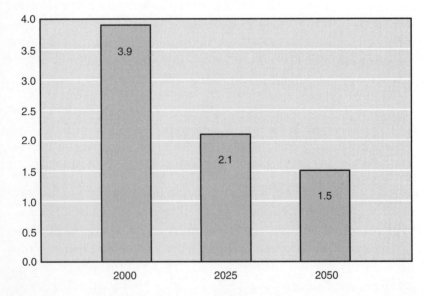

Figure 4.4 Japan's Old-Age Dependency Ratio (Number of Workers Supporting Each Citizen Aged 65 or Older)

the year 2025. Remember, when old-age dependency approaches 50 percent, only two workers are supporting every one senior citizen. But it doesn't stop there. Look what happens next. Twenty-five years later, by 2050, Japan's old-age dependency ratio will be above 67 percent. That means there will only be 1.5 workers supporting every one senior citizen (see Figure 4.4).

JAPAN'S LIFE EXPECTANCY

Let's take a closer look at the "axis of evil" in demographics that causes a country to have an aging population: Life expectancy rises, fertility rates decline, and migration is nonexistent. Let's focus first on life expectancy.

In 1950, Japanese life expectancy was only 56 years of age, whereas in the United States, it was 66 years of age. But today, Japanese life expectancy is 81, and in the United States it is 77. Somewhere during the past 50 some years, life expectancy numbers crossed and now Japan has the highest life expectancy in the world. How did that happen?

Several factors coalesced to push Japan's life expectancy higher:

- Infectious and chronic diseases no longer cause as many premature deaths.
- Sanitation and general quality-of-life issues have improved.
- Preventive health care is much better, with a more nutritious diet, adequate exercise, and the avoidance of smoking or drinking excessively.
- Housing and general living conditions have improved.
- An improved health care system has created new treatments, medicines, and health care regimens that make people healthier than ever before.

Put all those factors together and they add up to an increase in life expectancy.

JAPAN'S FERTILITY

Before I focus on the drop in Japan's fertility rate or "birth bust," I want to put it into perspective by looking at the Japanese baby boom. Yes, that's right, they had one, too. The Japanese baby boom was very short; in fact, it only lasted three years from 1947 through 1949. Between 1947 and 1949, almost 3 million children were born every year. Thus, the Japanese baby boom lasted three years and produced less than 9 million children. The United States' baby boom lasted 19 years (1946 to 1964) and produced 76 million children.

After a short-lived baby boom between 1947 and 1949, Japanese fertility decreased by more than 50 percent over the next decade. This was the most dramatic drop in fertility in recorded history.

The Japanese economy was basically nonexistent until 1950. In that year, Japanese per capita income was $153. Back then, Mexico's per capita income was $181; so from an economic perspective, Japan was at the bottom looking up to the likes of Mexico. Meanwhile, per capita income in the United States, at $1,883, was more than 10 times higher than Japan's per capita income. So, in 1950, as Japan's economy began to rise, fertility began to fall.

In the early 1950s, fertility declines were achieved through abortion. In fact, over 75 percent of all pregnancies in the first half of the 1950s ended in abortion. In the second half of that same decade, over 50 percent of all pregnancies ended in abortion. In the first half of the 1960s, pregnancies were being prevented with contraceptives.

Because of this dramatic decline of fertility in the 1950s, Japan was able to save a lot. And when you save a lot as a nation, you quickly accumulate a good deal of capital.

FERTILITY AND JAPAN'S ECONOMIC BOOM

With all this capital because of a high rate of savings in the 1950s, 1960 came in with a bang. Japanese per capita income was growing at close to 10 percent a year. The economy likewise was growing at almost 10 percent a year. These growth rates lasted throughout the 1960s.

It was just about that time, in the 1960s, that those Japanese baby boomers from 1947 to 1949 were coming into the workforce, and with so many of them, labor became very cheap. In addition to the increase in cheaper labor, more wealth had been accumulated throughout the 1950s. The international trade picture was improving and demand for Japanese-made products was soaring. By the end of the 1960s, Japan's per capita income was now the second highest in the world, trailing only the United States.

SINGLE BOOM

In the 1950s, Japanese fertility rates dropped through abortion and contraceptives. Enter the 1960s and other factors came into play. One of them is that Japanese women were staying single longer. In short, Japanese marriage patterns began to change.

Currently, over 50 percent of Japanese women in their late 20s are single. A decade ago, only 40 percent of Japanese women in their late 20s were single. And a decade prior to that, only 30 percent of Japanese women in their late 20s were single.

This big change in values is being driven by both education and employment opportunities. A larger number of Japanese women are now receiving a college education. More and more women are being hired, and because of this boom in female employment, the pay differences between male and female employees have all but disappeared.

As these women then get promoted and make even more money, they move up the corporate ladder. They also have more financial autonomy and less economic need to get married right away.

LATER CHILDREN

Another factor driving lower fertility is that Japanese women are waiting longer after marriage to have children. The average interval between marriage and having a first child was under 1½ years a decade ago. Now that number has grown to over 2½ years. It stands to reason that if women are waiting longer to get married and then are waiting even longer after marriage to have their first child, fertility rates have nowhere to go but down.

MIGRATION

Recall that migration is the long-term or permanent movement either into or out of a country. Immigration means "in-migration" into a country. Immigration becomes important if life expectancy is rising and fertility rates are falling, as in Japan, and you have a rapidly aging population, also as in Japan. Young immigrants then present a possible solution. In Japan, however, immigration is basically nonexistent.

The Japanese society is 99 percent ethnically pure. Only 1 percent of its population consists of immigrants, mainly Chinese and Koreans. The Japanese society is also pure linguistically—99 percent of the population speaks Japanese.

The Japanese government does not acknowledge the full citizenship of many foreigners who have lived in Japan for generations. Only children born in Japan to married parents, both holding Japanese citizenship, are considered "naturally Japanese" and can be entered into the family's *koseki* (Japanese family tree spanning generations).

KOSEKI

The significance of koseki is that if you are not in it, you really don't exist in Japan, which means that you are not eligible for any government programs or benefits.

Here is how the koseki works: The laws in Japan require that every household must report every birth, death, marriage, divorce, and criminal conviction to the local government. The local government then compiles the information into a detailed family tree for everyone in its jurisdiction. The koseki fills the role that birth certificates, death certificates, marriage licenses, and the census play in other countries. In Japan, the koseki puts it all at your fingertips.

Japan does not issue birth certificates to authenticate a person's identity because each Japanese person has an entry in their family koseki. A non-Japanese may not be noted in a koseki, even if married to a Japanese (although now some local government municipalities are compromising by allowing such marriages to be recorded in the "notes" section of the koseki).

Most government services cannot be rendered without authentication and the only way to be authenticated is to have an entry in a koseki.

MINORITIES

Because of this homogeneous ideology, Japanese society has been intolerant of ethnic and other differences. Thus, people who are not ethnic Japanese will not find acceptance as full members of society.

Because Japanese citizenship is based on the nationality of the parent rather than the place of birth, subsequent generations are not automatically Japanese. In fact, they have to be naturalized to claim citizenship despite being born, raised, and educated in Japan. This has been the case with most Koreans in Japan.

ECONOMIC IMPACT

Now that we have a clear view of the aging population trend of Japan, let's see what kind of impact an aging population will have on a country's economy.

If a country's working-age population is getting smaller, then a country's potential for economic growth must also get smaller. The broadest measure of a nation's economy is its gross domestic product (GDP). The GDP is the sum of a country's labor force times the average production per worker. So if a country has a shrinking number of workers, their economy is soon going to shrink as well. The only way around it is for productivity to rise faster than the labor force declines.

From a historical perspective, for a 20-year period in Japan from 1970 to 1990, the expanding labor force added 1 percent a year to Japan's gross domestic product. That stopped in the 1990s, which is one of the main reasons the Japanese economy stopped in the 1990s as well. Now Japan's labor force is actually declining. In fact, for the next 50 years, from 2000 to 2050, Japan's workforce will decline each year on average between 0.7 and 0.9 percent. Thus, the aging of Japan will have a negative influence on its economy.

FISCAL IMPACT

Now let's consider the potential fiscal impact that the aging population may have in Japan.

First, a little perspective: Japan's public finances worsened dramatically in the 1990s, which now makes dealing with its aging population even more challenging. Tax revenues across the board spiraled lower when the housing and stock market bubbles both burst at the same time. To make matters worse, in an attempt to recover from those bursting bubbles, government expenditures rose to stimulate the economy, especially through infrastructure and big public works projects. As if that was not bad enough, they had to pay for the costs of the Japanese government having to assume the financial liabilities of numerous failed financial services companies.

There is at least one bright spot. The government pension system still runs a surplus and controls a huge amount of assets. It is a little over 50 percent of Japan's gross domestic product. Except for its social security system, the general government deficit of Japan is close to 10 percent of GDP. Furthermore, net debt is now equal to total GDP, or looked at another way, net debt is now 100 percent, making it the highest for any industrialized country on the face of the earth.

REFORM

The Japanese government is trying to prepare for this aging population crisis. In March 2000, Japan adopted a pension reform that unbelievably contained provisions to slash pension benefits by more than 20 percent for future retirees. This will be accomplished through three factors. The first factor is an across-the-board 4 percent reduction in benefit levels. Second is a step-up increase in pension eligibility from 60 years of age to 65 that will start in 2013. Third is the indexing of future pension increases to the consumer price index instead of to disposable income.

In addition, the Japanese government's transfers to the social security system have just been raised to one-half of the basic pension benefits. It used to be one-third. This increase from one-third to one-half has reduced the Japanese government's unfunded pension liability by a third. But that is not enough. Japan will have to continue along this path of contribution rate increases to prevent social security assets from being depleted. To make matters worse, major structural reforms will be needed to get a handle on exploding health care expenditures.

RETIREMENT CRISIS

Japan's retirement crisis can only be solved in a couple of ways. The Japanese government can raise taxes, which is an unlikely choice as the Japanese economic recovery remains extremely fragile. Second, companies could increase their retirement contribution levels. This is not very likely either as very few, if any, Japanese companies have the free cash flow to absorb this additional burden. Third, and finally, they could shift more of the burden onto the employees. This is exactly what will happen.

Japan has to look no further than the United States or England for two primary examples about what to do with the pension system. Both the United States and England have moved from a defined benefit to a defined contribution system. As companies in both England and the United States made this shift, they placed more of the burden on the individual employee. For Japanese businesses to embrace this model, Japanese employees must have some incentive to become more responsible for their retirement. The most likely incentive will be a series of tax breaks and tax incentives for individuals to participate in defined contribution systems.

This system must be adapted to fit the profile of Japanese employees. In the United States, the 401(k) defined contribution model provides the employee with an almost unlimited choice of investment options. In addition, the employee assumes full responsibility. In England, there is considerably less choice. Also in England, the individual companies are still actively involved in determining the appropriate asset allocation levels for employees. Japan will most likely embrace the English model because individual Japanese investors are less experienced than individual investors in the United States. Thus, there will be a reluctance to let them go off completely on their own.

"OLD" ECONOMY VERSUS "NEW" ECONOMY

An aging population like Japan's can have a very different ending if the employee is working under the old economy model or is embracing the new economy model. The key difference lies in the role and the impact of productivity. The term *productivity* refers to the output (or stuff) that is created (in terms of goods produced or services rendered) per unit of input (how much labor, people, and hours) used. Everyone knows why productivity is important to business. If a business improves its productivity, it means that it will have lower costs and a business that has lower costs is better positioned to compete and increase profits.

What we sometimes don't focus enough on is the impact productivity has on the overall economy, which equates to the impact productivity can have on society.

Increases in productivity will also improve the standard of living. In addition, productivity improvements create income opportunities. And when new income opportunities are created, the economy grows.

Old Economy Model

The so-called old economy model is centered on manufacturing, which usually means mass production. With mass production, there tends to be mass consumption as well. Under this old economy model, products tend to have very long product life cycles. Where productivity is concerned in an old economy model, workers' productivity generally stays at current levels with no big swing up or down. Think of it as the status quo.

In this model, workers receive better than average and, for the most part, high wages. In addition to high wages, they also have job security. The best examples of the industries of the old economy model would be the steel industry, the airline industry, and the automotive industry.

New Economy Model

The new economy model is just the opposite. It is an information-based economy, and technology is the foundation of any information-based economy. This model is centered on flexibility in production schedules and in the products that will be produced. All these decisions are based on the information about what products and services consumers are likely to buy.

The need to focus on innovations to improve products puts new and different pressures on the workforce. Workers in the new economy feel the impact of two key changes. First, they must constantly upgrade and improve their skills and ability. A consequence of this constant focus on improving skills is that while your productivity is improving, you are also making yourself a candidate for a different job at a different company. The second factor is that workers now must adjust to extremely flexible and changing production schedules. Nothing is for certain anymore.

Industry examples of this so-called new economy would be technology, telecommunications, and biotechnology.

THE AMERICAN FARMER

The old economy/new economy debate is critical for Japan because aging in each of these two economic models will have a different impact on the overall economy. When a new economy greatly changes and influences consumption patterns and production schedules, it also changes the importance of the old-age dependency that demographic experts are so worried about.

The single best example of what I am talking about is what happened to the American farmer. In 1900, more than one-third (37.6 percent) of the American workforce worked in agriculture. It took almost 40 percent of the entire workforce of the United States to feed the United States. That was an old economy model.

In the new economy, the American farmer has gone high-tech. And it's not just by using all the latest and greatest pieces of farm equipment that can do the work of 10 men. There were other technological improvements as well. Because of this new information-based economy, farmers are now better equipped to protect their crops from disease and pests. This, in turn, has led to a dramatic improvement in crop yields. Today less than 2 percent of the American workforce is agriculturally based. And these few workers are not just feeding the entire United States; they are feeding people around the world as well.

So, should we focus on the number of people (workers) on the farm or should we be more focused on what the farm produces? Agriculture is not the only industry where these trends exist. Just about every industry is using some form of technology and information to boost productivity. More and more processes everywhere are becoming automated, and if we continue to boost productivity, it means that fewer workers can support a larger number of old-age dependents.

The new economy is driven by productivity, which means the ratio of individual workers to senior citizens is not as important as it once was. In the new economy model, we should be focusing on the output of workers, not the number of workers, to determine if the aging population is a problem. Maybe one of the most famous one-liners in U.S. presidential politics applies here. It was former President Bill Clinton's close political advisor and strategist who made this catchy one-liner famous. What James Carville said was, "It's the economy, stupid."

So what does all this mean? It means that productivity improvements can create other new and exciting economic growth. Instead of focusing on how to maintain the old-age dependency ratio, Japan should instead be focusing on how to restructure its economy to raise productivity.

NEW JAPAN LIFE CYCLE

In this new economy model, everything changes, even the employee's life cycle. The old economy life cycle of stable and secure employment with one company until retirement doesn't apply anymore. Instead, there will be numerous jobs and numerous careers, some of them intermittent. The one constant will be the continuous education, training, and development of old and new skills and abilities.

There will be more mixing of part-time and full-time jobs, and retirement may not be absolute but more gradual. The traditional life cycle is gone; the lines will be blurred as people transition into retirement.

For this new life cycle to work effectively, the Japanese government must make some changes. It needs to embrace and support the creation of new companies, and it has to stop supporting and bailing out failed companies and industries. It also must push for the creation of more part-time positions and contractor and subcontractor positions as well.

Japanese businesses have to play a key role. The labor market needs more flexibility. Because Japan is still too centered on seniority-based promotions and advancement, businesses do not use the skills of the current workforce as effectively as possible. In addition, these policies stop workers from flowing into other more productive subindustries.

In Japan, lateral movement within the same company is almost nonexistent. This must change. Corporations must recruit more midlevel people to work on focused short-term projects.

INTERNATIONAL TRADE

With the possible solution to Japan's aging population being the country's economy, it is more important than ever to take a close look at key areas, the first being international trade.

Because of its relatively small size geographically, Japan has always looked beyond its borders to do business. It wasn't always easy. After World War II, Japanese products had a poor reputation for quality that led to very low trading. Who wants to buy inferior products? The trend began to change in the mid-1960s; and by the late 1960s and early 1970s, it had reversed itself completely. Japanese companies have adopted the strictest quality control measures around the globe, and their high standards led to a turn-around in manufacturing. All of a sudden, automobiles, televisions, and semiconductors made in Japan had the highest quality standard anywhere. Japan had become the quality leader, and trade exploded. In the 1960s, exports grew at an annual rate of 17 percent, and in the decade of the 1970s, trade grew annually at an astounding 21 percent. Japan had one of the largest trade surpluses anywhere in the world.

However, trade deficits aren't necessarily bad, and trade surpluses aren't always good.

One has to go all the way back to the historical roots for why nations wanted to trade in the first place. The simple answer was gold. The strategy was straightforward—export a lot (sell things for gold) and import very little (to avoid using gold to buy things). That strategy ensured that the kingdom would have plenty of gold. And if there was plenty of gold, the kingdom could develop a great army and the royal family would become extremely wealthy as well.

The problem with this misguided strategy was that while it was great for the king to have all the gold that he could horde, such a situation led to poverty outside the royal castle. In fact, a case can be made that this misguided strategy of all exports and no imports led to the beginning of the end of royalty ruling the world.

A trade surplus that promotes exports while constantly letting the importing consumer lag behind is a formula for disaster today, just as it was in medieval times. The future of Japan depends on developing a balance that allows the importing consumer to emerge as an equally important link in the trading boom that historically has fueled Japan's growth.

BANK REFORM

The quickest way to jump-start importing consumers is to instill consumer confidence, and there is no better way to establish consumer confidence than to strengthen the nation's banking system. In 1998, the Financial System Reform Law was enacted in Japan. This reform will deregulate and energize the banking, insurance, and brokerage sectors by opening them up to foreign investment and ownership while implementing a series of regulatory reforms.

This so called Big Bang reform of the financial markets in Japan allowed individual Japanese investors to invest in non-yen-denominated investments that would provide higher returns. The name was derived from the explosion of Japanese assets that would start flowing into other countries, especially the United States, in search of higher yielding investments.

The bank bailouts that were put in place to fix Japan's ailing banking system were a major part of this reform package. Called the *Bank Revitalization Law,* this legislation called for the infusion of public taxpayers' money into the failing and beleaguered banks as well as the nationalization of insolvent banks. Close to $100 billion in taxpayers' money has been spent to prop up the failing banking system. The banks that did not want to accept the strings attached to the public money looked for other sources of capital infusion in the form of bank mergers. When the Japanese government opened the financial and banking sector to foreign investment and ownership, the Japanese government was actually encouraging the merger of weak banks as well as the outright purchase of the nationalized insolvent banks. The reason was simple. It wanted to limit the taxpayers' cost of this bank revitalization program.

The Long Term Credit Bank of Japan was one of the first banks to be nationalized. A U.S. investment firm ultimately purchased it. After the Long Term Credit Bank deal, the floodgates opened and a series of major and strategic mergers rapidly changed the structure of the banking system. Fuji Bank, Dai-Ichi Kangyo Bank, and the Industrial Bank of Japan decided to join forces to create the world's largest bank, with over 140 trillion yen in assets. Sumitomo and Sakura merged as well making them the second largest bank in the world, with 99 trillion yen in assets. And the banking landscape continues to evolve. Now Mitsubishi Tokyo Financial Group has acquired UFJ Holdings so Mitsubishi Tokyo Financial Group with assets of 190 trillion yen is the largest bank in the world.

The historical significance of all this is mind-boggling. Japan is a proud business community and does not take failure lightly. Japanese bank reform was a public admission that the entire banking system had failed. By setting its proud tradition to the side, Japan addressed its most serious problem in a most compelling way. It let the poorly managed, bad banks fail. The banks that could be saved, the government helped bail out. And finally, it encouraged mergers and acquisitions to create even stronger banks. Its bank reform strategy almost mirrors a similar strategy the United States adopted in the early 1980s when it bailed out its savings and loan institutions in one of the biggest financial crises ever. Back then, no one wanted to invest in a U.S. financial services company. Today, U.S. financial services companies are the envy of the world. I expect a similar result for Japan. Its financial system has already risen from the ashes, and 20 years from now, it will regain its place as one of the soundest financial services industries anywhere in the world.

SAVINGS BOOM

After consumer confidence is restored by fixing the ailing banking system, consumers still need to save and invest money. Enter the Japanese Post Office. Post offices around the world are not all the same. In the United States, the post office is used solely for delivering mail. In Japan, the post office—besides carrying the mail—has an investment product called postal savings accounts. These are, in essence, time deposits that pay guaranteed rates of return of 6 percent or more. In addition to delivering the mail, the Japanese post office lets you invest in its postal savings account. A decade ago when the Japanese stock market was crashing and interest rates were soaring, investors flocked to the post office not to mail letters but to get in on the best investment deal around—a time deposit with guaranteed returns of 6 percent or more. These time deposit accounts had a duration of 10 years.

Because this rush started a decade ago, we are about to witness an explosion in cash as these time deposits come due. Over the next two years, hundreds of thousands of postal savings accounts will mature with a value of more than $3 trillion yen. Investors can then decide to put the money in another time deposit at the post office or they may look for higher investment returns on their money. Or they might decide to spend some of the money. The answer is probably a little bit of each. This newfound pot of gold at the post office should provide strong fundamental support for both the Japanese stock market and the Japanese economy, which, in turn, addresses the aging population crisis in Japan. And with the recent landslide victory of Prime Minister Koizumi, these postal savings accounts will be privatized as well. Many investors don't realize it, but the combination of the insurance aspects (guarantees) of the postal system with the actual savings accounts has made the Japanese Postal Service system one of the world's largest financial institutions. Not anymore; it is time to get back to the basics of simply delivering the mail.

THE WORLD'S OLDEST NATION

There is no stopping the demographics of Japan. By the year 2025, the proportion of the Japanese population aged 65 or older will be higher than any other age category. That will make Japan the oldest nation in the world.

How can this be? Why is everyone talking about the U.S. aging baby boomers when Japan is becoming the oldest nation? Keep in mind why this is happening. Even though the United States is aging, in relative terms, the United States will be much younger than Japan. The reason is the baby boom difference. After World War II, the baby boom only lasted three years in Japan, from 1947 to 1949, whereas in the United States the baby boom lasted 19 years, from 1946 to 1964. Nineteen years versus three years makes a big difference in the next century.

OLD AND HEALTHY

In demographic studies, old age is a net negative because, as a population ages, it places more demands on the health care system. As people age, even with improved health care, physical problems increase.

But what would happen if you were healthy and old at the same time? That is exactly what is going on in Japan today.

For the first time ever, the World Health Organization is measuring "healthy" life expectancy. Previously, all we ever looked at was life expectancy. This demographic indicator is actually called *Disability Adjusted Life Expectancy* (DALE). Here is how DALE works: It summarizes the expected number of years to be living in what would be considered "full health" and subtracts from that the number of years of ill health to come up with a healthy life expectancy figure.

DALE takes into account not just a person's age but the health issues of blindness, paralysis, malaria, cancer, heart disease, crime, and violence.

The DALE system doesn't measure life expectancy based simply on the average number of years a person is expected to live. People don't live all those years in good health. At some point in life, people develop some level of disability. These years with disability are then weighted according to their level of severity to estimate the total equivalent lost years of good health. Subtracting this result from total life expectancy gives the number of years the person can expect to live a healthy life.

Eight of the Top 10 countries based on healthy life expectancy are in Europe: They are France, Sweden, Spain, Italy, Greece, Switzerland, Monaco, and Andorra (Andorra is a small landlocked principality bordered between Spain and France, with only 70,000 citizens). The country with the second highest healthy life expectancy is Australia (see Table 4.1).

But here are two surprises: First, the United States did not make the Top 10 or even the Top 20; its rank is 24. The second surprise is that the top-ranking country in healthy life expectancy is Japan. A key reason that Japan is number one is its low rate of heart disease, which is associated with the citizens' traditional low-fat diet.

So if you are both old and healthy, does that change things? I think it does; before now, this was an overlooked trend that will have a great impact on how we analyze aging populations in the future. The health of that aging population can have as big an impact as the age itself.

Senior citizens are a vital resource to an economy. If they stay healthy longer, they become even more vital. These are not simply

Table 4.1 The Top 10 Nations: Disability-Adjusted Life Expectancy (Healthy Life Expectancy)

Rank	Country	Healthy Years
1	Japan	74.5
2	Australia	73.2
3	France	73.1
4	Sweden	73.0
5	Spain	72.8
6	Italy	72.7
7	Greece	72.5
8	Switzerland	72.5
9	Monaco	72.4
10	Andorra	72.3

senior citizens—they are volunteers, grandparents (child-care providers), and caregivers. All these activities add economic value.

People who are healthier longer, volunteer longer, provide child-care services longer, and are caregivers longer, and if they do all that longer, they will also stay a consumer longer, which means there are still investment opportunities in the land of the setting sun! You just have to know where to look.

CHAPTER FIVE

GLOBAL SHIFT 4: NAPOLEON WAS RIGHT

THE CHINESE CONSUMER GENERATION

Some 200 years ago, Napoleon III likened China to a "sleeping lion" and warned that when China awakes "she will shake the world." Now awakening from a long economic hibernation, China is certainly shaking the entire world, especially Chinese consumers. Within 10 years, these Chinese consumers will replace U.S. consumers as the largest and most important buying group anywhere in the world. All it takes is money. Today only four million Chinese consumers earn more than $10,000 per year. Within 10 years, over 150 million Chinese consumers will earn over $10,000 annually. Maybe what Napoleon should have said is that when the Chinese consumer awakes, it will change the world!

CHINA AND CONSUMERS

There are two parts to this global shift: China and consumers, Together, they are fueling this dramatic shift.

CHINA PERSPECTIVE

Many people seem unaware that China is one of the world's oldest civilizations. Its history has been marked by violent dynasty changes, war and peace, and territorial divisions and then reunifications.

For centuries, China was one of the world's most advanced civilizations, especially from a technological standpoint. It also was the most dominant cultural influence on both Asia and Europe. But eventually China weakened and fell behind economically and politically.

As the nineteenth century began, China was too weak to stop the Japanese invasion of China. The Imperial Monarchy (where the head of state holds their office for life) ended when the Republic of China was established in 1912. Then, in 1949, the Chinese Civil War ended when the Communists claimed victory over the Republic of China's government. In that same year, the Communist Party established the People's Republic of China, which has since governed China's mainland. The People's Republic of China assumed sovereignty over Hong Kong in 1997.

The defeated government of the Republic of China fled the mainland and retreated to Taiwan. The Republic of China has been governing Taiwan since the end of World War II; however, the government now refers to and characterizes itself simply as *Taiwan*.

Meanwhile, the People's Republic of China does not recognize the Republic of China and claims to represent all of China, including Taiwan, as a result of its victory in China's Civil War. The matter of Taiwan's independence and China's reunification with the island remains a deeply divided political issue.

CONSUMER PERSPECTIVE

In economic circles, a *consumer* is an individual or a group of individuals who consume goods and services in an economy. Consumers are thought to have a budgeted income that they can spend on any number of different goods or services available in an economy. It is assumed that consumers will behave rationally and will spend their budget only on goods and services that best fill their needs. In addition to buying goods and services, consumers also should invest part of their budget to increase future spending power.

The biggest change with consumers is the way that the business world now views them. Consumers used to be looked at globally as a commodity—simply a group that either buys something or doesn't buy something. There was never much individuality among consumers.

That has all changed, and it is no longer sufficient for businesses to recognize that they have consumers; they need to know their consumers' demographics. Where do they come from? How old are they? How many are men, and how many are women? Marketers must ask and answer many similar questions.

This push for consumer segmentation and customized marketing has everyone focused on the same consumers. No matter what you want to sell to what age group with whatever demographic features, chances are you will find more of them in China than anywhere else in the world. The 1.3 billion Chinese consumers represent the greatest consumption bubble in the history of time.

CURRENT DEMOGRAPHICS OF CHINA

The overall population in China is 1,306,313,812, the largest in the world. Put into perspective, China's population is 3 times larger than the 25-country European Union, which has a population of 450 million. It is 4 times larger than the United States, with its population of a little under 300 million; and it is more than 10 times larger than Japan's population of 127 million people (see Figure 5.1).

China's population growth rate is 0.58 percent, a little more than half the population growth rate of the United States (0.90 percent). However, it is almost three times faster than the European Union's growth rate of 0.20 percent, and it is almost 12 times higher than Japan's growth rate of 0.05 percent.

The age groups break down in China as follows: 21 percent of its population is under 15 years of age, which puts it just ahead of

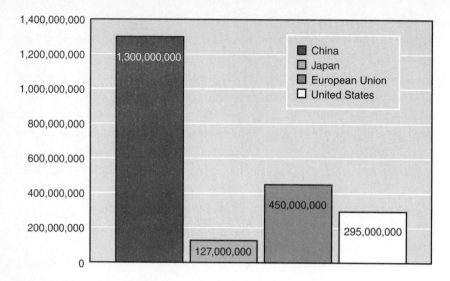

Figure 5.1 Current Total Population Comparisons: China, Japan, European Union, and United States

the United States (20 percent under age 15) and 5 percent ahead of the entire European Union (16 percent under 15).

Seventy-one percent of China's population is between the ages of 15 and 65, which is 4 percent higher than both the United States and the European Union and 5 percent higher than Japan (see Figure 5.2).

Only 8 percent of China's population is aged 65 years or older, 4 percent less than the United States, where 12 percent is 65 or older. It is 9 percent less than the European Union, where 17 percent is 65 or older. Last, it is amazingly 12 percent lower than Japan, where 20 percent of the population is 65 years of age or older.

China has a birthrate of 13.14 births per 1,000 population, exactly one birth per 1,000 lower than the United States, which has a rate of 14.14 births per 1,000 population, and almost 3 births higher per 1,000 population than the European Union, which has 10.2 births per 1,000 population. It is almost 4 births more per 1,000 population than Japan, which has a birthrate of 9.47 births per 1,000 population.

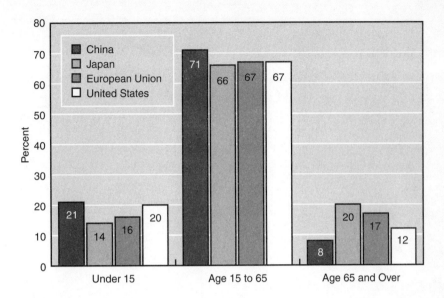

Figure 5.2 Current Age Structure: China, Japan, European Union, and United States

China's death rate is only 6.94 deaths per 1,000 population. That is lower than the U.S. rate of 8.25 deaths per 1,000 population and also lower than Japan's 8.95 deaths per 1,000 population. It is more than 3 deaths per 1,000 population lower than the European Union's 10.0 deaths per 1,000 population.

The net migration rate for China is negative at −0.40 migrants per 1,000 population, which is virtually at the other end of the spectrum from the United States with its net migration rate of 3.31 migrants per 1,000 population. China's net migration rate is even lower than Japan's zero migrants per 1,000 population rate. It is also at the other end of the spectrum from the European Union, which has a net migration rate of 1.5 migrants per 1,000 population (see Figure 5.3).

Life expectancy in China is only 72.27 years or almost 10 years less than the Japanese life expectancy of 81.15 years. It is 5 years lower than the United States life expectancy of 77.6 years, and almost 6 full years lower than the European Union's 78.1 year level.

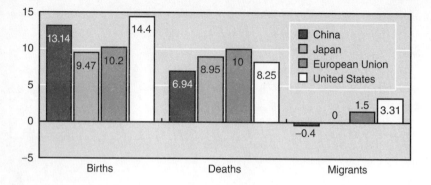

Figure 5.3 Current Births, Deaths, and Migrants per 1,000 Population: China, Japan, European Union, and United States

Within the entire European Union, only three countries have a life expectancy rate worse than China: Estonia, Latvia, and Hungary (see Figure 5.4).

Life expectancy for the male population is only 70.65 years, which is 7 years less than the life expectancy for the male population of Japan, which is 77.86 years. It is 4 years less than the life ex-

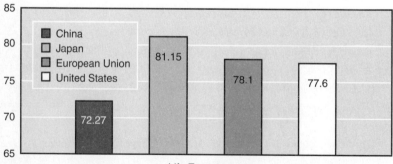

Figure 5.4 Current Life Expectancy: China, Japan, European Union, and United States

pectancy level for the male population of the European Union and the United States, where the rates are 74.9 years and 74.8 years, respectively.

The female population life expectancy is 74.09 years or more than 10 years lower than the female life expectancy rate of Japan at 84.61 years. It is also 7 years less than the female population in both the European Union and the United States which both have life expectancy levels for females above 81 years of age. In the United States, life expectancy for females is exactly 81 years of age and in the European Union it is 81.4 years.

China has an infant mortality of an almost unheard of 24.18 deaths per 1,000 live births. The U.S. infant mortality rate is 6.5 deaths per 1,000 live births, which means that China's rate is 4 times higher than the United States. Of the 25-member European Union, only two countries—Hungary and Poland—have infant mortality rates higher than 8 deaths per 1,000 live births (see Figure 5.5).

Literacy in China is only 90.9 percent. In Japan, it is 99 percent. In the United States, it is 97 percent. The lowest literacy rate for the entire 25-member European Union is Malta, which means the lowest literacy rate in the European Union is still 2 percent higher than China's literacy rate (see Figure 5.6).

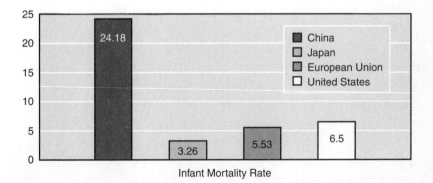

Figure 5.5 Current Infant Mortality Rate: China, Japan, European Union, and United States

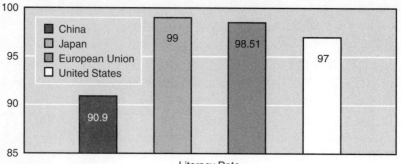

Figure 5.6 Current Literacy Rate: China, Japan, European Union, and United States

CHINA'S "ONE-CHILD" POLICY

No current snapshot of China's demographics could be complete without a discussion of the one-child policy. This policy was developed in 1979 when China's government began encouraging only one child per couple. The government was hoping that smaller families would become the norm. While the Chinese government encouraged the policy, it was originally not a law. Chinese Vice-Premier Chen Muhua described the one-child policy in this fashion in 1979: "A policy of encouragement and punishment for maternity, with encouragement as the main feature, will be implemented. Parents having one child will be encouraged, and strict measures will be enforced to control the birth of two or more babies. Everything should be done to insure that the natural population growth rate in China falls to zero by 2000."

"Encouragement and punishment" did not lead to sufficient reductions, and China's population growth rate didn't fall to zero. Thus, when the policy didn't work, it was turned into law. In September 2002, the Chinese government passed the law of Population and Birth Planning. Its purpose was to uphold the intent of the single-child policy for married couples. Unmarried persons were already restricted by law from having children.

The shift from policy to law marks an extremely important change in China's approach to population control. It brings together the greater legal force of law and legislation that was fraught with inconsistently applied features when it was just a policy. Now it is the law. This new law defines having more than one child as a criminal act.

WEALTH CREATION

If you think of all the Chinese people as a source of wealth creation, China is constructing the largest wealth-creation engine in history. Using the country's poverty level as a foundation puts this wealth-creation engine in perspective. In the past 20 years alone, over 170 million Chinese have escaped from or risen above the poverty level. What is especially impressive about this number is that it is 40 million larger than the entire population of Japan.

Now that these Chinese people are above the poverty level, they become candidates for saving. Saving is a key to China's economic engine. Over the past 20 years, China's economy has averaged a whopping 10 percent growth rate. This explosive rate is fueled by an unbelievable 35 percent personal savings rate. China has done a remarkable job of using this pool of capital to finance productive capital investment.

This rate of savings is one of the reasons that China's economy continues to explode. Currently the number three global economy, China will overtake number two, Japan, and number one, the United States, within the first quarter of this century.

With a population four times larger than that of the United States, China only needs to achieve one-fourth the per capita production levels of each American worker to outpace the United States. If instead of working at one-fourth the production levels of U.S. workers, Chinese workers could match the output per worker of their major economic and political competitors in Taiwan (which is likely), China's gross domestic product (GDP, the broadest measure of the economy) would pass not only the GDP of the United States and Japan, but would exceed that of all the rest of the industrialized world combined within the next 25 years.

HOW YA GONNA KEEP THEM DOWN ON THE FARM?

One of the underlying demographic shifts supporting this tremendous wealth creation machine is the movement of Chinese citizens away from the farm. Urban migration is the real story inside Chinese demographics. Today, less than 40 percent of the Chinese population lives in an urban area. Ten years from now, over 50 percent will live in an urban area; in 20 years that number will reach more than 60 percent.

This fundamental shift from rural life means that, over the next 20 years, the urban population will grow from its current level of 520 million people to 780 million; 260 million more people, close to the population of the entire United States, will move into cities. On an annual basis over 20 years, 13 million people, roughly the populations of Denmark and Sweden will move from rural environments into urban settings. No matter how you view it, China's population shift will be a landmark. And again, one of the real keys to this shift is the wealth that it can create. People living in urban areas will find better paying jobs than people living in rural areas. Urban incomes rise twice as fast as rural incomes because of the opportunity and flow of capital that come into the urban area.

THE LITTLE EMPERORS

Over the next 20 years, the majority of the population under the age of 15 (21 percent of the entire population) will be located in cities. Most of these children are single children, with all their parents' hopes and dreams pinned on them instead of being dispersed among several offspring. This sole child is the center of attention. I call them "little emperors." My analysis suggests that the desires, tastes, and spending habits of this generation will radically reshape the business climate, social fabric, and political institutions, not just of China, but potentially of the entire world.

The crucial point in understanding the potential impact of the Little Emperor Generation is that it was born into a world radically different from the one its parents grew up in. The parents of this age group, for the most part, were left scarred and desolated by World War II. The postwar era for these Chinese parents required hard work, dedication, individual sacrifice, and high savings, production, and conformity. These attributes have underpinned the industrial rise of China over the past half-century and have dramatically reshaped the world for China's teeming population of youths.

The little emperors are growing up in an era of prosperity, not poverty, and have opportunities and wealth that their parents did not have. Shopping is more characteristic of this group than saving. Their parents drank tea, wore sandals, ate rice, and bought things with cash, and their life centered around Buddhism

Not so for this under-15 generation. While their parents drank tea, they drink Coca-Cola. Their parents wore sandals; they wear Nike running shoes. Their parents ate rice; they eat chicken fingers at Kentucky Fried Chicken. Their parents bought everything with cash; they will probably buy everything with a credit card as more and more Chinese merchants embrace the world of purchases with plastic.

A by-product of China's economic success, this Little Emperor Generation is also better educated and more willing and able to travel abroad than their parents were. Leisure time, convenience, individualism, indulgence, spending, and other Western habits (or vices) permeate this generation. This is a radical change in mindset and actions from their parents' generation.

To put this potential consumer generation into perspective: Even if an unthinkable 25 percent of this under-15 generation never buys a single thing in its entire life, it would still be one of the greatest demographic consumption bubbles ever. For argument's sake, assume that 25 percent of this age group will never buy a Coca-Cola, or ever see a Nike swoosh and want a new pair of running shoes. We would still have 75 percent or 205 million young consumers (China's current population is 1.3 billion; the under-age-15 group accounts for 21 percent, or 273 million people; and 75 percent of 273 million is 205 million). This demographic group is the same size as the combined populations of Germany, France, the United Kingdom, and Ireland.

The situation begs investors to answer this question: Do you own the consumer-related companies positioned to satisfy the wants and needs of China's Little Emperor Generation? Think of what it is soon going to be purchasing—beverages, fast food, cigarettes, jeans, cars, shampoo, and cosmetic products.

ENTER THE "CHUPPIES"

First there was the "hippie," the name given to the rebellious youth of the 1960s in the United States. Hippies believed that corporate industry was greedy and all they really wanted to do was meditate and drop out of mainstream society. In the late 1960s and early 1970s, we had the "yippies," also in the United States. Yippies were much more outspoken and high profile; they were antiwar, antiestablishment, and pretty much antieverything.

Fast-forward, and today the children of these American hippies and yippies are classified as yuppies. *Yuppie* is short for "young urban professional." These so-called yuppies are in their 20s and 30s; they hold good jobs in the professional service sector. They tend to value material goods and seek convenience goods and services as their fast-paced urban lifestyle leaves them strapped for time. The "u" in the word yuppie has also been interpreted as meaning "upwardly mobile."

Chuppies, then, are young, urban, Chinese consumers. But here's the interesting part: They are young, they are affluent, and they want American products.

In 2005, United Parcel Service sponsored a survey conducted by Research International. It focused on urban Chinese consumers between the ages of 20 and 59. Everyone knows that the spending power of these chuppies, as well as the spending power of the entire middle class in China, is exploding. But we need to identify what they want to spend their money on. The United Parcel Service survey provides some interesting insights for American companies wanting to do business with the chuppies.

Here are a few highlights from the survey about the products most in demand:

- *American toiletries:* Fifty-three percent of all respondents would like to see a broader selection of U.S. products such as shampoo, shower gel, and dental care items.

- *American consumer electronics:* Fifty-three percent of those polled want a broader selection of American electronics. The most likely purchases are digital cameras, laptop computers, and video/digital recording devices.

- *Apparel/fashion accessories:* Fifty-two percent said they want more American fashions, especially athletic shoes, sandals, t-shirts with American logos, sportswear, and blue jeans.

- *American books, music, and videos:* Fifty percent would like to see a broader product selection of American entertainment. The most likely purchases are American videos/DVDs and music compact discs (CDs).

- *Home appliances:* Forty-five percent would like to see more U.S. durable products including refrigerators, washers/dryers, and microwaves.

In general, China's emerging urban middle class wants to buy certain American products. High-quality personal care toiletries and consumer electronics lead the list of what chuppies want the most (which might explain why Chinese computer maker Lenovo just brought IBM's personal computer division). They are also extremely interested in apparel, fashion accessories, music, and videos.

Maybe just as interesting was what they had no interest in buying from an American company, and that was liquor and cigarettes.

TELECOMMUNICATIONS BOOM

Telecommunications is an industry that is closely tied to all the consumer electronics that chuppies want to buy. Possibly the single most fundamental reason telecommunications will be a good investment in the next decade hinges around what is about to happen in China. The recent World Trade Organization (WTO) agreement between the United States and China will bring sweeping changes to many industries but none as dramatic as what will happen to telecommunications.

The WTO agreement is truly a landmark event for the telecommunications sector. Before this agreement, China severely restricted the sale of telecommunications services, and no company outside China could invest in telecommunications within China under any circumstance. This agreement opens up the telecommunications sector to a full array of services and to direct investment in telecommunications businesses in China.

These changes will alter the face of telecommunications in China forever, starting with the scope of services provided. First, the golden goose of China telecommunications services is the corridor between Beijing, Shanghai, and Guangzhou, which represents over 75 percent of all domestic traffic for telecommunications service. China will open that corridor immediately. Then, over time, the rest of the geographic restrictions will be lifted for the remaining somewhat rural parts of China. In three years, the paging services restriction will be lifted. In five years, the mobile phone service ban will be lifted, and in six years the local phone service ban will be removed as well. Anyone will be able to provide any telecommunications service anywhere in China.

Second, before the Chinese ratified this agreement, foreign investors were forbidden from investing in telecommunications services. China will now allow up to 49 percent of foreign investments in every type of telecommunication services. The floodgates will open, and capital will flow into China like never before.

Third, China will become a member of the Basic Telecommunications Agreement. That means China will implement the principles of this agreement, which will encourage competition, especially in pricing. Also, China will not be able to regulate technology. Under this agreement, China has no voice whatsoever regarding technology, which means that foreign telecommunication suppliers can use any technology they choose to provide their services.

In many ways, this may be one of the most far-reaching agreements from an investment perspective in the past one hundred years.

WORLD TRADE ORGANIZATION IMPACT

The impact that the WTO has had on China cannot be overlooked. One of the reasons investors have not wanted exposure to commodities is the fear that if one of the biggest users (namely China) reduces consumption, commodity prices will collapse. Having been to mainland China earlier this year, I can help put that country's growth story in perspective. China's need for commodities is unlikely to slow noticeably any time soon.

In 2001, China joined the WTO. Once China became part of the WTO, they began building an economic infrastructure. As they pursue this goal, they are consuming unprecedented amounts of raw materials and commodities. China trade (imports and exports) now totals over $50 billion a month—more than double the volume when they became part of WTO and an astonishing 10-fold increase over a decade ago. This trade growth has led to decreasing prices for China's exports and increasing prices for China's imports. China is consuming and importing a vast amount of commodities . . . you do the math.

No discussion of commodities would be complete without at least a brief focus on oil, the bellwether of all commodities. One of the concerns of individual investors is that with the price of oil hovering at all-time highs, it may be too late to invest in that commodity. But my analysis suggests otherwise. There are two interesting developments in the supply and demand of oil that could keep prices high for a long time. First, there simply is no spare capacity. Currently, OPEC (Organization of Petroleum Exporting Countries) spare capacity is just 2 percent of global demand, whereas in the early 1980s they had spare capacity of 30 percent.

The lack of spare capacity is long-term bullish for the price of oil. Second, demand continues to be high and should, given the exploding Chinese consumer, only go higher. Because of the real possibility of a major supply disruption caused by irregular events, from hurricanes to a terrorist act, many countries are now looking to build their own strategic petroleum reserves. While this has always been a focus in the United States, which attempts to have one year's supply of oil in strategic oil reserves, many other nations are nowhere near that level. Europe has strategic reserves that will last only 90 days (even though they are discussing increasing that to 120 days). China only has enough reserves for 7 days. As both Europe and China move to increase their oil reserves, demand will remain strong, which will be extremely bullish for the price of oil as well.

THE CONVERGENCE OF TECHNOLOGY AND TELECOMMUNICATIONS

With all these rapid changes going on in China and around the world as well, don't forget what will happen as technology and telecommunications (T&T) converge at a rapid pace. During the next decade, the division between the technology sector and the telecommunications sector will continue to blur, and as they converge, it will become harder and harder to tell one from the other. Nowhere is this dichotomy more prevalent than with the Internet. If your access to the Internet is "wired" (do you have to plug it in?), then it is considered technology; but if your access is "wireless," your Internet is no longer considered technology, but is now telecommunications.

The future of the Internet and likely the future of most technology will be wireless. The reason is convenience. Once people are hooked on something like the Internet, they want it all the time. The only way to have it all the time, no matter where the user may be, is for it to be wireless. To understand this issue of technology versus telecommunications and to get a sense of the potential of wireless, look no further than Asia.

China is the largest, most dominant country in Asia, with the most people as well. In China, mobile phone subscriptions are beating out Internet subscriptions by a six-to-one ratio. But the trend is not limited to China. It is happening throughout Asia. In Korea, mobile phone subscriptions are beating out Internet subscriptions by a five-to-one ratio. In Taiwan, it is a four-to-one ratio. And even in Hong Kong, mobile phone subscriptions are still outdistancing Internet subscribers by three to one. With all the new technology and technological advancements, what will happen when all these mobile phone users become Internet users because wireless technology will enable them to quickly, cost-efficiently, and reliably access the Internet through their mobile phones? Will it be a technology revolution or a telecommunications revolution?

China has about 79 million Internet users. Over half of them are college students, and a majority of these students don't even own a computer. In fact, there are less than 16 million computers in China. By comparison, the United States has 164 million computers, or 10 times more.

Most Chinese college students access the Internet through personal computers at their schools. And don't forget what it is like in college; students seldom have any money. The average college student in China earns under $200 a month. Eventually they will graduate and earn a decent income, but that transition from poor college student to free-spending young professional is sometimes a long transition.

Meanwhile, let's look at what is happening on the wireless mobile phone front in China, where there are over 325 million mobile phone subscriptions. Mobile phones in China are used by China's wealthiest consumers. Now, consider the dichotomy between those who use the Internet and those who have mobile phone subscriptions. The Internet users are primarily college students with no money. The mobile phone users are China's most influential and wealthiest consumers, and there are five times as many of them.

For a real peek at the future, consider this. Because of their heritage, tradition, culture, and pride, Chinese consumers do not like to buy things on credit. The typical Chinese consumer has little if any use for a credit card. The major reason that shopping on the Internet in China has been a real bust is that to shop online you need a credit card. Imagine what will happen to Chinese shopping online when the following development occurs: Chinese consumers who access the Internet through their wireless mobile phone can purchase anything they want online and instead of using or needing credit cards, simply bill the purchase to their mobile phone account.

Will it have been technology or telecommunications that finally got the Chinese consumer to shop online?

TECHNOLOGY PRODUCER AS WELL

China is not simply a consumer of technology; it is also a major producer of technology. China exports $160 billion annually in technology products—and it imports the same amount annually. Of that amount, almost half of the imports are semiconductors. As a result, semiconductor fabrication plants are popping up as fast as high-rises and highways.

Let's look at telecommunications again, a story that is incredibly compelling. At 325 million and counting, China now has the largest group of mobile phone users in the world. Compare this figure with the approximately 300 million fixed-line phone users in China, and you can see that China has already hit the tipping point of more mobile phone users than fixed line users.

A primary reason for the fixed-line phone is Internet access. Of the 79 million Internet users, many still access the Internet through their fixed-line telephone company. China remains the number two market in the world for computers and the number one market for cell phones.

There are close to 1,000 models of cell phones available for sale in China today. In contrast there are less than 100 different cell phone models available in the United States. Further, many of these trend-driven chuppies replace their mobile phone three or four times a year (the global average for cell phone replacement is once every two years). As you can imagine, this forces phone makers to keep coming up with new and innovative features, and because of all the competition, it keeps pressure on prices as well.

POWER NEEDS

China's energy needs will continue to be strong. Computers, cell phones, and appliances all run on energy, in particular, electric energy.

To get some idea how much electric capacity will need to be added around the world, look no further than China and its major Asian partners. Over the past 30 years the trends have been going straight up in terms of kilowatt-hours of electricity consumed by each person. In China, consumption of kilowatt-hours of electricity per person has gone up over 400 percent. In Hong Kong it is up 300 percent. In Singapore it is up over 600 percent. In Thailand and South Korea it is up over 1,000 percent. Increases in demand are impressive, but when we compare Asian electric consumption with that in the United States, we get a sense of future trends.

Per person electricity consumption in the United States stands at approximately 12,000-kilowatt hours. In Singapore it is 8,000, or only 66 percent of U.S. usage. Hong Kong stands at 5,000, which means that its usage is merely 40 percent of the United States' consumption pattern. And China is currently under 1,000 kilowatt-hours per person, which is only 8 percent compared with the United States. As the Asian countries become more industrialized, they will consume more electricity and their kilowatt-hour consumption patterns will look more and more like that of the United States. As this demand evolves, the world may not be able to build power-generating plants fast enough. I hope you can turn it on after you plug it in!

The only obstacle that could slow the China boom is insufficient power. The Chinese government knows that. Electric power is, without a doubt, the key to China's economic future. Remember all those appliances, from computers and cell phones to refrigerators, need to be plugged into something.

Energy demand offers both opportunity and the potential for problems. Of the 31 electric power grids that cover mainland China, 24 of them suffered major shortages in 2005. To remedy that problem, the Chinese government plans to double its electric power capacity within the next five years. It may well be the biggest power buildup in modern history.

WOMEN AND COSMETICS

Thus far, we have discussed gadgets and energy—bigger ticket items and larger trends. But the face of China is changing, too—literally.

Traditionally, a pale complexion has been considered desirable by most Asian women. Women with dark skin tones or a tanned complexion were viewed as farmworkers. In fact, sporting a tan in China was commonly referred to as having the "peasant" look.

In addition, it was believed that anyone who wore makeup was trying to hide something. The practice was truly shunned. Not so any longer. China has also experienced a cultural revolution. As colored televisions and television programming increasingly made their way into China, people quickly realized that America, Europe, and even Japan had different ideas of beauty. Further, as more Chinese women traveled outside China, they gained a new perspective firsthand.

Fast-forward to today, and the market for cosmetics in China is booming. The total value of China's beauty and cosmetic market today approaches $6 billion, and is now the fourth largest consumer category in China.

The cosmetic market jumped to number four because of its unprecedented growth rate of over 25 percent annually for the past five years. This boom has been driven by two factors. First, the overall rise in the standard of living has boosted consumer spending across the board. Second, the chuppies are willing to spend much more of their hard-earned disposable income to look better.

To underscore the point and the strength of the trend, the Chinese government has even relented on previous policy and has lifted its prohibition on beauty pageants. After a 54-year ban, both local and national beauty pageants have returned. The Chinese are not only focusing on beauty but are even becoming obsessed with it.

CHANGING VALUES

The trend in the cosmetics industry is just the tip of the evolving Chinese consumer iceberg. In what is, without a doubt, the most comprehensive survey and study of young Chinese consumers comes the first real look at how values are changing. This survey was conducted by the British Council, a government arm that promotes the education of different cultures. In the summer of 2005, they surveyed 70,000 chuppies, aged 16 to 39, living in 30 major urban areas of China. The most unique aspect of the survey is that they focused a good deal on values and what is important to these young adults.

Here are a few key findings of the British Council Survey:

- *Experimenters:* Seventeen percent of those surveyed consider themselves "experimenters." They want to be the first to buy a new cell phone, or laptop, or a personal digital assistant (PDA). As a subset, 11 percent said they are both young and hip. They want trendy designer-labeled clothes and the latest gadgets (for example, iPods).

- *Individualism:* Sixty-seven percent said that given a choice of relying on others or doing things themselves, they would rather do things themselves. The same 67 percent said that they do not pass judgment on how other people choose to live their lives.

- *Women's rights:* Sixty-four percent said the men should also do housework.

- *Ambitious:* Eighty percent stated that they are working "very hard" for their career. Only 39 percent are happy with their life as it is; 59 percent said they need to take risks to be successful. Only 18 percent say they have enough money to enjoy life; 67 percent think that it is important for their own family to think they are successful.

- *Knowledgeable:* Seventy-five percent felt it was important to be well informed. They view knowledge as the link to a better quality of life.

- *Fitness:* Thirty-three percent said they exercise regularly and 62 percent said they spend time outdoors walking, hiking, and exploring nature.

- *Global:* Sixty-seven percent expressed interest in other countries, cultures, traditions, and international news events. In addition, 52 percent said that they were attracted to the lifestyles of people in developed and industrialized countries.

Do not make the mistake of thinking all Chinese consumers are the same. The Chinese consumer is becoming extremely sophisticated. To be successful in this market, businesses must quickly learn how to segment and customize all the varieties of Chinese consumers.

Instead of thinking of chuppies simply as young urban Chinese consumers, think of them as young urban, individualist, women's activist, ambitious, knowledgeable, fitness focused, and global-minded Chinese consumers. That is how you can get inside the mind of a chuppie.

THE "YUEGUANGZU" CONSUMERS

An important subset of chuppie consumers in China is referred to as the *Yueguangzu* consumers. Yueguangzu means that they spend all that they earn every month without saving a single penny. These Yueguangzu consumers are not saving for a rainy day. In fact, they are willing to spend tomorrow's money today on luxury goods and products because they desire a better quality of life today, not next week, next year, or five years from now. They want it all and they want it now.

These Yueguangzu consumers are well educated and most have decent paying jobs; 60 percent of them are willing to buy things with "tomorrow's money." In other words, 60 percent do not view debt negatively as previous generations have. They want brand-name suits; jewelry and quality cosmetics; and cool electronic gadgets. They want to look successful even if they had to go into debt to get that look now.

These Yueguangzu consumers are confident about China's future. They feel that there is no need to wait to buy something later that they can use and enjoy today by buying it on credit. The Chinese Academy of Social Sciences did a study of personal debt in the major cities of Beijing and Shanghai to find the personal debt ratio in those two major urban areas. (If a person has debts of $20,000 and assets of $10,000, the personal debt ratio would be 200 percent—20,000 divided by 10,000.) In Beijing, the personal debt ratio is 122 percent; and in Shanghai it is 155 percent. In contrast, the so-called debt-ridden United States consumer has a personal debt ratio of 115 percent.

MADE IN JAPAN

Another interesting trend developing with young Chinese consumers is that they are also buying things made in Japan. That is very different from the consumer patterns of their parents.

Their parents still think a great deal about World War II. They remember how Japan invaded and occupied China in the 1930s and has yet to publicly apologize for the invasion and harsh occupation. These parents view politics and business as one and the same, and they still boycott anything made in Japan. Of course, the boycott is hardly total. Most of the steel in many of the high-rises in China today came from Japan. Likewise, many components in mobile phones come from Japan. Chinese consumers of a certain age may wish to boycott Japan on a personal level, but the Chinese government has ignored that tradition when it has made business sense to engage in trade.

To the young Chinese consumer, it doesn't matter. First of all, they don't think about World War II. Second, to them, politics is politics and business is business. Their shopping decisions are based on the quality, price, and brand reputation of a product—not on the politics of the country producing that product.

While Japanese companies have less than a 10 percent market share in China, their position will change as the chuppies continue to distance themselves from Japanese/Chinese political history issues.

HISTORY REPEATS ITSELF

In thinking about the history of Japan and China, another link to ponder is that an Olympic tie can create long-term investment opportunities. The 2008 Olympics will be held in Beijing, China, and that is a compelling reason to invest in the Chinese consumer boom.

First, a quick history lesson on why you would want to invest in the Beijing Olympics in 2008. On one of my trips to Asia, I was in Kobe, Japan, and needed to get to Kyoto. I was running late, and it was clear that I would never make it by car. Everyone in Japan told me that even though they have an awesome national highway system—developed in the late 1950s in preparation for the 1964 Olympics in Tokyo—I would never get to Kyoto fast enough. I would have to take the bullet train.

Well, I take the train to work in Chicago, and the last thing I wanted to do was hop on a train in Japan. But, I am glad I did. The bullet train in Japan was also created for the 1964 Olympics just in case all the highway construction projects were not completed on time. In the late 1950s, most of the roads in Japan were dirt. Does it sound like anywhere you know today? Like maybe China? Then it hit me: History does repeat itself. If you want a peek into the future, look at the past.

The story of the great economic and market boom in Japan in the 1960s through the 1980s was not about some unique Japanese business management model or quality circles, or about their new-found Just in Time Inventory (JITI) concept. It was all about one simple impetus—the economic boom leading up to the 1964 Olympics in Tokyo, Japan, which at the time was one of the biggest infrastructure buildups ever. For the following 20 years, the Japanese economy and market benefited from that economic boom.

I am convinced that history is about to repeat itself in China. This economic boom is all about the Beijing Olympics in 2008. The benefits to the global economy and global demand have the potential to play out for the next 20 years in China just as they did in Japan after the Tokyo Olympics in 1964.

Short-Term Olympic Boom

China's current consumption levels are unprecedented. China is consuming 50 percent of the world's cement, 40 percent of the world's steel, and 30 percent of the world's coal.

To glimpse how China is using all those raw materials, look no further than the infrastructure projects being built for the Beijing Olympics in 2008. As of 2005, China has over 15,000 different highway projects underway that will add 162,000 kilometers (or 100,000 miles) of road in China. This is enough new road to circle the globe at the equator four times. With all these pending projects, the talk of a slowdown is overdone.

Olympic Strategy

The question to investors is clear: How does one develop a strategy to benefit from the Chinese Olympic trends? The answer is simple. Think back to *The Graduate* and one of the most famous one-liners in film history, when Mr. McGuire said, "There's a great future in plastics. Think about it." Today, the word is "commodities." There is a great future in commodities.

When the short-term commodity boom of the Beijing Olympics in 2008 is combined with the longer-term boom in commodities around the globe, the old investment strategy asset allocation model that finds the optimal level of stocks, bonds, and cash will need to incorporate commodities as well.

Let me end where I began. Three simple facts put this commodity boom in the proper perspective. First, China consumes 50 percent of the world's cement. Second, China consumes 40 percent of the world's steel. Third, China consumes 30 percent of the world's coal. The consumption levels show no sign of slowing down in the next five years. China is in the early stages of a major economic boom that will take it through 2008 (which just happens to coincide with the 2008 Olympics in Beijing). I have never seen a nation, anywhere at any time, more focused on a single event than the 1.3 billion Chinese who are obsessed with their big chance to showcase China to the world through the Beijing Olympics in 2008. When the Chinese focus on something, they can do amazing things—remember that wall they built over there. (Come to think of it, that used quite a bit of commodities as well.) Go for the gold . . . go for commodities.

More Olympics

Beijing has three separate subway systems. Seven new subway systems are being added. By the time of the Olympics, Beijing will have 10 separate subway systems. It will be one of the world's most comprehensive mass transit systems. And it's not just the subways. Let me describe for you in more detail what is going on with the highway infrastructure. Most major U.S. cities incorporate a beltway system that encircles the cities so that drivers can drive around and into city centers. In Beijing, not one beltway, or two, or even three, but five separate beltways surround the city, with each new beltway making a bigger circle around the city. No U.S. city has two beltways circling the same city but Beijing has five. And they are building four more beltways before the Olympics. Nine separate beltways will circle the entire city of Beijing with each one taking people closer to the city. There is no system like it anywhere in the world.

A final thought on the Olympics: They are not just about Beijing. Olympic events will be hosted in cities as far away as Shanghai and Hong Kong. We should call 2008 the Chinese Olympics, not just the Beijing Olympics.

THE WORLD'S FAIR

Another point to ponder is the concern of many investors that China's economic growth may collapse after the Olympics in 2008. I don't think China will have time to slow down, let alone collapse, after 2008, because two short years after the Olympics, Shanghai will host the World's Fair! That's right. The next World's Fair is scheduled from May 1 to October 31, 2010, in Shanghai, China. The theme for this World's Fair is "Better City, Better Life." As an investor, don't underestimate what a World's Fair can do for a city or a country. In 1893, Chicago (my hometown) hosted the World's Fair, with the theme, "Fourth Centennial of the Discovery of America." Many historians have asserted that the World's Fair began the transformation of Chicago from a hog-slaughtering cow town to the cosmopolitan city it is today. That World's Fair unveiled many great new products and inventions including electrified street lighting, modern sewer systems, the Ferris wheel, Juicy Fruit gum, and much, much more. One can only imagine what will be unveiled at the World's Fair in Shanghai.

Every investor wants to know the next big thing. The 1990s were all about each new next big thing. First, the decade ushered in the European Union. Then came the Internet, the dot-com craze, and the tech boom. The first decade of the twenty-first century has brought us the China boom. What's next? I think I may know the next big thing after China. It will be China. And I believe I also know what the next big thing after that will be. You guessed it: China once again.

WHAT ABOUT HONG KONG AND TAIWAN?

No discussion about China and the Chinese consumer would be complete without a brief look at the biggest issue still facing China today—Hong Kong. International investors around the globe are still holding their collective breath, hoping that the return of Hong Kong to China will not disrupt the global financial emerging markets. Its importance transcends all markets, as Hong Kong has become the benchmark of what every economy and every market around the world would like to become. And while many have tried to mirror Hong Kong's success, no one has been able to do it.

In 1984, Britain and China agreed that all of Hong Kong would revert to Chinese rule. At that time, the Hong Kong stock market was valued at $30 billion. Twenty years later, the Hong Kong stock market has a market capitalization of over $500 billion. No one will ever duplicate Hong Kong's success because the Hong Kong story is unique. The confluence of three factors fueled Hong Kong's success, and no country on earth can duplicate those three factors.

First, there's that age-old real estate key—location, location, location. Hong Kong is next door to the largest source of labor in the world as well as the largest consumer market (China). Hong Kong can tap into both of these unbelievable benefits without paying any of the costs. Hong Kong does not have to pay any of the social costs of sustaining the world's largest labor and consumption market. That problem and all of the costs associated with it are China's problem to bear.

Second, Hong Kong found itself in the unique position of not expending any of its precious financial or economic resources on national defense. Because Hong Kong was a British colony, national defense was Britain's problem to worry about and Britain's problem to fund, not Hong Kong's.

Third, as a result of the first two factors, Hong Kong's tax burden is among the lowest anywhere. If, as a country, you don't have to worry about huge social problems and you don't have to worry about national defense, you don't need higher taxes.

Do not worry about this unique and truly unbelievable economic miracle that Hong Kong has put together. It will be just fine under Chinese rule. China will not destroy the golden economic goose.

This does not mean that there will not be major bumps in the road over the free and honest flow of financial and political information. And it does not mean that there will not be potential pitfalls as the civil service system evolves and changes. The human rights issue will also be with us for some time, as will the memory of Tiananmen Square, along with the fear that the next demonstration might turn into another disaster scene. While all these factors may be legitimate short-term concerns, none will stop the successful transformation of Hong Kong and China into "one country, two systems."

Nervous investors around the globe are still searching for clues to the future for the Hong Kong market now that China has regained control of Hong Kong, ending 156 years of colonial rule by Britain. Perhaps the biggest clue to the future reunification of Hong Kong with China can be found in the past, in the title of the 1950s' Doris Day movie—*Tea for Two*.

The real reason that the reunification of Hong Kong will be successful is because it is not just about Hong Kong; it is about Taiwan as well. Hong Kong is only the first step in getting what China really wants and that is reunification with Taiwan. Unless the Hong Kong reunification is a rousing success, China can never hope to get Taiwan to the table to talk about reunification. While the celebration over the return of Hong Kong fulfills a dream of every patriotic Chinese, that dream is only halfway complete. Taiwan is what they are really dreaming about.

Once investors realize that China's ultimate goal never was just regaining control of Hong Kong, they will quickly realize that despite potential problems in the short run, in the long run China will not allow the reunification with Hong Kong to fail. After all, who wants to have a tea party with only one guest (Hong Kong)? It's much more fun having Tea for Two (Hong Kong and Taiwan).

MONEY AND FIREWORKS

Too many investors simply look at China as a third-world country trying to become a first world or modern country like a lot of other emerging markets around the world. That is not the case with China.

Remember that prior to the Communist Revolution, China was a sophisticated world leader. But that sophistication only included a few: Most of the population in China lived in poverty on farms. So instead of thinking of China as a third-world country trying to become a first-world modern country, think of it as a once modern and sophisticated society now moving to allow the masses to enjoy and be part of that modern country. It is important to remember just how ingenious the Chinese people have been through history.

The Chinese invented paper money. Because of a shortage of copper and other metals to strike into coins, the Song Dynasty, in A.D. 960, issued the first paper money in the world.

Somewhat earlier, during the Tang Dynasty, around A.D. 800, the Chinese invented fireworks. And 600 years prior to that, they invented firecrackers by roasting bamboo to produce loud "pops" in the fire. With the discovery of gunpowder, also in China, the first true fireworks came along as well.

These two Chinese inventions offer an interesting insight about Chinese consumers. First, they have the money to shop. Second, they are going to celebrate, not with impressive fireworks displays, but by shopping. Maybe in the future, the Chinese New Year will be less about fireworks and more about shopping.

CHAPTER SIX

HOW TO DEVELOP AN INVESTMENT MEGATRENDS PORTFOLIO

N ow it is time to make some money. Let's connect the dots between these global demographic shifts—my Investment Megatrends—and the investment opportunities these shifts are creating.

After briefly summarizing my investment perspective on each of the four global shifts presented in this book, I identify the five companies best positioned to benefit from each shift. You will then have a portfolio of the 20 global companies best positioned to make money from these four demographic shifts.

Consider these companies your Investment Megatrends Portfolio for the next decade.

GLOBAL SHIFT 1: THE PONCE DE LEÓN EFFECT—THE AMERICAN BABY BOOMERS

Several dominant themes emerge when focusing on American baby boomers. The first is that these baby boomers are going to continue to be big savers, and they are going to be looking for some financial advice. These baby boomers want to spend their retirement years looking at their grandchildren, not stock charts. The best way to invest in this theme is through brokerage and investment banking stocks because through the firm's investment banking arm, it can provide its brokers unique opportunities that other brokers cannot access. One of the largest and most trusted brokerage firms in the world, Merrill Lynch, is best poised to benefit from this trend.

MERRILL LYNCH (STOCK SYMBOL: MER)

Merrill Lynch is one of the world's leading brokerage and financial management firms. The firm offers financial advice to individuals, corporations, and governments.

Merrill Lynch's business model is divided into three operating units. The first unit is called the Global Private Client Group. It was recently created by combining the U.S. Private Client Group with the International Private Client Group. This global group provides investors around the world with brokerage services as well as investment products that include mutual funds, annuities, and life insurance. This group offers the kind of one-stop shopping that these American baby boomers are looking for.

The second operating unit is called the Global Markets and Investment Banking Group. This group deals primarily with big institutional clients. It offers both investment banking and capital market services to governments, corporations, and foundations around the world.

The third operating unit is Merrill Lynch Investment Management. It is one of the largest asset managers in the world with over a half trillion dollars under management. In an attempt to provide one-stop shopping for these baby boomers, this unit also offers credit cards and banking services.

Merrill Lynch is a global powerhouse with locations in 35 countries. In addition to serving customers outside the United States, they also can service the American baby boomers when they travel. Over 50,000 employees are ready to provide services to clients on behalf of Merrill Lynch. Finally, its brand "the bull" is one of the best recognized logos for one of the most coveted brands anywhere.

The second theme among American baby boomers is that they are tech savvy. These baby boomers already use the Internet as much as Generation X and Generation Y that followed them. These baby boomers are wealthy and highly educated, which means that they have the money to buy and the knowledge to use technology. Also, don't forget, as these baby boomers age, the easiest and quickest way to stay connected to children, grandchildren, extended family, and friends is through technology. The best way to invest in this theme is through Dell, the world's number one direct seller of computers. And Dell's positioning just got stronger with these American baby boomers because IBM (an American computer giant these boomers grew up with) sold its personal computer division to Chinese computer maker Lenovo.

DELL, INC. (STOCK SYMBOL: DELL)

Dell Computers has one of the best and simplest business models anywhere. Simply eliminate the middleman and sell your products for less. Dell's computers are all custom-ordered and built specifically for the individual consumer. This plays well with baby boomers who always want things customized to their specific wants and needs. But it's not just about the customer. Because everything is built to order, Dell has lower inventories, which in turn means lower costs, which leads to higher profit margins.

Don't make the mistake of assuming that Dell is just about selling desktop and notebook computers. It also offers network services, storage systems, workstations, and handheld computers, as well as an integrated support and training team.

Dell is one of the most customer-service friendly firms anywhere. It never loses touch with what its customers want because it sells to them directly. Dell has over 60,000 employees worldwide waiting to customize a computer for picky baby boomers.

The third theme in this baby boomer shift is that the boomers are going to be travelers. The globalization of the world's economies and markets has opened new avenues to travel and new ways to explore the world. Tourism is now being embraced as a way of life in almost every corner of the globe. Baby boomers want to see and experience it all in their lifetimes. They have the disposable income and wealth to travel anywhere they want. The best way to invest in the travel theme is through the world's number one cruise operator, Carnival Corporation.

CARNIVAL CORPORATION (STOCK SYMBOL: CCL)

Carnival Corporation operates 12 cruise lines with almost 100 ships. You will probably recognize the following lines: Princess Cruise, Holland America, Seabourn Cruise, Windstar Cruise, Cunard Cruise (they operate *Queen Mary II* and *Queen Elizabeth II*) and, of course, Carnival Cruise.

No matter where the baby boomers want to travel and vacation, Carnival goes there. They are in the Caribbean, the Mexican Riviera, Alaska, the Mediterranean, Scandinavia, New England, Canada, throughout Asia, and just about everywhere in Europe as well.

But the real reason that Carnival will be so successful with these baby boomers is that its management recognizes that not all the baby boomers will retire with the same amount of wealth and income. It doesn't matter to Carnival: They have a cruise line for everyone. They have deep discount cruises targeting middle-class and baby boomer retirees on a tight budget, as well as super high-end luxury *Windstar* and *Seabourn* liners with the finest wines and food and exotic destinations for the well-to-do baby boomer who wants to see it all in first class. In 2004, over 6,000,000 passengers took a cruise with Carnival.

The fourth theme evolving in this baby boomer shift is that they like to drink alcoholic beverages. These baby boomers spend more on alcoholic beverages than every other age group except the under-25 crowd. And it is not just that they are drinking more, they will pay more as well . . . meaning imported beer.

The best way to invest in this theme is through one of the largest brewers in the world, Molson Coors Brewing Company.

MOLSON COORS BREWING COMPANY (STOCK SYMBOL: TAP)

The merger of Coors and Molson's created this dominant brewer. The company now offers over a dozen brands of beer. The baby boomers are going to like this company for two reasons.

First, one of the reasons that baby boomers spend so much on alcoholic beverages is that they pay more for imported beer. Now these boomers can order an imported Molson Canadian or a Richard's Red Ale or even a Black Ice. All these imports came along with the Molson merger.

The second reason Molson Coors remains the boomers' number one brand and top seller is the "Silver Bullet," or Coors Light. When you get older, your metabolism slows and you cannot consume what you did when you were 25 or 30 and maintain the same weight. When you were in your 20s, you could drink beer and not gain a pound. In your 50s and 60s, when you drink a beer the pounds come easier and stay longer. One solution is to consume reduced calorie beverages. The Silver Bullet is popular among calorie-counting beer drinkers.

The fifth and final theme with this baby boomer shift is that they are extremely health and nutrition conscious. Not only do they want to take care of themselves for a very long time, but they also want to look good and be healthy.

The best way to invest in this health and nutrition theme is through Johnson & Johnson, one of the world's largest health-care product manufacturers.

JOHNSON & JOHNSON (STOCK SYMBOL: JNJ)

Johnson & Johnson is without a doubt one of the most diversified health-care product manufacturers anywhere in the world. No matter what these baby boomers want or need regarding health-care products, Johnson & Johnson makes it.

Johnson & Johnson has three operating units. Its consumer products unit makes over-the-counter drugs and products for first aid, dental care, skin care, hair care, infants' health and nutrition, and women's health and nutrition.

Its second operating unit is the medical devices and diagnostics division, which produces monitoring devices and surgical equipment. In the eighteenth century, Benjamin Franklin uttered these now-famous words: "Nothing is certain in life except death and taxes." I have taken the liberty of updating Franklin's words so they relate to baby boomers. As these baby boomers get older, "Nothing is certain in life except they are probably going to have some sort of surgery and they are going to be monitored for something." When that happens, it will be Johnson & Johnson surgical equipment and monitoring devices products.

Their third unit is a pharmaceutical division that makes one of the widest arrays of drugs of any drug company. Recall that prescription drug usage begins to trend upward at age 45 and never reverses course. As these baby boomers age, pharmaceutical demand will boom.

Johnson & Johnson will serve baby boomers in all aspects of their lives. When they baby-sit the grandkids and one of the kids falls and scrapes a knee, the baby boomers will reach for a Band-Aid—a Johnson & Johnson product. When the grandkids don't stop screaming and the baby boomers reach for Tylenol, that's a Johnson & Johnson product as well.

As these baby boomers continue to watch their waistlines and pick a no-calorie, noncarbohydrate sweetener like Splenda, that's a Johnson & Johnson product as well.

Promising Investments for Global Shift 1

The five individual companies best positioned to benefit from the aging of the baby boomers are Merrill Lynch; Dell, Inc.; Carnival Corporation; Molson Coors Brewing Company; and Johnson & Johnson.

GLOBAL SHIFT 2: THE WALLS KEEP TUMBLING DOWN—EASTERN EUROPEAN WORKERS

Several dominant themes emerge when focusing on Eastern European workers and their likely impact on Europe. The first theme is that these low-cost Eastern European workers will provide a spark to economic growth, not just to Eastern Europe but to Western Europe as well, which will serve to further integrate trade and commerce among the 25-member European Union (EU) countries. The best way to invest in this increasing trade and commerce theme is in shipping, specifically Dryships, Inc., a global shipping company from Athens, Greece.

DRYSHIPS, INC. (STOCK SYMBOL: DRYS)

When trade and commerce pick up in Europe, the first issue becomes, "How do you get all the stuff from one place to another?" The answer is, "Ship it."

Dryships are carriers of dry bulk commodities such as coal, iron ore, and grains. They also ship fertilizers and steel products. In addition, they have what are referred to in the industry as combination carriers that can transport crude oil and other oil products.

Here is what uniquely positions Dryships, Inc., in Europe. Think back to the population ranges within the European Union. The largest of the 25-member EU countries is Germany with over 82 million people and the smallest is Malta with less than 400,000 people, while the other 23 fall somewhere in between. Within Europe and within these countries, there will sometimes be demand to move a lot of commodities; other times, the demand may only be to move limited commodities. The range in demand will be very wide.

Dryships serves the complete spectrum of sizes in the shipping industry. They fill the large fleet category with their Capersize Line. They fill the medium fleet category with their Panamax Line and the small fleet category with both their Handymax and

Handysize Lines. What is even more remarkable is that they can employ their shipping capabilities in any combination to suit the cargo. Think of the diverse sizes and needs of the 25 EU members and then think about Dryships' ability to fill every order, big or small, from grain to oil to steel.

Let's stay on this trade and commerce theme. Another great way to invest in this theme is Mittal Steel Company, headquartered in the Netherlands.

Mittal Steel Company N.V. (Stock Symbol: MT)

If Dryships, Inc., ships a lot of commodities, especially steel, it only stands to reason that the largest steel producer in the world would be a good investment as well.

Mittal Steel was formed when Ispat International (70 percent owned by the Mittal family) purchased LNM Holdings (wholly owned by the Mittal family), and that combined company then bought U.S.-based International Steel Group. Combining these three companies has made Mittal Steel the largest steel company in the world, producing more than 50 million metric tons annually.

Economic growth as a result of increased trade and commerce usually means more stuff is going to be built, and when we build more stuff, we use more steel. A company with 180,000 employees serving 5,000 customers in 120 countries is in a place of strength and market dominance.

Another reason I like this investment is that, in a sense, it represents a microcosm of the Eastern European workers' global shift. Here is why: Prior to 2005, Mittal Steel had two operating units in Europe—a Western Europe unit and an Eastern Europe unit. It is now one consolidated Mittal Steel Europe unit.

Mittal Steel recently acquired Polish steel company Huta Czestochowa and merged it into its operations of Mittal Steel in Poland, further leveraging the cheap labor in Eastern Europe to increase the profitability of selling steel throughout Europe.

I am one of those people who believe three is a charm, so I am staying with this trade and commerce boom theme to give you the third and final company to benefit from this theme—Germany's BASF, the largest chemical company in the world.

BASF (Stock Symbol: BF)

If trade and commerce pick up in Europe, then the largest chemical company in the world should stand to benefit as well. Especially one as diversified as BASF. They have over 100 major manufacturing plants around the world.

They operate five separate units: (1) They have a plastics unit, (2) they have an agricultural products and nutrition unit dealing in herbicides and fertilizers, (3) they have a basic chemicals unit, (4) they have a "performance products" unit that deals with dyes and coatings, and (5) they have an oil and gas exploration and production unit. They have over 82,000 employees working on five continents.

But here is why I really like them for our European trade and commerce theme: Even though they are the largest chemical company in the world with operations and clients spanning the globe, half of all their sales still come from Europe. As Europe goes, so goes BASF.

The second theme is that as the standard of living improves, consumers will have more disposable income. These Eastern European country economies get strong as more companies locate there, and Western European country economies also get stronger as their companies become more profitable and labor standards become more flexible. The standard of living and disposable income will rise for both Eastern and Western Europe. The best way to invest in this increasing standard of living theme is through Ericsson, from Sweden, the world's largest maker of wireless telecommunications equipment.

Ericsson (Stock Symbol: ERICY)

If your standard of living increases you are more likely to buy that mobile phone, and if you buy a mobile phone, Ericsson wins.

Ericsson is the largest supplier of mobile systems in the world. They support every standard for wireless communications. But here's the real catch: The world's 10 largest mobile operators are customers of Ericsson. Almost 50 percent of the calls in the world go through an Ericsson system, which is why they have operations in 140 countries.

Mobile phone service providers use Ericsson's antennas, transmitters, and other wireless infrastructure gear to build and expand networks. As economic and political walls continue to crumble and there is more trade, commerce, and travel between the 25 EU countries, a mobile phone becomes a necessity. You may not buy a mobile phone with your first paycheck, but you surely will buy it within that first year of paychecks.

The third and final theme within this global shift focuses on the large component of senior citizens aged 65 or older. Seventeen percent of the entire EU population is in the senior citizen age group, which means that there are roughly as many senior citizens in Europe as there are baby boomers in the United States—76 million. The best way to invest in the European senior citizen theme is through a leading drug company such as Shire Pharmacueticals Group from the United Kingdom.

SHIRE PHARMACEUTICALS GROUP (STOCK SYMBOL: SHPGY)

As the population of Europe continues to age, Shire's two-pronged business approach should benefit on two fronts.

First, they are a drug company. They are the European leader of drug treatments for the central nervous system, gastrointestinal and renal diseases. These are all ailments that plague senior citizens.

Second, their unique business and marketing strategy focuses on the specialty physician. Shire focuses on the therapies that are prescribed by specialist doctors as opposed to primary care physicians. As more and more patients go to specialist physicians, this in turn will increase the demand for Shire products. When a population like

Europe ages, it will need and demand more specialist physicians. The more this trend evolves, the greater the potential market share increases for Shire. Think of it as more share for Shire!

PROMISING INVESTMENTS FOR GLOBAL SHIFT 2

The five individual companies best positioned to benefit from the shift in Eastern European Workers are Dryships, Inc.; Mittal Steel Company; BASF; Ericsson; and Shire Pharmaceuticals Group.

GLOBAL SHIFT 3: THE RISING SUN IS CLEARLY SETTING—THE AGING JAPANESE POPULATION

Four dominant themes emerge when focusing on the aging Japanese population. The first is that not only does Japan have one of the oldest populations in the world but these senior citizens are the healthiest as well. Japan is ranked number one for healthy life expectancy.

That means that in addition to being around to baby-sit for their grandchildren, they also may be around and healthy enough to baby-sit for their great grandchildren. As we age, we become more nostalgic about life and memories, especially when it comes to grandchildren and great grandchildren. I will give you two great ways to play the Japanese healthy life expectancy theme. The first is Canon, a leading camera and camcorder manufacturer from Japan.

CANON, INC. (STOCK SYMBOL: CAJ)

There is simply no way these healthy aging Japanese senior citizens are going to let all these memories go by without capturing them on camera or with a camcorder.

Canon still operates its original camera business in addition to being the leader in the high-end digital camera market. They also manufacture camcorders so these grandparents can record their grandbaby's first step.

What is interesting about Canon is that they are also making great inroads into another line of business—the document reproduction market. The company makes printers and other computer peripherals mostly for home use, but some for small office use as well. When these healthy aging Japanese senior citizens are done taking their photographs with their digital camera from Canon, they can download them on their computer and then print copies for all their friends on their, you guessed it, Canon printer.

The second company to benefit from this theme is Fuji Photo Film Company, from Japan, the world's largest photographic film and paper producer.

Fuji Photo Film Company (Stock Symbol: FUJIY)

Fuji offers a different angle for playing the same memory theme. Not only is Fuji the number one photographic film and paper producer in Japan, but it has finally passed Eastman Kodak to become the world's leader as well.

Fuji has operations in North America, South America, Europe, Asia, and Australia. However, I like this company as a way to invest in the aging Japanese theme because, even though they are the global leader, a majority of their sales comes from one place, Japan. There is nothing negative (except thc film) about this company or this theme.

The second dominant theme that emerges from Japan is that women are staying single longer. Over 50 percent of Japanese women in their late 20s are single. Twenty years ago, only 30 percent of Japanese women in their late 20s were single.

Delayed marriage means that there are also more men who are single as well, which means that everyone has more time to play and be entertained. The best way to play this staying-single-for-longer theme is Konami Corporation, a leader in making video games for personal computers, Sony PlayStation, and other services. Konami Corporation is also from Japan.

KONAMI CORPORATION (STOCK SYMBOL: KNM)

People in their late 20s who are still single have more time to be entertained. Without the burdens of family and home, they have more free time. No company is in a better position to fill their needs than Konami Corporation.

Konami has three business units. The first is their digital entertainment business. This business produces and sells video game software for computers and cell phones as well as for Sony PlayStations. You are young, single, and tired of the bar scene. You just want to go home and chill out by playing some video games. When Japanese singles do that, they are paying Konami.

Let's say they don't want to play video games at home all by themselves. They want to go out and be entertained and maybe even go to a casino. That's where Konami's second business unit comes in—their Gaming Business Unit. They design and manufacture video games and token-operated games for amusement facilities as well as gaming machines for casinos.

What if you're not a couch potato and, instead, want to stay healthy? As one of these staying-single-for-longer Japanese with time to kill, you might decide to buy some exercise or fitness equipment. However, with most living quarters so small, it is more likely you would go to a fitness center. It doesn't matter; either way Konami wins. Enter their third and final unit, the Health & Fitness Business. Not only do they design, manufacture, and sell fitness machines and health-related products, they also manage fitness centers; they get their consumers coming and going.

The third dominant theme that emerges from Japan is that after these Japanese women who stay single longer, finally get married, they then decide to wait to have children. Japanese women are now waiting 2½ years after marriage to have that first child. That means 2½ years of a two-income marriage with no children to spend their disposable income on. If you aren't spending it on your children, you spend it on yourself by buying cool and hip stuff. The best way to invest in this having-children-later theme is through Sony Corporation, one of the world's top consumer electronics firms.

SONY CORPORATION (STOCK SYMBOL: SNE)

If you are married, without children, and have disposable income to spend on electronic gadgets, Sony will probably stand to benefit. Most investors make the mistake of thinking that Sony is just about their PlayStation home video system (which, by the way, these young married couples without children will buy). In fact, more than 60 percent of Sony sales come from something other than PlayStation.

Let's say these having-children-later Japanese want to buy a personal computer, Sony offers desktop and laptop computers. It also sells digital cameras. Sony also makes Walkman stereos. And it makes a mobile phone, called a Sony Ericsson phone, which is a joint venture with Ericsson (I bet you are liking my Ericsson stock pick even more right about now).

But the best is yet to come. Sony is currently developing a computer chip for use in cell phones so that they can be used as a train pass and for personal identification. These having-children-later Japanese will buy two of those hip and cool gadgets as soon as they are available.

The fourth and final dominant theme that emerges from Japan is the potential saving boom coming from their post office. Post offices in Japan also offer investment savings accounts. When the Japanese markets and economy crashed a decade ago, most Japanese put their money in these postal accounts, which had a duration of 10 years. The 10 years is up now, so money can finally be taken out of these accounts. The best way to invest in this savings boom is through the largest banking company in Japan, Mitsubishi UFJ Financial Group.

Mitsubishi UFJ Financial Group (Stock Symbol: MTU)

Not only is Mitsubishi Tokyo Financial Group one of the largest banks in Japan, it is also merging with another Japanese bank, UFJ Holding, and they will become the largest bank in the world. When all these Japanese investors are looking for a new home for their money coming out of these postal accounts, many will look no further than that largest bank in the world, right in their own backyard. Mitsubishi Tokyo has deposit, lending, leasing, investment advice, and trust services, not just in Japan, but in 40 other countries as well. They also provide brokerage services through their subsidiary, Mitsubishi Securities, in 70 branches all across Japan. These 70 branches are focused on a single objective: Get as much as possible of the nearly three trillion yen that is coming out of the post office looking for a new home. Mitsubishi Tokyo Financial Group will be the new home for much of that money.

Promising Investments for Global Shift 3

The five individual companies best positioned to benefit from this shift are Canon, Inc.; Fuji Photo Film Company; Konami Corporation; Sony Corporation; and Mitsubishi UFJ Financial Group.

GLOBAL SHIFT 4: NAPOLEON WAS RIGHT— THE CHINESE CONSUMER GENERATION

Five dominant themes emerge when focusing on the Chinese Consumer Generation. The first is that young Chinese consumers are buying things made in Japan, unlike their parents who still boycott such products because of the Japanese invasion and occupation of China in the 1930s. To these young Chinese consumers, that doesn't matter. They make their shopping decisions based on the quality of the product along with the price and that product's brand reputation. The political history of the country that produces the product does not matter to them. The best way to invest in these young Chinese consumers is through one of the world's leading automakers, Japan's Toyota Motor Corporation.

TOYOTA MOTOR CORPORATION (STOCK SYMBOL: TM)

These young Chinese consumers are evolving from riding bicycles to mopeds to automobiles. As they look for quality automotive products with strong brand recognition, no company is better positioned to serve them than Toyota.

Toyota is a global powerhouse; it has 51 manufacturing facilities in 26 countries. It employs close to 275,000 workers worldwide and its vehicles are sold in more than 140 countries.

But more importantly, it is a company that is focused on these Chinese consumers. Toyota has already entered into an agreement with the Chinese government to produce passenger cars for sale in China. These cars are going to be built by Tianjin Toyota Motor Corporation, which is a joint venture between Chinese automaker Tianjin Automobile Xiali and Toyota.

Toyota is also establishing between 15 and 20 Lexus dealerships in China (Lexus is part of Toyota Motor Corporation). They have another joint venture to build engines in China. This joint venture agreement is with Guangzhou Automobile Group.

As more and more Chinese consumers continue to distance themselves from the bad blood in Japanese and Chinese political history, more and more Japanese companies like Toyota will be embraced by these young Chinese consumers (I bet you like my Sony pick even better right about now because you are probably thinking, after they buy a Toyota vehicle, they will probably buy a Sony PlayStation).

And one more thing. As these consumers go from bikes to mopeds to cars, Toyota also wins in that progression. Toyota already owns a 5 percent stake in Yamaha, the world's number two motorcycle maker.

The second powerful theme to develop out of China is the commodity boom that is occurring as a result of increased Chinese consumption. Chinese consumers will be driving commodity prices higher for the next decade, especially oil and chemicals that are used in the production and manufacturing of many products as well as all the oil that will be used to transport these products throughout China. The best way to invest in this Chinese consumer commodity boom is through PetroChina Company, the largest petroleum, chemical, and natural gas company in China.

PetroChina Company (Stock Symbol: PTR)

PetroChina produces over two-thirds of China's oil and gas. It has its own domestic exploration business and already owns close to 10,000 miles of natural gas pipeline in China, in addition to its 29 refineries and 11 chemical plants.

But what really interests me about PetroChina is that it was created as part of a restructuring of the Chinese government-owned and operated China National Petroleum Corporation and is actually a subsidiary of that corporation. Now think about national strategic oil reserves. The U.S. government has strategic oil reserves to last 365 days without obtaining more oil. Europe has strategic oil reserves to carry them through 90 days, and they are proposing increasing it to 120 days. Meanwhile, the government of China has only enough reserves for 7 days. When the Chinese government begins to increase their reserves first to match Europe's level and then to match the U.S. level, you can bet they will be buying all that oil from a subsidiary of the Chinese government, PetroChina.

And finally, recall the roads that are being built to accommodate the cars and the urbanization of China. There are 15,000 highway projects underway in China that will add 162,000 kilometers (100,000 miles) of road in China. Once the new roads are built even more consumers will buy new cars. (I can see you smiling about my Toyota pick because we both know these Chinese consumers will be buying Toyota automobiles.) To ride the roads, you need to fill up the tank, which helps big oil companies like PetroChina. But this one gets even better. PetroChina also owns or has interest in more than 15,000 gas stations in China. So you get to fill up the tank and push up the stock at the same time.

The third dominant theme that develops when focusing on these young Chinese consumers is that they are wireless consumers. Mobile phone subscriptions in China are beating out Internet subscriptions through a fixed line by a six-to-one ratio. The best way to invest in the wireless Chinese consumer theme is through China's leading mobile phone provider out of Hong Kong, China Mobile.

CHINA MOBILE (STOCK SYMBOL: CHL)

China has the largest group of mobile phone users anywhere in the world at 325 million (more cell phone users than the entire population of the United States) and counting. China has more mobile phone users than fixed phone line users. China is the number one market in the world for cell phones.

China Mobile is all about China. China Mobile provides mobile service to all 31 provinces in China. They have a mobile phone subscriber base of close to 225 million, which gives them an almost unbelievable 70 percent market share of the mobile phone industry in China.

And do you want to know why? It's all about the service. China Mobile's domestic service network has coverage of more than 99 percent of all the cities and towns in China. In addition, China Mobile's global roaming service has coverage when these young Chinese consumers travel to over 184 countries around the globe. And it has a staff of almost 90,000 employees to support its customer base.

Don't forget about the underlying city migration shift that is occurring as Chinese citizens move away from farms and into urban areas. Ten years from now, 50 percent of China's population of 1.3 billion will live in a major urban area. As they move into urban China, they will realize that a mobile phone is a necessity. If 50 percent of 1.3 billion (650 million) will be using a cell phone in 10 years, and all China Mobile does is keep its market share where it is today at 70 percent, they will have 455 million subscribers (which would be larger than the present population of the entire European Union). China Mobile's subscription will double from its current 225 million member base. If the world is going wireless, then China Mobile will rule the stock market.

The fourth dominant theme that develops when focusing on these Chinese consumers is the impact of the "little emperors." An almost unbelievable 21 percent of the Chinese population is under the age of 15. Because of China's one-child policy, most of these little emperors are the only royalty in the family, meaning that they 6are always the center of attention and get basically whatever they want. The best way to invest in the little emperor theme is through Yum Brands, Inc., the world's largest fast-food franchiser. They have over 34,000 fast-food restaurants in 100 countries.

Yum Brands, Inc. (Stock Symbol: YUM)

You will probably better recognize Yum Brands by the flagship brands it operates under: Kentucky Fried Chicken, Pizza Hut, Taco Bell, A&W (Root Beer) Restaurants, and Long John Silver's.

When all these little emperors want something to eat, they want it right now, which means eating out, which to them means going to a fast-food restaurant. When that happens, no one is positioned better in China than Yum Brands.

The top five international brands in China today are McDonald's (number 5), Coca-Cola (number 4), Lux body soap (number 3), and Safeguard body soap (number 2); the top-ranking brand is Kentucky Fried Chicken (part of Yum Brands), which was the very first quick-service restaurant chain to enter China in 1987. Then in 2002, Kentucky Fried Chicken opened the first-ever drive-through restaurant (so you can drive through in your Toyota) in China. There are now almost 1,500 Kentucky Fried Chicken Restaurants located in almost 300 cities in Mainland China (see Table 6.1).

Think about this intuitively for a minute. First think about the Chinese people: What type of meat do they eat the most? The

Table 6.1   Top 10 Brands in China

Rank	Brand	Product
1	Kentucky Fried Chicken	Fast food
2	Safeguard	Body soap
3	Lux	Body soap
4	Coca-Cola	Soft drink
5	McDonald's	Fast food
6	Rejoice	Shampoo
7	Colgate	Toothpaste
8	Kodak	Film
9	Contac	Cold medicine
10	Nestle	Instant coffee

answer is chicken, so no wonder they love Kentucky Fried Chicken. Second, these little emperors have an unbelievable thirst for information about American culture and traditions. So Yum Brands slaps up a life-size picture of Colonel Sanders on the front of all their restaurants, and the young people go inside because Colonel Sanders represents the United States to them.

It is not just about the chicken though. In 1990, Pizza Hut opened the first pizza restaurant chain in China. Now more than 180 Pizza Huts are located in 40 cities in Mainland China. But what I really like about Yum Brands is that they are the world's leader in multibranding restaurants. They combine two or three restaurants under one roof in one location. Thus, no matter what these little emperors want to eat, they can go to one place to get it.

First it was the fried chicken, next it was the pizza, and it will not be long before these young consumers are eating tacos at Taco Bell. It all adds up to profits for Yum Brands.

The fifth and final theme when focusing on this Chinese consumer generation is the women-and-cosmetics theme. The traditional fashion for Chinese women was to have a pale complexion. A tan complexion indicated the woman worked outside under the sun on the farm. It was referred to as the peasant look. Now the cosmetic industry is booming in China. And the single best way to play this theme is through the world's largest direct seller of cosmetics, Avon Products, Inc.

AVON PRODUCTS, INC. (STOCK SYMBOL: AVP)

The total value of China's beauty and cosmetic market is approaching $6 billion. It is now the fourth largest consumer category in China behind real estate, automobiles, and tourism. But why Avon?

Remember what the chuppies said in the United Parcel Service survey—53 percent want to buy more American toiletries. It simply doesn't get any more American than Avon, located in New York City.

Watch how this is working in China. Avon is the world's largest direct seller, meaning that the Avon Lady comes to you. But there has been no such thing as a Chinese Avon lady because in 1998 China banned direct selling out of concern that Chinese consumers found it too difficult to distinguish between companies that direct sell and those that are simply a pyramid or Ponzi scheme.

That didn't stop Avon. They devised a different distribution plan in China. They sell their products in small beauty boutiques. They have over 5,000 of these in China, located in every single province. Store representatives sell Avon products at these fixed locations. Avon also has counters in many major department stores in China.

Don't forget that the rise in the overall standard of living in China serves as a foundation for a rise in disposable income that can be spent on cosmetics. More and more Chinese women are traveling outside China and seeing firsthand how other women around the world use cosmetics.

But here is why I really like Avon. Because these Chinese women traveling around the world have run into some of the almost 5 million Avon Ladies around the globe (there are more Avon Ladies than there are people in Ireland with a population a little over 4 million), they came back to China and asked, why not here? Well, China's government has changed its mind and is now allowing Avon to test the direct selling of Avon products in three locations— the cities of Beijing, Tianjin, and the province of Guandong.

It just doesn't get any better than this. I wonder how you say "Ding-Dong, Avon's calling" in Chinese?

PROMISING INVESTMENTS FOR GLOBAL SHIFT 4

In focusing on the Chinese Consumer Generation, the five individual companies best positioned to benefit from this shift are Toyota Motor Corporation; PetroChina Company; China Mobile; Yum Brands, Inc.; and Avon Products, Inc.

Now that you have my Investment Megatrends Portfolio made up of 20 companies, it is time to find out what Wall Street thinks of it.

WHAT WALL STREET THINKS

Finding out what Wall Street thinks is not as difficult as it might seem, and you don't have to travel all the way to New York to do it.

Just go on the Internet. One of the easiest sites for finding out what Wall Street thinks is www.moneycentral.com. Go to their main page, type in the symbols of the stock you are interested in, and it will pull up the latest stock price. From there, look at the menu choices on the left. One of them is called "analyst rating." Click on that, and it will tell you what Wall Street thinks of that stock.

Zach's Investment Research compiles all of Wall Street analysts' recommendations on each company's stock and will give you a "mean" recommendation number.

Here is how the grading system works: Stock recommendations fall into one of five categories—Strong Buy, Moderate Buy, Hold, Moderate Sell, and Strong Sell. A point value is then applied to each recommendation:

> Strong Buy = 1.0
> Moderate Buy = 1.1 through 2.0
> Hold = 2.1 through 3.0
> Moderate Sell = 3.1 through 4.0
> Strong Sell = 4.1 through 5.0

The lower the number and the closer to 1.0, the more Wall street likes the stock and the higher the number and the closer to 5.0 the more Wall Street hates the stock.

So let's see what Wall Street thinks of the 20 stocks in my portfolio:

- *Merrill Lynch:* Mean recommendation of 1.97, which makes it a Moderate Buy. (Remember that *mean* is the sum of all the recommendations divided by the number of recommendations; the slang term is "average.")
- *Dell, Inc.:* Mean recommendation of 1.70, also a Moderate Buy.
- *Carnival Corporation:* Mean recommendation of 1.72, a Moderate Buy.
- *Molson Coors Brewing Company:* Mean recommendation of 2.85, a Hold.
- *Johnson & Johnson:* Mean recommendation of 2.26, also a Hold.
- *Dryships, Inc.:* Mean recommendation of 1.0, a Strong Buy.
- *Mittal Steel Company:* Mean recommendation of 2.00, a Moderate Buy.
- *BASF:* Mean recommendation of 2.67, a Hold.
- *Ericsson:* Mean recommendation of 2.11, a Hold.
- *Shire Pharmaceuticals Group:* Mean recommendation of 2.00 a Moderate Buy.
- *Canon:* Mean recommendation of 1.50, a Moderate Buy.
- *Fuji Photo Film:* Mean recommendation of 3.00, which is a Hold.
- *Konami Corporation:* Mean recommendation of 5.00, a Strong Sell.
- *Sony:* Mean recommendation of 4.00, a Moderate Sell.
- *Mitsubishi UFJ Financial:* Mean recommendation of 1.00, a Strong Buy.
- *Toyota Motor Corporation:* Mean recommendation of 2.67, a Hold.
- *PetroChina Company:* Mean recommendation of 2.33, a Hold.

- *China Mobile:* Mean recommendation of 3.25, a Moderate Sell.
- *Yum Brands:* Mean recommendation of 2.61, a Hold.
- *Avon Products:* Mean recommendation of 2.81, a Hold.

So there you have it, now you, too, know what Wall Street thinks. Keep in mind that Wall Street tends to change its mind a lot, so these recommendations are simply a snapshot of analysts' recommendations during one point in time in late 2005. Analysts' recommendations are just that, recommendations based on their analysis for that point in time. These recommendations should only serve as one data point. You should never make an investment decision solely on a Wall Street analyst's recommendation. Remember all the positive ratings that Wall Street analysts were giving Enron right up until it collapsed.

My entire Investment Megatrends Portfolio has a mean recommendation of 2.42, which is a Hold (see Table 6.2).

WHAT DO YOU THINK?

The important question is not what Wall Street thinks, but rather what you think about this portfolio. To answer this question, you need to ask your financial advisor and if you don't have one, you should get one.

I have a financial advisor because I recognize the value of that assistance.

Without a financial advisor, you don't have a plan; and without a plan, you cannot succeed. Investing successfully isn't just about picking certain stocks. It is about fitting them into your overall investment plan. Your current portfolio could already have too much exposure to some of the themes and issues I have discussed, and you may not even know it. In addition, your financial plan will address tax strategies and take into account your risk tolerance as well as the cash flow you need. Simply picking an individual stock is not a financial plan.

Table 6.2 Megatrend Investment Portfolio

Company	Location	Stock Symbol	Listed Exchange	Zach's Recommendation
Merrill Lynch	New York, NY	MER	NYSE	Moderate Buy
Dell, Inc.	Round Rock, TX	DELL	NASDAQ	Moderate Buy
Carnival Corporation	Miami, FL	CCL	NYSE	Moderate Buy
Molson Coors Brewing Company	Golden, CO	TAP	NYSE	Hold
Johnson & Johnson	New Brunswick, NJ	JNJ	NYSE	Hold
Dryships, Inc.	Athens, Greece	DRYS	NASDAQ	Strong Buy
Mittal Steel Company	Rotterdam, Netherlands	MT	NYSE	Moderate Buy
BASF	Ludwinshafen, Germany	BF	NYSE	Hold
Ericsson	Stockholm, Sweden	ERICY	NASDAQ	Hold
Shire Pharmaceuticals Group	Hampshire, United Kingdom	SHPGY	NASDAQ	Moderate Buy
Canon, Inc.	Tokyo, Japan	CAJ	NYSE	Moderate Buy
Fuji Photo Film Company	Tokyo, Japan	FUJIY	NASDAQ	Hold
Konami Corporation	Tokyo, Japan	KNM	NYSE	Strong Sell
Sony Corporation	Tokyo, Japan	SNE	NYSE	Moderate Sell
Mitsubishi UFJ Financial Group	Tokyo, Japan	MTU	NYSE	Strong Buy
Toyota Motor Corporation	Toyota City, Japan	TM	NYSE	Hold
PetroChina Company	Beijing, China	PTR	NYSE	Hold
China Mobile	Hong Kong, China	CHL	NYSE	Moderate Sell
Yum Brands, Inc.	Louisville, KY	YUM	NYSE	Hold
Avon Products, Inc.	New York, NY	AVP	NYSE	Hold

In closing, therefore, I want you to do two things. First, go see your financial advisor today. If you don't have one, go get one. Second, when you meet with your financial advisor, see if it makes sense for you to fit my Investment Megatrends Portfolio into your overall investment plan.

◆

DEMOGRAPHIC WEB SITES

Some of the best demographic information in the world is at your fingertips on the Internet. All you need to know is where to search for it. I have picked out some of the best web sites for you and have categorized them in five areas; demographic articles and commentaries, child demographics, health demographics, U.S. demographics, and international demographics.

In addition, I have rated them for you. But instead of using stars, like the restaurant and hotel rating system, I have used my caricature: 1 means it's a useful web site, 2 means it's a good web site, and 3 means this is a great web site. Have fun surfing the net.

DEMOGRAPHIC ARTICLES AND COMMENTARIES

Advertising Age's American Demographics Magazine 😀
www.AdAge.com

Access to numerous articles on demographics as well as links to other sites.

Council of Professional Associations on Federal Statistics 😀
www.members.aol.com/copafs

Great web site for a wide variety of articles and also provides a great link to other demographic sources.

Cyberatlas/ClickZ 😀 😀
www.clickz.com/stats

Great Source for demographic articles and summaries. No basic demographic statistics.

Rand Corporation 😐 😐 😐

www.rand.org

The Rand Corporation is a nonprofit research organization providing objective analysis and effective solutions that address the challenges facing the public and private sectors around the world. For more than 50 years, the Rand Corporation has pursued its nonprofit mission by conducting research on important and complicated problems. Initially, Rand (the name is a contraction of the term **r**esearch **and** **d**evelopment) focused on issues of national security. Eventually, Rand expanded its intellectual reserves to offer insight into other areas, such as business, educational, health, law, and science. One of their 15 core areas of research is population and aging. Rand research on population and aging includes family planning policy, vulnerable populations such as the elderly, demographic trends, environmental effects, security implications, labor markets, and economic development.

U.S. Social Security Administration 😐 😐

www.ssa.gov

Great web site for articles and content on senior citizen demographic trends and issues.

Population Index of Princeton University 😐

http://popindex.princeton.edu

Population Index is the primary reference tool to the world's population literature. It presents an annotated bibliography of recently published books, journal articles, working papers, and other materials on population topics. This web site provides a searchable and browsable database containing 46,035 abstracts of demographic literature published in Population Index in the period 1986 to 2000.

CHILD DEMOGRAPHICS

Annie E. Casey Foundation 😐

www.aecf.org

Since 1948, the Annie E. Casey Foundation has worked to build better futures for disadvantaged children and their families in the United States. It also has a great web site. At the main page drop-down menu, simply click on "Get State Census Data." It then has compiled indicators of child well-being from the 2000 U.S. Census, profiles, rankings, and raw data are available for the nation as a whole, states, cities, countries, and towns.

Federal Interagency Forum on Child and Family Statistics 😀 😀
www.childstats.gov

This web site offers easy access to statistics and reports of children and families, including: population and family characteristics, economic security, health, behavior and social environment, and education. The Federal Interagency Forum on Child and Family Statistics fosters coordination, collaboration, and integration of federal efforts to collect and report data on conditions and trends for children and families. The Forum is a working group of federal agencies that collect, analyze, and report data on issues related to children and families. The Forum has partners from 20 federal agencies as well as partners in private research organizations.

U.S. National Center for Education Statistics 😀 😀
www.nces.ed.gov

The National Center for Education Statistics is the primary federal entity for collecting and analyzing data that are related to education in the United States and other nations as well.

HEALTH DEMOGRAPHICS

Population Council 😀 😀
www.popcouncil.org

The Population Council is an international, nonprofit, nongovernmental organization that conducts biomedical, social science, and public health research. For more than 50 years, the Council has been evaluating and developing sustainable approaches to enhancing people's health and well-being in the following areas: biomedicine, gender and family dynamics, HIV/AIDS, infants and children, quality of care, reproductive health, social science, strengthening local resources, and transitions to adulthood. It is a great web site for a wide range of demographic issues.

Public Health Foundation 😀
www.phf.org

Great web site for health-related demographic trends and issues.

U.S. Centers for Disease Control and Prevention ☺ ☺ ☺
www.cdc.gov

As the lead federal agency for protecting the health and safety of people, CDC also compiles statistical information to guide actions and policies to improve the health of the nation. Working with partners throughout the health community, it uses a variety of approaches to efficiently obtain information from the sources most able to provide information. It collects data from birth and death records, medical records, interview surveys, and through direct physical exams and laboratory testing. CDC's national programs form key elements of the national public health infrastructure, providing credible information to enhance health decisions, and promoting health through strong partnerships. You can view statistics on aging activities; and births, deaths, and marriages as well.

U.S. Centers for Disease Control and Prevention—CDC Wonder ☺ ☺
http://wonder.cdc.gov

CDC Wonder is a wide-ranging online data source for epidemiologic research—an easy-to-use, menu-driven system that makes the information resources of the Centers for Disease Control and Prevention (CDC) available to the public at large. It provides access to a wide array of public health information. CDC Wonder, developed by the Centers for Disease Control and Prevention (CDC), is an integrated information and communication system for public health. With CDC Wonder you can search for and read published documents on public health concerns, including reports, recommendations and guidelines, articles and statistical research data published by CDC, as well as reference materials and bibliographies on health-related topics. You can also query numeric data sets on CDC's mainframe and other computers, via fill-in-the-blank web pages. Public-use data sets about mortality (deaths), cancer incidence, HIV and AIDS, behavioral risk factors, diabetes, nationality (births), census data, and many other topics are available for query, and the requested data are readily summarized and analyzed.

U.S. National Center for Health Statistics ☺ ☺
www.cdc.gov.nchs

Some NCHS data systems and surveys are ongoing annual systems while others are conducted periodically. NCHS has two major types of data systems: Systems based on populations, containing data collected through personal interviews or examinations; and systems based on records, containing data collected from vital and medical records. There is a drop-down menu on the National Vital Statistics System, where you can choose from the following; birth data, mortality data, fetal death data, linked births/infant deaths, national mortality follow-back survey, national survey of family growth, national maternal and infant health survey.

Urban Institute
www.urban.org

The most interesting of all the databases is the National Survey of America's Families—a major new survey focusing on the economic, health, and social characteristics of children, adults under the age of 65, and their families.

UNITED STATES DEMOGRAPHICS

CASI Marketing Systems
www.demographics.casi.com/free_menu.html

Detailed statistics with national comparisons for any zip code in the United States. Simply type in the word "demographics" and hit the search button and the whole world opens up to you.

Easi Demographics
www.easidemographics.com

Offers customized demographic reports. Reports on race, family incomes, and property ownership. Searchable by state, city, or zip code, and this web site just got better! This site, which makes it easy for users to access demographic analysis for business and personal use, now offers a new service. That service is free demographic site reports or ring studies. The user just enters the location of their site and can get a 1, 3, 5, or any mile radius size demographic ring study. They can do as many ring studies as they desire! The data includes: population, households, White population, Black population, Asian, pacific Islander population, Hispanic population, population by age distribution (0 to 5 years through 75 years and over), median age, total household income, median household income, average household income, per capita income, household income distribution (less than $15,000 through $150,000 and over), annual average temperature, average annual precipitation, and average annual snowfall.

Econ Data 😕 😕 😕
www.econdata.net

This web site has links to nearly every government and academic data source available. Great for detailed economic demographic statistics. This is clearly your guide to regional economic activity. It has 1,000 links to socioeconomic data sources, arranged by subject and provider, pointers to the Web's premiere data collections, and their own list of the 10 best sites for finding regional economic data. Here are the subcategories under "data collections." You simply click on any category heading to jump down to the corresponding list:

Access tools to multiple data series: Tools (often query-based) for gathering data from a variety of sources

Statistical compendia: Handy single volume data books, often downloadable

Indicies, Rankings, and Comparisons: Indicies, rankings, and comparisons of states and metro areas by various criteria

Economic analyses and forecasts: Reviews of recent and projections of future economic conditions and trends

Guides to data on the Web: Sites (in addition to this one) with annotated links to sources of socioeconomic data

Data intermediaries: Organizations assisting users in regional data access and interpretation

Search engines: Tools for searching government data sources

Microdata: Data series with observations for individual firms and people

Mapping resources: GIS and related tools for mapping socioeconomic data and geographic features

Geographic classifications and codes: Classifications, definitions, and numerical codes for states, metro areas, counties, places, and smaller geographic units.

Economic Information Systems 😕 😕
www.econ-line.com

Very good site for economic demographic statistics. Best profiles of economic conditions of major metropolitan areas in the United States.

FedStats

www.fedstats.gov

FedStats is the new window on the full range of official statistical information available to the public from the federal government. Use the Internet's powerful linking and searching capabilities to track economic and population trends, education, health care costs, aviation safety, foreign trade, energy use, farm production, and more. Access official statistics collected and published by more than 100 federal agencies without having to know in advance which agency produces them.

GeoStat

http://fisher.lib.virginia.edu

Very detailed demographic data searchable in numerous formats. At this site, you can examine state and county topics for individual census years. You can examine multiple topics within a census year or you can produce tables of data by state or county and sort data by selected categories as well as create ratios between any two data categories.

Minnesota Population Research Institute

www.ipums.umn.edu

This web site is a coherent national census database spanning 1850 to 2000. It has high precision samples, integrated microdata, comprehensive documentation, and free access and use! It also now has an international component dedicated to collecting and distributing census data from around the world. Its goals are to collect and preserve data and documentation, harmonize data, and disseminate the data.

Premier Insights

www.premierinsights.com

Good national data and it's free. It will also send free reports via e-mail or fax. Premier Insights, Inc., is a research consulting firm based in the Jackson, Mississippi, area. The firm specializes in research and statistical analysis for various industries. Premier Insights also specializes in demographic and geographic analysis.

U.S. Bureau of the Census

www.census.gov

The most comprehensive collection of demographic data anywhere. The Census Bureau serves as the leading source of quality data about the nation's people and economy.

U.S. Bureau of the Census—American Factfinder 😕 😕
www.factfinder.census.gov

One of the best sources for population, housing, economic, and geographic data. There are several drop-down menus to choose from. For age, education, income, and race, click "People." For home values, ownership, and mortgage, click "Housing." For foreign trade, governments, and housing starts, click "Business and Government."

U.S. Bureau of the Census—Housing and Household Economics 😕 😕
www.census.gov/hhes

The Census Bureau reports income and poverty estimates from several major national household surveys and programs: Annual Social and Economic Supplement to the Current Population Survey, American Community Survey, Survey of Income and Program Participation, Census 2000 (long form), and the Small Area Income and Poverty Estimates program. Each of these surveys differs from the others in various ways. Here is a brief summary:

> *Annual Social and Economic Supplement (ASEC) to the Current Population Survey (CPS):* Because of its detailed questionnaire and its experienced interviewing staff trained to explain concepts and answer questions, the CPS ASEC is the Source of timely official national estimates of poverty levels and rates and of widely used estimates of household income and individual earnings, as well as the distribution of that income. The CPS ASEC provides a consistent historical time series of many decades at the national level and can also be used to look at state-level trends and differences (through multiyear averages). The relatively large sampling errors of state-level estimates for smaller states somewhat limit their usefulness.
>
> *American Community Survey (ACS):* Starting with 2000, the ACS provides subnational estimates of income and poverty for essentially all places, countries, and metropolitan areas with a population of at least 250,000. Estimates have also been produced for the nation and the states. These estimates have a different reference period than the CPS and a different population universe. The sample size of this survey since 2000 (about 800,000 addresses per year) makes the ACS exceptionally useful for subnational analyses.
>
> The U.S. Census Bureau expects the fully implemented ACS to have an annual sample size of about three million housing unit addresses

across the country. That implementation will lead to release of annual estimates for the ACS in 2006 (and every year thereafter) for all geographic areas with a population of 65,000 or more. Three-year averages would then be available starting in 2008 for areas and subpopulations as small as 20,000. Five-year averages would then be available for census tract/block groups and for small subgroups of the population starting in 2010. Both will be updated every year after they are first available. Because of its large sample size, estimates from the fully implemented ACS will provide the best survey-based sub national income and poverty estimates. Under full implementation, time series trends for all geographic areas, and for small population subgroups, will be available.

Survey of Income and Program Participation (SIPP): The SIPP is useful mainly for understanding changes for the same households in income and poverty, that is the dynamics of income and poverty, over time (up to 3 or 4 years), and for examining the nature and frequency of poverty spells and periods of income receipt of less than a year. Census 2000 (long form)—The best measure of change over the decade of the 1990s for subnational areas, even small places, and for subpopulations, are the comparisons of Census 2000 results with those from the 1990 Census.

Small Area Income and Poverty Estimates (SAIPE) Program: For the geographic area it covers, the SAIPE program provides the most accurate subnational estimates of median household income and poverty for different age groups, but with a time lag. Its estimates are controlled to match the CPS ASEC annual estimates at the national level, and will soon use the ACS estimates as an additional input to improve its estimates yet further.

U.S. Bureau of the Census—Population Data 😵 😵
www.census.gov/population

This web site has a menu that contains data summaries and reports produced by the Population Division of the U.S. Bureau of the Census. The Population Division creates and develops programs that collect, process, and disseminate statistical data generated from population surveys and censuses. This statistical data describes the size, structure, distribution, and characteristics of the U.S. population. To respond to the evolving data needs of the nation, the population division conducts special surveys and applied demographic research, reporting its findings in analytical reports and graphs. A description of the menu options follow:

Estimates: This option contains data summaries of current estimates of the population of the United States. Geographic details of the estimates range from the entire nation to individual states to counties, also encompassing cities, metropolitan areas, and other geographic subdivisions. Estimates also cover the basic demographic characteristics (sex, race, etc.) of the population.

Projections: This option contains data summaries of national and state population projections.

U.S. Bureau of Labor Statistics 😕 😕 😕
www.bls.gov

This site has an extremely interesting demographic component. Several programs at the Bureau of Labor Statistics (BLS) make significant amounts of data available for specific demographic categories. Demographic categories used by BLS include sex, age, race, and ethnic origin. The data by age generally are limited to persons of working age, defined as 16 years and older. Data on race generally are for blacks and whites. Data on ethnicity are confined chiefly to information on persons of Hispanic origin. BLS statistics that are available by demographic category include:

Demographic characteristics of the labor force (current population survey): A monthly household survey that provides comprehensive information on the employment and unemployment of the population classified by age, sex, race, and ethnic origin, as well as other characteristics such as educational attainment and veteran status.

Geographic profile: Contains some demographic information from the current population survey for regions and divisions, 50 states, and the District of Columbia.

Consumer spending: Measures the spending habits of U.S. consumers and includes data on their expenditures, income, and demographic characteristics.

Injuries and illnesses: Includes demographic details for both fatal and nonfatal occupational injuries along with information about the event producing the injury, the industry in which it occurred, and other details of the incident.

Longitudinal studies (national longitudinal surveys): Provides information about many aspects of the lives and labor market experiences of six groups of men and women at multiple points in time, some stretching over several decades.

The American Time Use Survey (ATUS): Measures the amount of time people spend doing various activities, such as paid work, childcare, volunteering, commuting, and socializing.

U.S. Internal Revenue Service ☺

www.irs.gov

Great source for tax statistics. At the menu bar simply click on tax stats. The individual tax statistics are the most useful where you can find information on: filing season statistics, estate and gift tax, individual income tax, and finally personal wealth.

INTERNATIONAL DEMOGRAPHICS

Population Reference Bureau ☺ ☺

www.prb.org

This is one of the most customized research sites around. This database contains data on 95 demographic variables for more than 220 countries, 28 world regions and subregions, the world as a whole, the United States as a whole, and the U.S. states. (Not all countries have data on all variables.) You begin by selecting a region of the world, and then you select a country. Next you get to choose from eight variables that include population trends, education, employment, environment, health, HIV/AIDS, reproductive health, and youth.

Statistics Canada ☺

www.statcan.ca

Produces statistics that help people better understand the country of Canada—its population, resources, economy, society, and culture. As Canada's central statistical agency, Statistics Canada is legislated to serve this function for the whole of Canada and each of the provinces. In addition to conducting a census every five years, there are about 350 active surveys on virtually all aspects of Canadian life. This is the most comprehensive Canadian demographic web site around.

United Nations 😐 😐 😐

www.un.org

This is your best source for global demographic trends. At the main menu bar click on "publications, stamps, and databases." Then click on databases and the entire world opens up to you. The U.N. Statistics Division compiles statistics from many international sources and produces global updates, including the Statistical Yearbook, World Statistics Pocketbook, and yearbooks in specialized fields of statistics. It also provides to countries, specifications of the best methods of compiling information so that data from different sources can be readily compared. It also provides a global center for data on international trade, national accounts, energy, industry, environment, transportation, and demographic and social statistics gathered from many national and international sources.

University of Texas—Demographic Data Link 😐

www.lib.utexas.edu/government

This site is a list of links to every possible demographic data web site. It begins with a browsable list of frequently used online government reference sources and web sites, including the recently revised CIA World Factbook. It also includes links to census data, including American Factfinder and the Texas State Data Center. And finally, it links to the United Nations, international agency and country information including the United Nations Official Documents Online.

U.S. Bureau of the Census—International Data Base 😐 😐

www.census.gov/ipc/www/idbnew.html

The International Data Base (IDB) is a computerized data bank containing statistical tables of demographic and socioeconomic data for 227 countries and areas of the world. It has a menu of six drop-down categories:

1. *Summary demographic data:* Displays data for selected countries.
2. *Online access:* Displays data for selected tables, countries, and years.
3. *Online demographic aggregation:* Displays demographic data for user-selected regions and/or countries.

4. *Population pyramids:* Displays graphs of the population, by age and sex.

5. *Countries ranked by total population:* Lets you find the largest countries for any year 1950 to 2050.

6. *World population information:* Provides overall world population data.

The IDB combines data from country sources (especially censuses and surveys) with IPC's estimates and projections to provide information dating back as far as 1950 and as far ahead as 2050. Because the IDB is maintained at IPC as a research tool in response to sponsor requirements, the amount of information available for each country may vary. The major types of data available in the IDB include population by age and sex, vital rates, infant mortality, and life tables, fertility and child survivorship, migration, marital status, family planning, ethnicity, religion and language, literacy, labor force, employment, and income and households.

U.S. Bureau of Economic Analysis

www.bea.doc.gov

Great web site for national, international, and regional economic statistics. From the national perspective you can get statistics on gross domestic product, personal income and outlays, corporate profits and fixed assets. From an international perspective you get balance of payments, trade in goods and services, international investment position, and direct investment. And finally, from a regional perspective you get state and local personal income, gross state product, and regional input-output multipliers.

U.S. Department of Homeland Security

www.uscis.gov/graphics/shared/statistics/index.htm

This web site is managed by the Office of Immigration Statistics (OIS), within the Management Directorate of the Department of Homeland Security (DHS). It is responsible for developing, analyzing, and disseminating statistical information needed to assess the effects of immigration in the United States. You can access information in six categories for any given year:

1. *Naturalizations in the United States:* Presents information on the number and characteristics of foreign nationals who were naturalized during the fiscal year.

2. *Data on naturalizations:* Provides data on foreign nationals who naturalized in the fiscal year by country of birth, state of residence, and other characteristics.

3. *Legal permanent residents:* Presents information on the number and characteristics of persons who become legal permanent residents in the United States during the fiscal year.

4. *Data on legal permanent:* Provides data on immigrants who became legal permanent residents in the fiscal year by class of admission, country of birth, state of residence, and other characteristics.

5. *Temporary admissions of nonimmigrants to the United States:* Examines the number and characteristics of nonimmigrant admissions in the fiscal year.

6. *Data on nonimmigrant admissions:* Contains data tables on nonimmigrants by class of admission, country of citizenship, and other characteristics for the fiscal year.

U.S. Central Intelligence Agency—World Factbook

www.cia.gov/cia/publications/factbook

The World Factbook is one of the very best sources for a wide range of international demographic information. It has individual country profiles that cover geographic coordinates, land boundaries, climate, land use, natural resources, and environment. The population information covers age structure, birthrate and death rate and life expectancy. It also has information on the type of government and legal system. It has an economic component that gives an economic overview as well as composition by sector (i.e., industry, agriculture). It also has household income and consumption data, including debt. It also has a very comprehensive employment analysis. If you want a demographic look at any one country, this is where you need to go first.

APPENDIX 2

EUROPEAN UNION

COUNTRY BY COUNTRY
DEMOGRAPHIC RANKINGS

European Union Population Rankings

Rank	Country	Population
1	Germany	82,431,390
2	France	60,656,178
3	United Kingdom	60,441,457
4	Italy	58,103,033
5	Spain	40,341,462
6	Poland	38,635,144
7	Netherlands	16,407,491
8	Greece	10,668,354
9	Portugal	10,566,212
10	Belgium	10,364,388
11	Czech Republic	10,241,138
12	Hungary	10,006,835
13	Sweden	9,001,774
14	Austria	8,184,691
15	Denmark	5,432,335
16	Slovakia	5,431,363
17	Finland	5,223,442
18	Ireland	4,015,676
19	Lithuania	3,596,617
20	Latvia	2,290,237
21	Slovenia	2,011,070
22	Estonia	1,332,893
23	Cyprus	780,133
24	Luxembourg	468,571
25	Malta	398,534

European Union Population Growth Rankings

Rank	Country	Percentage
1	Luxembourg	+1.25
2	Ireland	+1.16
3	Cyprus	+0.54
4	Netherlands	+0.53
5	Malta	+0.42
6	Portugal	+0.39
7	France	+0.37
8	Denmark	+0.34
9	United Kingdom	+0.28
	European Union Average	**+0.20**
10	Greece	+0.19
11	Sweden	+0.17
12	Finland	+0.16
13	Belgium	+0.15
14	Slovakia	+0.15
15	Spain	+0.15
16	Austria	+0.11
17	Italy	+0.07
18	Poland	+0.03
19	Germany	0
20	Slovenia	−0.03
21	Czech Republic	−0.05
22	Hungary	−0.26
23	Lithuania	−0.30
24	Estonia	−0.65
25	Latvia	−0.69

European Union Age Structure—Population below
15 Years of Age Rankings

Rank	Country	Percentage
1	Cyprus	21
2	Ireland	21
3	Denmark	19
4	France	19
5	Luxembourg	19
6	Malta	18
7	Netherlands	18
8	United Kingdom	18
9	Belgium	17
10	Finland	17
11	Poland	17
12	Portugal	17
13	Slovakia	17
14	Sweden	17
15	Austria	16
16	Hungary	16
17	Lithuania	16
	European Union Average	**16**
18	Czech Republic	15
19	Estonia	15
20	Germany	14
21	Greece	14
22	Italy	14
23	Latvia	14
24	Slovenia	14
25	Spain	14

European Union Age Structure—Population
between 15 and 65 Years of Age Ranking

Rank	Country	Percentage
1	Czech Republic	71
2	Slovakia	71
3	Slovenia	71
4	Latvia	70
5	Poland	70
6	Hungary	69
7	Lithuania	69
8	Malta	69
9	Cyprus	68
10	Estonia	68
11	Ireland	68
12	Netherlands	68
13	Spain	68
14	Australia	67
15	Finland	67
16	Germany	67
17	Greece	67
18	Italy	67
	European Union Average	**67**
19	Belgium	66
20	Denmark	66
21	Luxembourg	66
22	Portugal	66
23	Sweden	66
24	United Kingdom	66
25	France	65

European Union Age Structure—Population over 65 Years of Age Ranking

Rank	Country	Percentage
1	Germany	19
2	Greece	19
3	Italy	19
4	Spain	18
5	Austria	17
6	Belgium	17
7	Estonia	17
8	Portugal	17
9	Sweden	17
10	Finland	16
11	France	16
12	Latvia	16
13	United Kingdom	16
14	Denmark	15
15	Hungary	15
16	Lithuania	15
17	Luxembourg	15
18	Slovenia	15
	European Union Average	**15**
19	Czech Republic	14
20	Netherlands	14
21	Malta	13
22	Poland	13
23	Slovakia	12
24	Cyprus	11
25	Ireland	11

European Union Birth Rates per 1,000
Population Rankings

Rank	Country	Rate/1,000
1	Ireland	14.47
2	Cyprus	12.57
3	France	12.15
4	Luxembourg	12.06
5	Denmark	11.36
6	Netherlands	11.14
7	Portugal	10.82
8	Poland	10.78
9	United Kingdom	10.78
10	Slovakia	10.62
11	Finland	10.50
12	Belgium	10.48
13	Sweden	10.36
	European Union Average	**10.20**
14	Malta	10.17
15	Spain	10.10
16	Estonia	9.91
17	Hungary	9.76
18	Greece	9.72
19	Czech Republic	9.07
20	Latvia	9.04
21	Slovenia	8.95
22	Italy	8.89
23	Austria	8.81
24	Lithuania	8.62
25	Germany	8.33

European Union Death Rates per 1,000
Population Rank

Rank	Country	Rate/1,000
1	Latvia	13.70
2	Estonia	13.21
3	Hungary	13.19
4	Lithuania	10.92
5	Germany	10.55
6	Czech Republic	10.54
7	Denmark	10.43
8	Portugal	10.43
9	Sweden	10.36
10	Italy	10.30
11	Belgium	10.22
12	Slovenia	10.22
13	United Kingdom	10.18
14	Greece	10.15
15	Poland	10.01
	European Union Average	**10.00**
16	Finland	9.79
17	Austria	9.70
18	Spain	9.63
19	Slovakia	9.43
20	France	9.08
21	Netherlands	8.68
22	Luxembourg	8.41
23	Malta	8.00
24	Ireland	7.85
25	Cyprus	7.64

European Union Migrants per 1,000
Population Ranking

Rank	Country	Rate/1,000
1	Luxembourg	8.86
2	Ireland	4.93
3	Portugal	3.49
4	Netherlands	2.80
5	Denmark	2.53
6	Greece	2.34
7	Germany	2.18
8	United Kingdom	2.18
9	Italy	2.07
10	Malta	2.06
11	Austria	1.97
12	Sweden	1.67
	European Union Average	**1.50**
13	Belgium	1.23
14	Slovenia	1.00
15	Spain	0.99
16	Czech Republic	0.97
17	Finland	0.89
18	Hungary	0.86
19	France	0.66
20	Cyprus	0.43
21	Slovakia	0.30
22	Poland	−0.49
23	Lithuania	−0.71
24	Latvia	−2.24
25	Estonia	−3.18

European Union Life Expectancy Rankings

Rank	Country	Years
1	Sweden	80.40
2	Italy	79.68
3	France	79.60
4	Spain	79.52
5	Greece	79.09
6	Austria	78.92
7	Malta	78.86
8	Netherlands	78.81
9	Luxembourg	78.74
10	Germany	78.65
11	Belgium	78.62
12	United Kingdom	78.38
13	Finland	78.35
	European Union Average	**78.10**
14	Cyprus	77.65
15	Denmark	77.62
16	Ireland	77.56
17	Portugal	77.53
18	Slovenia	76.14
19	Czech Republic	76.02
20	Slovakia	74.50
21	Poland	74.41
22	Lithuania	73.97
23	Hungary	72.40
24	Estonia	71.77
25	Latvia	71.05

European Union Infant Mortality Rate per 1,000
Live Births Rankings

Rank	Country	Rate/1,000
1	Latvia	9.55
2	Hungary	8.57
3	Poland	8.51
4	Estonia	7.87
5	Slovakia	7.41
6	Cyprus	7.18
7	Lithuania	6.89
8	Italy	5.94
9	Greece	5.53
	European Union Average	**5.53**
10	Ireland	5.39
11	United Kingdom	5.16
12	Portugal	5.05
13	Netherlands	5.04
14	Luxembourg	4.81
15	Belgium	4.68
16	Austria	4.66
17	Denmark	4.56
18	Slovenia	4.45
19	Spain	4.42
20	France	4.26
21	Germany	4.16
22	Czech Republic	3.93
23	Malta	3.89
24	Finland	3.57
25	Sweden	2.77

European Union Literacy Rate Ranking

Rank	Country	Percentage
1	Denmark	100
2	Finland	100
3	Luxembourg	100
4	Czech Republic	99.9
5	Estonia	99.8
6	Latvia	99.8
7	Poland	99.8
8	Slovenia	99.7
9	Lithuania	99.6
10	Hungary	99.4
11	France	99.0
12	Germany	99.0
13	Netherlands	99.0
14	Sweden	99.0
15	United Kingdom	99.0
16	Italy	98.6
	European Union Average	**98.5**
17	Austria	98.0
18	Belgium	98.0
19	Ireland	98.0
20	Slovakia	98.0
21	Spain	97.9
22	Cyprus	97.9
23	Greece	97.5
24	Portugal	93.3
25	Malta	92.8

APPENDIX 3

◆

BOBSPEAK

A UNIQUE GLOSSARY OF DR. BOB'S INVESTMENT AND DEMOGRAPHIC TERMS AND OPINIONS

Accountant's Opinion: A letter that typically precedes a detailed financial report. It is prepared and signed by an independent accountant (who is nonetheless paid by the company). However, most if not all of the information provided to the accountant was provided by the company's employees, so how independent can the figures, their representation, or the accountant's opinion be? The opinion goes on to describe the scope of the financial statement and presents a judgment on the quality of the data presented. Never ever make an investment decision on the quality of the data presented. Never ever make an investment decision based on an accountant's opinion. Information is only as good as the source and the source of the information is the company that the accountant is rendering an opinion on. Accountants can be lied to and mislead. An accountant's letter is like a letter of recommendation—if you look long enough you will find someone to give you one.

Accounts Payable: The money that a company owes to other companies and various vendors for products and services purchased on credit. When this number is rising, it is a signal to dig deeper. A rising accounts payable number can be either good or bad. If business is growing and expanding you will obviously buy more on credit, thus, in this case it's a good thing. If business is flat and you don't have much cash, you might begin to purchase more and more on credit to hide your current problems. This is a very bad thing. A rising accounts payable number on its own isn't good or bad, rather it's a sign you need to dig deeper.

Accounts Receivable: The dollar amount that is owed to a company by its customers or clients for products or services that have already been provided on credit. This is an extremely critical number to watch because it is out of the control of the company. Sometimes you can get so focused on the company that you are investing in that you forget about the companies that buy the products your company makes. This number is really a measurement of the financial strength of your customer base. Any company can make sales go up if they don't have to worry about getting paid. Always, always check this number.

Age Distribution: The percentage of a given population that falls into certain age categories. The three most popular categories to determine a country's age distribution are: (1) Under 15 years of age, (2) 15 years of age to 65 years of age, and (3) Over 65 years of age. The actual percent of the population that falls into these categories is called the age distribution and tells how the "ages" are "distributed" throughout the population.

Agency Bonds: These are securities that are typically issued by a government agency. They do not have the full faith and credit of the U.S. government behind them. The most popular and well-known of these are the bonds of the mortgage associations that go by the nicknames: **Ginnie Mae,** which stands for the Government National Mortgage Association; **Fannie Mae,** which stands for the Federal National Mortgage Association; and **Freddie Mac,** which stands for the Federal Home Loan Mortgage Corporation. Even though these securities are not backed by the full faith and credit of the U.S. government from a risk perspective, they are pretty secure. I would consider them just one small notch below Treasuries, which are backed by the full faith and credit of the U.S. government. The best thing about these bonds are their names—at cocktail parties you can name-drop Ginnie Mae and Fannie Mae and Freddie Mac and impress the heck out of your guests.

American Depository Receipt (ADR): This investment vehicle was created in the United States in 1927. It is a stock that trades in the United States but actually represents a specified number of shares in a foreign corporation. American Depository Receipts are bought and sold every day on U.S. stock markets just like U.S. stocks. ADRs were introduced as a result of the extreme complexity involved in buying stock shares in a foreign country that trade at different prices and different currency values. For this reason, U.S. banks purchase a large lot of foreign stock shares from the company, bundle the shares into groups, and reissue them on either the New York Stock Exchange (NYSE) or NASDAQ as American Depository Receipts.

Annuity: A legal contract that is typically sold or underwritten by an insurance company. The insurance company will then make payments over time to the person who holds the contract. Payments usually begin at retirement. There are different types of annuities. A fixed annuity will pay an individual a guaranteed rate spelled out in the contract. A variable annuity pays a rate that is determined by the investment returns that are tied to the performance of the market. Possibly the best thing about an annuity is that your investment grows and you don't have to pay any taxes on it until you receive withdrawals. Anytime you can avoid paying taxes, do it. Not only is it good for you, it's good for your country as well. The less money paid in taxes means less money for politicians to waste. You need to buy an annuity today!

Asset Allocation: The technique of spreading an investment portfolio among the various asset classes of stocks, bonds, and cash. What used to be a relatively simple thing to do has now become much more difficult because the complexity and choices of investments has grown. Will your asset allocation consider domestic and international stocks? If it does include international stocks, how much should be allocated to emerging markets? You also need to decide if you want growth stocks, value stocks, or a blend of both? Then, you must chose between large capitalized stocks, mid-capitalized stocks, small-capitalized stocks, or micro-capitalized stocks. And this just covers stocks. You have yet to determine which bond and cash options are best from almost as long a list of choices. The best asset allocation plan is to call your financial advisor.

Bankruptcy: A legal proceeding in federal court for either a person or a business. The bankruptcy court can declare that person or business insolvent, that is, bankrupt. Once this happens, the individual or business is freed from making any additional payments on all of their outstanding debts. This doesn't occur, however, without a cost associated with it. To get out of paying all of your debts, whether you are an individual or a business, you have to actually surrender all of your assets to a court appointed trustee. Bankruptcy can either be voluntary or involuntary. In a voluntary bankruptcy, *you* start the proceeding. In an involuntary bankruptcy, *someone that you owe money to* initiates the proceeding. The real reason individuals use bankruptcy as an option, especially from a personal bankruptcy standpoint, is to stop debt collection and legal actions against them. This means that all lawsuits, eviction notices, the shutting off of utilities, and other actions must cease. The bankruptcy trustee that you turned everything over to divides up all of your stuff among everyone that you owe money to except for a portion of it which you get to keep. What property you get to keep and how much of it varies from state to state. In many states, certain property is exempt from bankruptcy proceedings. Most of your personal belongings such as your clothes are exempt. Typically, your home and car are exempt as well. All retirement accounts are also exempt from bankruptcy proceedings. The reason that we have such an increase in bankruptcy filings is not because individuals or businesses are in that much worse shape today than prior years. It's the lawyers. Instead of chasing ambulances to file a lawsuit, they now chase spending.

Basis Point: Is one hundredth of 1 percent. It is typically used in discussing the yields on bonds. For example, 25 basis points is equivalent to ¼ of 1 percent. So if yields increase from 5.50 percent to 5.75 percent that would be a 25 basis point increase or, looked at another way, yields increased one-quarter of 1 percent. I think this term was created by bond market "geeks" just to confuse investors. I think we should throw it away and simply talk about percentages. It would be less confusing and maybe even get people to invest in bonds.

Beige Book: An economic release that reports on the current economic conditions. It is published by the Federal Reserve Board eight times a year. The actual report has a beige-colored cover, which is why it is referred to as the Beige Book. Each of the 12 Federal Reserve Banks—Boston, New York, Philadelphia, Cleveland, Richmond, Atlanta, Chicago, St. Louis, Minneapolis, Kansas City, Dallas, and San Francisco—gather information on current economic conditions. The final report then summarizes all of this information. One of the reasons this is such a great release is not just because you get a sense of the overall strengths and weaknesses in each geographic region but it's the comprehensive nature of the report itself. Every report touches on consumer spending, manufacturing, real estate and construction, agriculture, natural resources, financial services and credit, employment and wages, and finally, prices. Instead of the Beige Book, I always thought it should be the black and red book. If things are bad (in the red if you will) we could use a red cover. On the other hand, if things are good (or in the black) we would use a black cover. This would greatly help those investors who hate details and wouldn't even have to read the report. They could simply look at the color of the cover.

Beta: This is one of those terms in the investment world that half of the people misunderstand and the other half misuse. I wish it would go away. However, until it does here is what it means: Beta is a technical analysis tool that measures the volatility of your stocks' return relative to the overall market, which is captured by using the Standard & Poor 500 Index. The Beta is based on a three-year historical regression analysis of the return of your individual stock compared to the return of the Standard & Poor 500 Index. Here's how it works. If your stock has a Beta of 1.5 that means that your stock tends to move 50 percent more than the Standard & Poor's 500 Index in the same direction. A Beta of 1.0 is exactly the same as the Standard & Poor's 500 Index. Your stock is moving in lock step with the Index. A 1.5 Beta means that your stock will be moving 50 percent more than the Standard & Poor's Index. When the Standard & Poor's Index rises 10 percent your stock should rise 15 percent (or 50 percent more). Conversely, when the Standard & Poor's Index falls 10 percent your stock is expected to fall 15 percent (again 50 percent more). When your investment moves more than the overall market in either direction it is considered a riskier investment. So, the higher the Beta is, the higher the risk. I urge you to never place an investment Bet(a) simply on this lone factor.

Birthrate: Typically used as one word, it is the number of childbirths in a given year, usually expressed as childbirths per 1,000 persons per year.

Bond: A type of investment or security that represents debt of the corporation that issues it. Typically, the issuer is required to pay the person who holds the bond (bondholder) a specified rate of interest for a specified time and then the issuer repays the entire debt. Because every rate is predetermined or fixed, bonds are also called fixed income securities. For example, if you have a $100,000 10-year corporate bond that pays 8 percent interest here is what will happen: For each of the next 10 years you will receive your annual 8 percent interest payment of $8,000. Then, at the end of the 10th year you receive your $100,000 back as well. Bonds such as this are typically viewed as a safe investment; however, their biggest shortcoming is inflation. The interest that you receive is fixed so inflation really determines the true value of your investment each year. If you receive 8 percent and inflation is only 2 percent (it cost 2 percent more to live) your investment was really worth 6 percent (8 percent – 2 percent = 6 percent). However, if inflation jumps to 5 percent your 8 percent bond would effectively only be yielding you 3 percent (8 percent – 5 percent = 3 percent).

Bond Rating: Is a measure of the quality and safety of a bond. Bond ratings are given to both foreign and domestic corporations as well as state and local governments and foreign countries. There are a lot of bond ratings out there. The two biggest bond-rating agencies are Moody's and Standard & Poors (S&P). Combined, they have bond ratings for over

20,000 companies and almost 40,000 municipal bonds (which include state school districts, water district, etc.). The rating is actually given with a letter. It goes in descending order from A to D. The higher the rating, the safer that bond is thought to be. In other words, the higher the rating, the greater the likelihood that they will meet their scheduled principal and interest payments. The highest quality is AAA. Then it goes to AA, A, BBB, BB, B, CCC, CC, and C. D is used when the bond is actually in default. That means they are not paying you. Bond ratings change over time and can be upgraded or downgraded. Two things that you need to be leery of as an investor: First, if you are a company and need a bond rating, you must pay for it. In other words, you are now a customer of the rating agency. You pay their salaries. They can't upset you too much can they? There is an inherent conflict of interest in this business. Second, there are so many bonds outstanding that it is impossible for the rating agencies to keep track of them all. Often, by the time they get around to downgrading a bond, the whole world already knows about it. If you are making investment decisions based on bond ratings you are making a big mistake. Most ratings aren't worth the paper that they are written on. If you want to focus on letters, focus on your children's report card. The report card from bond rating agencies should be written with disappearing ink.

Book Value: Is an investment measurement that takes the net worth of a company (which is its assets minus its liabilities) and divides it by the total number of shares outstanding. That price is then considered a company's book value. Let's say that a company has a net worth of $950 million and it has 37 million shares of stock outstanding. It would have a book value of $25.67 ($950,000,000 \div 37,000,000 = 25.67). This measurement is important because you then compare it to a company's stock price. If a company's stock price is lower than its book value it's a bargain. In this example if the company's stock were trading at $19.50 buy it. It's like paying $19.50 for $25.67 worth of assets. If it were cash, you would do it in a minute. Anyone would give $19.50 in cash to receive $25.67 in cash. What's good for cash is good for stocks. Follow the book value—it's better than the yellow brick road.

Business Cycle: Is the periodic changes and long-term patterns of economic activity. These activities are driven by employment, production prices, and interest rates. This cycle is either going up or down. When economic growth is going up, we call it a recovery. When economic growth is going down, we call it a recession. The typical business cycle was thought to last 8 to 10 years. That's why most businesses required 5-year business plans, because it would get you through most of the cycle. Today, economists debate whether the business cycle is dead or not. The answer is that it is not. You cannot kill the business cycle. You can, however, change it so it is tougher to recognize—which is exactly what we have done. Because of technology and the interconnected global market, the 8- to 10-year business cycle has been replaced by the 2- to 3-year business cycle. It's not dead. Maybe we should call the business cycle "lite" instead.

Capacity Utilization: Is a monthly economic indicator that measures how much industrial output is currently being used. As this rate moves up or down it is a great sign of where industry is trying to take the economy. This number is given as a percentage, and as a rule of thumb, the closer it approaches 90 percent, it is virtually at full capacity and inflation concerns will take center stage. Conversely, when the number approaches 70 percent it's a sure sign that industry is slowing to the point that could be recessionary. While I have watched this number over time, I've often wondered how much better 84 percent is than 82 percent. I don't think the absolute numbers are as important as the direction the number is heading. The importance of this indicator is the trend line, not the percentage.

Capital Gain: Is determined by looking at the initial price you paid for your investment, let's say $10,000, and the value of that investment today. Let's say $12,000. Thus, you have a $2,000 capital gain (current value $12,000 − $10,000 purchase price = $2,000 capital gain). A capital gain can either be realized or unrealized. A realized capital gain means that you actually sold your investment and you have the $2,000 difference in your hand today. You have "realized" the gain. An unrealized capital gain is one in which it hasn't actually been sold yet but if you sold it you would have a capital gain. In this example, if you don't sell the investment that you purchased for $10,000 and you still have it, you have an unrealized capital gain of $2,000 that you will realize once you sell it. Capital gains can also be long term or short term. A long-term capital gain is any investment that you have owned longer than a year while a short-term capital gain is for anything that you owned for less than one year. Call your financial advisor and he or she can explain it to you. If you don't have a financial advisor, get one!

Capitalism: Is an economic system in which most of what is produced is privately owned and controlled, which means the prices of what is produced are determined by market forces. Those in control of production in a capitalist society generally run those productions for profit. This is also referred to as a *free market system.*

Census: Is the process of obtaining information about every member of a given population. In most countries, a census is taken every 10 years. A census can cover a variety of information like, age, sex, employment, income, and other factors.

Census Tract: Is a section of a population defined for the purpose of taking a census. A census tract typically coincides with the boundaries of a city or village. In the case of larger unincorporated areas, the census tract usually coincides with county lines.

Communism: Is an economic and political system based on communal ownership of all property. In a communist system, all of what is produced is communally owned and controlled by the government. There is little, if any, private ownership and nothing is run with an attempt to make a profit.

Compound Interest: The amount of interest that is earned on the original principal plus the accumulated interest. It's the magic that makes money grow. When you start receiving interest on your interest in addition to interest on your principal, your investment will grow much faster. The catch is that you can't touch your interest; you need to keep reinvesting it . . . no exception. The most important element to the concept is time. The more time you give your investment, the greater the impact compound interest will have. This is one of the cornerstone concepts of investing.

Consumer Price Index (CPI): This is a monthly economic indicator that is religiously followed by most market watchers as the key to where inflation is headed. This index is commonly referred to simply by the initials CPI. It is supposed to be an indicator of the general level of prices. Just about everything is included in this index from energy to food and beverages, housing, apparel, transportation, and medical care, to list just a few factors. The CPI is simply not what it is cracked up to be. It overstates inflation and makes things actually look worse than they are. While there are numerous technical and statistical issues that converge to overstate inflation, the basic fundamental reason that the CPI overstates inflation is because it does not take into account the retail consumers' behavior regarding changes in prices. When the price of peaches rise faster than the price of bananas, most consumers will simply put more bananas in their fruit salad and less peaches. The kids can expect bananas cut up over their cereal instead of peaches. In other words, people will change their buying habits because of price and buy more bananas than peaches. That doesn't mean that the consumer is spending more on food even if the price of peaches is rising dramatically. The CPI simply doesn't understand the psychology of the retail price-conscious shopper. The CPI assumes that the consumer who wants a peach will buy a peach at any coast when, in reality, that simply is not so. This index drives me bananas. I don't care about it and neither should you.

Contrarian: An investor who goes against the crowd. Someone who does just the opposite of the consensus on Wall Street most of the time. Someone who sees value in a particular investment when no one else wants it. The true contrarian tends to focus on everything that is currently out of favor. The greatest contrarian investor ever is my good friend, David Dreman.

Credit Card: A card that is issued by a bank or other financial institution that gives the person who holds the card (cardholder) access to a specified line of credit to purchase products, services, or receive cash. The slang term is *plastic* because these cards are plastic cards. Credit cards are possibly the greatest invention ever in the financial services industry. They allow you to never need to worry about having cash and act like a personal accountant who follows you around and keeps track of every penny you spend. Before credit cards, people had a far more difficult time keeping track of their spending. All the hype about consumers taking on too much debt is a bunch of bologna. Credit card usage should not be confused with debt. After all, many consumers, myself included, pay their credit card balances off monthly. They use them for the convenience. Who knows, maybe the future is in plastic.

Crude Death Rate: It is the simplest and most basic measure of mortality. You don't even need to take a statistics course to calculate a crude death rate. It is a simple calculation of the total number of deaths in a given period (usually one year) divided by the total population. The number you get is called the crude death rate. However, not only is it crude, but it's almost useless as well because death is a relatively rare event (can only happen to someone once). The crude death rate is a very, very small number that goes out a few decimal points like 0.00021 or something. That's why mortality rates are expressed as the number of deaths per 1,000 people, which is far easier for comparison purposes.

Defined Benefit Plan: A type of a pension plan that guarantees a pre-specified amount to employees who work a certain number of years. (Also known as "I don't care about the stock market." If you haven't read the book, this will make absolutely no sense to you.) In a defined benefit plan, the employer makes all of the financial contributions and is responsible for investing them as well. The world is changing and more and more and companies around the globe are moving away from these plans. They will soon become the dinosaur of pensions.

Defined Contribution Plan: A type of pension plan that has no guarantees regarding what it will pay at retirement. Typically, both employers and employees contribute to this plan. The employee then decides how all of the money will be invested. (Also known as the "I am a stock market junkie" plan.) These investments will then grow tax free. However, that only matters if you make the right investments. This type of plan is the wave of the future. It makes individuals solely responsible for their retirement assets. Unless, of course, they are smart enough to seek the advice of a financial advisor.

Demographics: Are the social and economic characteristics of a nation. They are characterized by age, sex, income level, education, and occupation. In my opinion, demographics are the single most influential factor on investing. They are also the most misunderstood. Unlock the mystery of demographics and you will also unlock the secrets to investing.

Deportation: Is the expelling of foreigners from a country. Every country has the right to deport foreigners. In most circumstances, it is used against a foreigner who has committed a serious crime or is wanted in another country. Generally, deportation is quick and swift. There typically is no trial, no lawyers, and no appeals.

Dividend: This is a taxable payment that is made to stockholders. A dividend payment must be declared by a company's board of directors. Most dividends are paid out of a company's earnings. Dividends are typically paid quarterly in the form of cash. However, more and more companies are moving to pay out their dividends in the form of their company's stock. Dividends are a good thing and they help boost the total return of your investment.

Disability Adjusted Life Expectancy (DALE): A new demographic indicator by the World Health Organization that actually measures "healthy" life expectancy. It works like this: the World Health Organization summarizes the expected number of years to be living in what is considered "full health" and subtracts from that the number of ill-health years to come up with a healthy life expectancy figure. This indicator takes into account not just a person's age, but various health issues as well. This is a great indicator because it doesn't measure life expectancy simply on the average number of years a person is expected to live. We all know that people don't live all years in good health. At some point in your life, you have some level of disability. That's when DALE kicks in. DALE takes these years with a disability and then assigns a weight to them according to their level of severity to estimate the total equivalent lost years of good health. You subtract this from total life expectancy and what you have left is the number of years you can expect to live a healthy life. This is a real demographic breakthrough for strategic planning purposes for health care organizations.

Dollar Cost Averaging: One of the simplest and wisest investment strategies around. You select a fixed dollar amount ($100 for example) to invest at regular intervals (weekly, for example). And you do this regardless of whether the market is up or whether the market is down. What this strategy enables you to do is average the purchase of your shares over the long run. Thus, you will make some purchases when the market is cheap and you will make some purchases while the market is expensive; however, on average, you will be much better off than the investor who attempts to time the market. Did you ever notice how sometimes the simplest things are also the best things? Everyone should have a dollar cost averaging plan. . . . I do! Why don't you?

Dow Jones Industrial Average (DJIA): Is the oldest and most widely used measure of the overall condition of the stock market. The DJIA began in 1896 with only 12 stocks. In 1916, the number of stocks was increased from 12 to 20. Then, in 1928, it was increased to 30 stocks, and it has remained a 30 stock average ever since. The 30 individual companies that comprise the DJIA change over time. You can be taken off or added to the list. There have been two substantial changes to the DJIA since the mid-1990s. On March 17, 1997, Hewlett Packard, Johnson & Johnson, Travelers, and Wal-Mart were added while Bethlehem Steel, Texaco, Westinghouse Electric, and Woolworth were deleted. Then on November 1, 1999, Home Depot, Intel, Microsoft, and SBC Communications were added and Union Carbide, Goodyear Tire & Rubber, Sears, and Chevron were dropped. While arguments will always reign whether this is the most accurate measure of the U.S. stock market or not, one thing that you can't argue about is that it is still the most widely watched and widely quoted. I believe it is the single most influential and watched stock market measure anywhere in the world.

Durable Goods Orders: Is a monthly economic indicator. This economic release is the best barometer of future manufacturing activity. Think of durable goods as the big-ticket items. Technically, a durable good would include any manufactured item with a normal life expectancy of three years or longer. Because it lasts at least three years, we call it durable. Even though this only measures future manufacturing activity, I like this release because I think it is a wonderful indicator regarding consumer and business confidence. Big-ticket durable good items like cars and airplanes and refrigerators tend to be purchased when consumers and businesses are confident about where the economy is going. This release is much more important than it first appears. It not only measures future manufacturing activity; it measures business and consumer confidence as well. Watch this indicator closely. I do.

Earnings: Quite simply put, it's the amount of money that corporations make over a certain period of time. Two of the most popular earnings periods to look at are quarterly and annually. Earnings are the reason that corporations are in business. Earnings are also the single greatest determinant of the future direction of a company's stock price. In real estate, the three most important factors are location, location, location. In investing, it's earnings, earnings, earnings.

Economic Indicator: Statistics that measure certain components of the economy. Some indicators focus on housing and others focus on employment or inflation. There are hundreds of economic indicators to choose from. Economic indicators can be classified into three different groups as follows: (1) Leading economic indicators, which have some predictive value, give you a clue about what will happen in the economy; (2) coincident economic indicators are occurring at the exact same time as the economic activity; and (3) lagging economic indicators only become apparent well after the economic activity has occurred. There are so many indicators that measure so many things it's no wonder why economists can never agree on anything.

Emigrants: One of the four types of migration. People who leave and whose move takes them to a different country are classified as emigrants. So for example, if I moved from Illinois to Frankfurt (meaning I have moved from one country to another, from the United States to Germany) I would be classified as an emigrant by Illinois. The other three types of migration are out-migrants, in-migrants, and immigrants.

Employment Cost Index: This is a quarterly U.S. economic indicator. It is the best and the broadest measure of employment cost. First, it covers both salaried and hourly employees. Second, it includes employees from the private (business) sector as well as the public (government) sector. Third, it includes the cost of all benefits paid to employees such as health and insurance benefits. Fourth, it covers the widest time frame of any of the employment numbers because it is quarterly. Fifth, and possibly most important, is the fact that this is one of the indicators that the Fed Chairman closely monitors. If it's important to them, it should be important to you because it will be important to the markets. And, yes, it is important to me as well. Don't fight the Fed.

Empty Nest: When the children are grown and move out of the house and are on their own, that house is referred to as an empty nest—similar to when baby birds grow up and fly away from the nest. The parents who are left behind in this house with no children are commonly referred to as "empty nesters."

European Monetary Union: A monetary union is where several countries have agreed to share a single currency among them. The European Monetary Union actually consists of three stages of integration beginning with coordinating economic and fiscal policy and culminating with the adoption of the euro, the European Union's single currency. Currently, there are 25 countries that comprise the European Union: Austria, Belgium, Cyprus, Czech Republic, Denmark, Estonia, Finland, France, Germany, Greece, Hungary, Ireland, Italy, Latvia, Lithuania, Luxembourg, Malta, Netherlands, Poland, Portugal, Slovakia, Slovenia, Spain, Sweden, and the United Kingdom.

Factory Orders: Is a monthly economic indicator that captures the pulse of the manufacturing industry. Factory orders are comprised of manufacturers' shipments, inventories, and any new or unfilled orders. This indicator has less and less relevance as we move from a manufacturing-driven economy to a service-driven economy. Very seldom if ever does this indicator move the markets.

Federal Reserve Board: A seven-member board of governors responsible for overseeing the Federal Reserve System. That system is in essence the central banking system for the United States and is made up of the 12 Federal Reserve Banks as well as national and state bank members. The Federal Reserve Board is commonly referred to as the Fed. As an investor, you know them best as the group that establishes monetary policy by moving interest rates in an attempt to influence economic growth. The Fed can raise rates by either increasing the discount rate (which is the interest rate charged by the Fed for short-term loans to member banks) or the federal funds rate (which is the interest rate that banks charge each other for the use of funds that have been deposited by commercial banks at Federal Reserve Banks). They do this to curb excessive growth in the money supply. This in turn should slow down the economy. The Fed can also ease rates (my favorite Fed action by the way). They do this when they feel that the economy is not growing fast enough so lowering rates will ease credit conditions which should stimulate the economy. Because the U.S. economy is the largest economy in the world, the Fed is the most highly watched and influential Central Bank in the world today. We focus on it a little too much in my opinion.

Fertility: Is the measurement of the ability to produce healthy offspring. From a demographic perspective, we usually talk about fertility in terms of fertility rate (which is the number of children per women). Fertility can be impacted by numerous factors including health, nutrition, culture, economic conditions, and quality of living. That's not to say that sexual behavior and timing don't have a role as well.

Financial Advisor: (See **Stockbroker.**)

Flat Tax: A tax system in which all levels of income are taxed at the same tax rate whether it's 10 percent or 15 percent or 20 percent. Flat means level; everyone pays the same level, flat tax rate.

G-7: The G-7 actually stands for the Group of 7. The G-7 is made up of the seven largest industrialized countries in the world. The G-7 is comprised of the United States, Japan, Great Britain, France, Germany, Italy, and Canada. The Finance Ministries (in the United States it's called the Secretary of the Treasury) attend meetings of the G-7 to formulate global economic policy issues. Pay attention to what they say and do. Even though none of them are elected, they exert more influence than all of the other politicians in the world combined.

Generation Gap: Any time there is a vast difference in cultural standards, values, desires, and traditions between a younger generation and an older generation. The difference in their views or feelings is called the generation gap. The cause of a generation gap is that younger and older people do not understand each other's views because of their different experiences, behaviors, values, habits, and opinions. The more diverse the views are, the bigger the generation gap is thought to be.

Gross Domestic Product (GDP): This is a quarterly U.S. economic indicator. And it is the broadest of all indicators as it measures economic pro-

duction for the entire nation. This number places a market value on all
of the newly produced goods and services. Without a doubt, this is the
best overall indicator regarding economic strength. Because it is re-
leased quarterly (after the quarter is over) you already have a pretty
good idea about the economy from the hundreds of economic indicators
that have preceded it that quarter. This is the one number that politicians know and watch the most.

Immigrant: Is one of the four types of migration. People who move into
a country from an entirely different country are classified as immigrants.
So for example, if I moved from Illinois to Frankfurt (meaning that I
have moved from one country and into another from the United States to
Germany) I would be classified as an immigrant by Germany. The other
three types of migration are out-migrants, emigrants, and in-migrants.

Industrial Production: This is a monthly economic indicator. It measures the level of activity in terms of the actual physical output of the key
industrial components of the economy. These include the manufacturing, mining, gas, and electric utility industries. It's a pretty good indicator of how the old economy or the smokestack economy is doing.

Infant Mortality Rate: Is the number of deaths of infants in the first year
of life. This infant mortality rate can be further defined as neonatal
death, which is death that occurred in the first 27 days of life and post-
neonatal death, referring to deaths after 28 days of life until one year.
The infant mortality rate has taken on added importance in recent years.
It is thought to be one way to measure the level of health care in a country because it is directly linked to the health status of infants, children,
and pregnant women. I think this rate is important because it gives you a
sense of access to medical care in a given country as well as living conditions and public health practices.

In-Migrants: Is one of the four types of migration. People who move into
a population from the same country but to a different location in that
country are classified as in-migrants. So for example, if I moved from
Illinois to California (meaning I am still in the same country, the United
States of America) I would be classified as an in-migrant by California.
The other three types of migration are; out-migrants, emigrants, and
immigrants.

Inventory: This number will appear in a company's financial statement.
Simply put from an accounting perspective, it measures the value of all of
a company's raw materials, anything that is in the pipeline or in process,

supplies that are being used in current operations and finished goods as well. While this number is important from a financial analysis perspective, it is even more important from an investment perspective. A company that has excess inventory on its balance sheet most likely is facing one of two problems. Problem number one is this is usually an indicator of a slow-down in sales. If you can't sell the stuff, it usually stays in your warehouse and is captured as inventory. This is a bad thing for investors. Problem number two is it could also be an indicator of no pricing power. In other words, customers are not willing to pay for your product; this is also a bad thing for investors. And while the inventory number is an accountant's term found on a balance sheet, savvy investors should watch this number closely because inventory doesn't lie.

IPO: Stands for an Initial Public Offering of a company's stock. Everyone loves to have something that they can't have and because an IPO represents the very first time investors can own this stock, it's usually preceded with a great deal of hype. Typically, an IPO is an extremely volatile investment. I think this is where the term "here today gone tomorrow" was discovered. Anyway, proceed with extreme caution. Not for the amateur investor.

Lifetime Approach: This is one of the ways to measure fertility. This is the measure of the number of births (fertility rate) in a person's lifetime. The good thing about this approach is that it smoothes out any one-year or two-year distortions because you are looking at this over someone's lifetime. But that is also the problem. Child-bearing years typically span 35 years from age 15 to 50. So that means when you use the Lifetime Approach, you have to collect the data for that entire 35-year period. Thus, the information is not very timely. The other approach to measuring fertility is called the Single Period Approach (which I think is the better approach to measure fertility).

Literacy: When someone talks about a country's literacy rate, they are talking about the number of people 15 years of age and older in that country who can read and write.

Lockup Period: This is one of the most important things to look for if you want to invest in the Initial Public Offering (IPO) market. The Lockup Period is actually a period of time, typically years, during which directors and employees of the IPO company are restricted from selling stock that they own in the company. The longer the lockup, the better it is. I like three years minimum to start. It is this provision that brought the so-called dot-com geniuses back to reality. They launch a new IPO, keep a couple million shares of stock, the stock price goes to the moon, and they are multimillionaires (on paper). Eventually investors forget about the hype, realize this company will never be profitable, they sell the stock crushing the stock price and by the time the Lockup Period is over, their holdings are worth a small fraction of what they once were on paper. Easy come, easy go. If you are going to invest in IPOs lock'em up Dano!

Maastricht Treaty: This treaty is officially called the Treaty on European Union. It is commonly referred to as the Maastricht Treaty because it was actually signed and agreed to between the members of the European community on February 7, 1992, in Maastricht, Netherlands. It led to the creation of the European Union and ultimately the euro.

Market Capitalization: Is the calculation to determine just how much money investors think that an individual company is worth. The higher the market capitalization, the more investors think the company is worth. You can figure out a company's market capitalization by multiplying the number of the shares of stock outstanding by the share price of the stock. A company with 5 million shares of stock outstanding with a stock price of $68.50 would have a market capitalization of $342 million (5,000,000 × $68.50 = $342,500,000). Market capitalization is typically broken down into four classes with the following general guidelines: **Micro-cap,** which has a capitalization between 0 and $300 million; **Small-cap,** which has a capitalization between $300 million and $1 billion; **Mid-cap,** which has a stock market capitalization of $1 billion to $5 billion; and **Large-cap,** which has a capitalization over $5 billion. In theory, the smaller the market capitalization, the riskier the investment. However, history has already proven this not to be true. Some Large-cap stocks can be just as risky as a Micro-cap stock the only difference is that a lot more people own the stock. Making investment decisions based on market capitalization is a waste of time.

Megatrends: Large social, economic, political, cultural, and demographic changes that are slow to form, however, once they are in place, their influence will last for decades. This term was first used by John Naisbitt, perhaps the greatest "futurist thinker" of our time. These Megatrends are not the lead story of the day on CNBC or Fox News, which are all about the here and now, what is happening this minute. Instead Megatrends will tell you what will happen a decade from now.

Merchandise Trade Balance: This is a monthly economic indicator. It simply measures the difference between imports and exports. When exports (things that are leaving the country) are higher than imports (things that are coming into the country), there is what is referred to in economic circles as a surplus in the balance of trade. Conversely, when imports are higher than exports, there is a trade deficit. We have been taught to be concerned with deficits, thus we are worried about trade deficits. I believe that this economic release that alarms investors about the trade deficit is the most useless of all economic releases. First of all, it doesn't account for the value of what you import and export. If the stuff you export has value (like software) but the stuff you import has little value (like coffee), you will always have a trade deficit. Also this number does not account for all of the multinational companies that are in essence trading with themselves—not other countries. Then when you add in the distortion of currency movement, you will realize what I did long ago: This economic release isn't worth the paper that it's written on.

Migration: Is a change in a person's permanent place of residence. You can migrate a few miles and actually just move into a new neighborhood. Or you can migrate a few hundred miles and move into a new state. Or you can migrate a few thousand miles and move to a new country and continent as well. People who migrate are classified into one of four types: out-migrants, emigrants, in-migrants, and immigrants.

Migration Rate: A country's migration rate will tell you if more people are moving into or moving out of a country. A positive migration rate means more people are moving into the country than are moving out of the country. Conversely, a negative migration rate means more people are moving out of the country than are moving in. Here's how it works: First you take the number of immigrants (people from another country moving into your country) and then you subtract the number of emigrants (people from your country moving to another country); the number left is the migration rate.

Mortality Rate: Is the number of deaths in a country's population each year. It is typically expressed as "deaths per 1,000 people." So a country that has a mortality rate of 98 deaths per 1,000 people means that for every 1,000 people in this country, 98 of them died last year.

Municipal Bond: Is an investment vehicle issued by a political entity. It can either be a state or city or county or school district or water and sewer district, or some other entity. There are more than one million different municipal bonds to choose from. There are more municipal bonds than there are corporate stocks and corporate bonds combined. Municipal bonds are typically used to either finance construction of a special project or they are used to pay for ongoing general expenses. The great thing about these investments is that they are exempt from federal taxes. The money you make, you keep. You don't have to send any of it to the federal government.

National Center for Health Statistics: The main health statistical agency in the United States. Their main function is to identify any disparities in health and any differences in the use of health care based on sex, race, economic, or geographical factors.

Non-Farm Payroll: This is a monthly economic indicator. It measures the total civilian workforce and captures the total number of people employed in all sectors, industries, and activities except agriculture. So I guess this means that no one cares if you work on a farm anymore. This is a somewhat useful number to get a general idea of movements in the employment market. However, it gives you no clue regarding whether the corn crop will be harvested on time or not.

Old Age Dependency Ratio: Is determined by dividing the aged population (defined as 65 and older) by the population of the working age group (defined as 15 to 65). For example, let's say there are 5 million people age 65 and older, and there are 20 million people age 15 to 65. This country would have an old age dependence ratio of 25 percent ($5 \div 20 = 25$ percent). Meaning there are four workers supporting every one person 65 years of age and older. An Old Age Dependency Ratio of 50 percent means there are only two workers supporting every one person 65 years of age and older. The lower the Old Age Dependency Ratio percentage the better off that country's retirement system will be.

Out-Migrants: Is one of the four types of migration. People who leave but whose move keeps them within the same country are classified as out-migrants. So for example, if I moved from Illinois to California (meaning I am still in the same country, the United States of America) I would be classified as an out-migrant by Illinois. The other three types of migration are emigrants, in-migrants, and immigrants.

Ponzi Scheme: An illegal investment scheme that is actually named after Charles Ponzi who ran such a scheme in 1920. The way a Ponzi scheme works is that all of the returns on your investment are paid to the earlier investor out of money paid into the scheme by newer investors. This is different than a pyramid scheme because a Ponzi scheme is operated by a central person or company that is lying about how the money is being invested and where the returns are coming from. Come to think of it, this sounds a little like the U.S. Social Security System.

Population Growth Rate: Is the comparison of a country's population between two points in time, typically, from one year to another. Here is how it works. Let's say on December 31 a country has a population of 1,000,000 people. Then on December 31 of the following year they have a population of 1,025,000 people. Your growth rate would be 25,000 people or 0.025 percent.

Price/Earnings (P/E) Ratio: A measurement whereby you take the price of the stock and divide it by its earnings per share. The number that remains is its P/E ratio. If a company's stock price was $36 and it was earning $3 per share its P/E ratio would be 12 ($36 ÷ $3 = 12). This would be considered a low P/E ratio. A company that has a stock price of $236 and is earning the same $3 per share has a P/E ratio of 78 ($236 ÷ $3 = 78). To most investors, this would be considered high. I think way too much time is spent worrying about P/E ratios. You should never, ever make an investment decision based solely on a company's P/E ratio. It can be one of the factors, but it should never be the only one, or the dominant one. You better get used to P/E ratio's going higher because the global marketplace is creating limitless opportunities for companies to grow their business and when the business grows the stock price grows and when the stock price grows, the P/E ratio grows. Don't worry about it. All of this newfound concern over P/E makes me yearn for the good old days when someone in the high school parking lot was discussing PE they were talking about physical education class, not price earnings!

Producer Price Index (PPI): This is a monthly economic indicator that is very closely watched in order to determine where inflation is headed. This index is commonly referred to simply as PPI. It actually measures the level or price that is paid for all goods produced and imported. Simply put, PPI tells you how much more it's costing to make stuff.

Prudent Man Rule: This is the most basic and fundamental principle for all professional money managers. Its roots actually date all the way back to 1830 when Judge Samuel Putnam uttered the now famous words "those with responsibility to invest money for others should act with prudence, discretion, intelligence, and regard for the safety of capital as well as income." Right on Judge! Now consider this, if you invest your own money this rule doesn't apply. You don't have to be prudent with your own money; you can make all the dumb mistakes that you want. If, however, you send your money to a stockbroker, the Prudent Man Rule applies. Prudent . . . Not Prudent. Do it yourself. . . . Get advice from a stockbroker. This is a no-brainer if I ever saw one. Pick up the phone and call a stockbroker. . . . It's the prudent thing to do.

Pyramid Scheme: An illegal investment scheme in which investors are promised ridiculous returns on their investments. The scheme works like this, a hierarchy is created in the shape of a pyramid. New investors who join the pyramid scheme join under others who have already joined and the new entrants pay money to those above them in the hopes that they will in turn get paid from the new entrants below them. Pyramid schemes are illegal. Remember if it sounds too good to be true, it probably is.

Refugee: A person seeking "refuge" in another country in order to escape persecution or prosecution. A person who is attempting to gain refugee status is commonly referred to as an "asylum" seeker. In addition, when a country accepts such a refugee, it is referred to as that country offering "political asylum."

Registered Representative: (See **Stockbroker.**)

Retail Sales: This is a monthly U.S. economic indicator. It captures every single sale transaction that occurred at the retail level. It is one of the most comprehensive economic releases. The following types of retail sales are included as part of this number: automobiles, building materials, clothing, drugstores, food, furniture, gasoline, and restaurants, to name a few. The reason that this number is so important is that the consumer accounts for over ⅔ of the U.S. economy. Retail sales give you an excellent idea of just how healthy the consumer is. Thus, it gives you an excellent idea of just how healthy the overall economy is as well.

Single Period Approach: This is one of the ways to measure fertility. All you do with the Single Period Approach is to look at how many births occurred in any one year or single period, which is where the name "single period" comes from. This is the most popular way to measure fertility. It's easy to use this approach because most government agencies produce fertility data classified by year. And second, it's timely. You don't wait decades for the information, you simply wait one year. The other approach to measuring fertility is called the Lifetime Approach, and yes, you have to wait a "lifetime" to gather all of the information, which is why I am not a big fan of the lifetime approach.

Stagflation: Is the economic term that was coined to explain high inflation, high unemployment, and a slowing economy—all occurring at the same time. Prices are going up while the economy is going down.

You don't have to be an economist to figure out that this is not a good thing.

Stagnation: Is the economic term that was actually coined in the United States in the 1970s to describe what was going on with its economy. It is used to describe a period of very little if any economic growth in a country's economy. This is not a good sign.

Stockbroker: An individual who is a professional investor. That is what he does for a living. He eats, drinks, and sleeps thinking about investments. They are also known as Financial Advisors or Registered Representatives. All stockbrokers must be registered before they can transact any business with the public. In addition, they must pass rigorous qualifying exams administered by the National Association of Securities Dealers. Possibly one of the most important decisions you will make in your lifetime is picking your stockbroker. After all, you are picking someone who will now be responsible for your financial future. In the decade ahead, the stockbroker will evolve into one of the most important and respected professions around the globe. And for all of you who don't have a stockbroker I say thank you. Because if it weren't for you, the stockbrokers wouldn't have any investment dummies to exploit to make money for their clients.

Sub-Replacement Fertility: The fertility rate of a population is the number of births per woman. Any country that has a fertility rate below 2.1 children is considered to have sub-replacement fertility. Here is why the minimum number of 2.1 children was chosen. The 2.1 children per woman includes two children to replace the two parents and one-tenth of a child to make up for the early death of children and women. In theory, a country with a fertility rate of 2.1 children (with no other changes such as immigration, etc.) would maintain the same population over time. Anything above 2.1 and the population will grow. Anything below 2.1 and the population will decrease,

The Street: Term used when talking about Wall Street. It's the name given to the financial district in New York City. It is also used to describe the stock market as a whole. When someone says the street thinks this or the street thinks that, they are not actually talking about some paved street. They are telling you what is the consensus of the brokerage and other financial services firms. When someone says the street is expecting a rate-cut, they are telling you what the consensus is of the experts on Wall Street. The problem with "The Street" is no one is accountable. If the street says it's still a good time to invest and it turns out it isn't, you have no recourse other than kneeling down and actually talking to the real concrete street. Who knows, maybe those people aren't crazy after all; they are just trying to get a hot stock tip from the street.

Ten-Bagger: This has nothing to do with baseball where a two-bagger is a double and a four-bagger is a home run (called a four-bagger because you touch all four bases; first, second, third, and home). A 10-bagger is when the stock you buy rises 10-fold. So if you buy a stock at $17 and it goes to $170, you have a 10-bagger ($17 × $10 = $170).

Total Return: Is a valuation measurement of your investments' performance. It is calculated by taking the interest or dividend income generated by your investment plus the capital gain. For example if your stock investment paid a dividend income of 4 percent and the value of the stock increased 10 percent (capital gains) your total return would actually be 14 percent (4 percent dividend + 10 percent capital gains = 14 percent total return). This is not only the best measurement of your investments' performance; it is the only one you should use. Anything else only gives you half the story.

Treasuries: These are fixed income securities issued by and backed by the full faith and credit of the U.S. government. Considered by many (myself included) to be the safest investment around. There are three types of Treasuries: (1) **Treasury bills,** which are commonly referred to on Wall Street as T-bills, are the shortest-term investments with maturities, which range from three months to one year. (2) **Treasury notes,** which are also called T-notes, are the government's medium-term securities with maturities that range from 2 years to 10 years. (3) Finally there are **Treasury bonds,** which are the government's longest-term securities that have maturities that range from 10 years to 30 years. The beauty of Treasuries is not only are they the safest investment around but the interest that you receive from the U.S. government is exempt from any state and local taxes. And remember any time you can avoid paying any taxes to anyone, do it.

Triple Witching: Occurs four times a year in the stock market. It happens on the third Friday in March, June, September, and December. On this day, the options contracts and futures contracts expire on all of the market indexes. The simultaneous expirations set off heavy trading of options (single witch), futures (double witch), as well as the individual underlying stocks (triple witch). These days are almost always accompanied with extreme volatility.

Unemployment Rate: This is a monthly U.S. economic indicator that is issued as a percent. It captures the number that is currently unemployed as a percentage of the total employment market. The problem with this release is if you are not actively seeking a job, you are not included in this number as unemployed. I'm not sure what you call it, but to me if you're not employed you are unemployed. Economists worry that if the unemployment rate goes too low we will have wage inflation because employers will have to pay employees more money (and this is a bad thing somehow). Anyway, that's not going to happen because of the low unemployment rate. This rate doesn't take into account the merger boom, which keeps employees nervous about job security and employees nervous about job security don't tend to demand higher wages.

U.S. Census Bureau: In 1902 the U.S. Congress created the U.S. Census Bureau. The sole purpose of the Census Bureau is to compile statistical information from both individuals and businesses in order to compile their statistical reports. Here is a little known fact about the Census Bureau: It is illegal for anyone from the Census Bureau to reveal any specific information that could identify any business, person, or household. The Census Bureau employs approximately 12,000 employees, however, when the census is taken every 10 years, there is a dramatic expansion of temporary employees. When the last census was taken in the year 2000, over 860,000 temporary employees were hired.

U.S. Immigration and Nautralization Service (INS): In 2003, the well-known INS was transitioned into the Department of Homeland Security as the U.S. Citizenship and Immigration Services (USCIS). It is responsible for the administration of all immigration and naturalization functions including immigrant visa petitions, naturalization petitions, as well as asylum and refugee applications.

Volatility: Is the rate at which your investment or a market index moves up or down. When an investment or market is highly volatile that means that it is typically characterized by large price swings both up and down. Volatility is not a bad thing; it is actually a good thing. For without volatility, you would never have the chance as an investor to buy low and sell high. Investors who don't understand volatility, end up buying high and selling low. Buying high and selling low is not how you make money.

Year of the Fiery Horse: Every 60 years in Japan is marked by the "year of the fiery horse." An old wives' superstition says that every 60 years the zodiac's year of the horse "turns fiery." The superstition goes on to say that unfortunate girls born in that year are not suitable as wives and will suffer from ill fortune. The last year of the fiery horse or "hinoe-uma" as the Japanese call it, was 1966. And sure enough, that year there was a birth bust in Japan. Superstitious parents did not want to risk having a daughter born in the year of the fiery horse. The Chinese Zodiac is thousands of years old. While Western astrology is based on the months of the year, Chinese astrology is based on a 12-year lunar cycle. Your sign is determined by the year in which you were born, not the month. Each sign and those born under it are represented by one of 12 animals, and are given a set of attributes the Chinese believe comprise the nature of each particular animal. Legend has it that the 12 animals of the Chinese Zodiac were chosen by Buddha. When Buddha was near death, he invited all animals to visit him. Only 12 came; the rat, ox, tiger, rabbit, dragon, snake, **horse,** goat, monkey, rooster, dog, and pig. For visiting him, Buddha honored each by using them to represent the 12 signs of the Zodiac.

Yield: Is how much your investment has earned you expressed as a percentage. You can determine the yield by taking the income earned on a security and divide it by that security's price. If for example you had a stock that was paying you an annual dividend of $2.40 and had a current stock price of $26.00 your yield would be 9.2 percent ($2.40 dividend/$26.00 stock price = 9.2 percent yield). Just another way to measure how much money you are making.

UNIVERSITY OF DAYTON

◆

ABOUT R • I • S • E

(REDEFINING INVESTMENT STRATEGY EDUCATION)

R.I.S.E. is an international forum that promotes an understanding of the global investment industry. I am donating the financial proceeds of this book to R.I.S.E.

The annual R.I.S.E. (Redefining Investment Strategy Education) forum, in its sixth year in 2006, brings together students, academics, leading financial institutions, and business leaders from around the world. This global student investment forum has become the largest student investment forum in the world. My firm, Deutsche Asset Management, is a strategic partner of R.I.S.E. along with the New York Stock Exchange, the Frankfurt Stock Exchange, the Singapore Stock Exchange, the Chicago Board of Trade, NASDAQ, the *Wall Street Journal*, CNBC, the CFA Institute, and the University of Dayton, which also acts as the host of this event every year on its campus in Dayton, Ohio. I was one of the co-founders of this event and I continue to play an active role as the forum moderator on keynote speaker day as well as program co-chair for the entire event.

First, I thought I would give you a little historical perspective of how R.I.S.E. has evolved, as it embarks on its milestone six-year anniversary forum.

As way of background, the first of its kind, interactive forum between students, professors, and the global investment industry has witnessed remarkable growth. In its inaugural year in 2001, R.I.S.E. attracted 200 students from 39 colleges and universities. It drew 400 students from 61 colleges and universities in its second year. In 2003, 600 students from 84 colleges and universities attended R.I.S.E. And in 2004, R.I.S.E. attracted almost 1,000 students from 108 colleges and universities and there was a satellite feed of the event to London. In 2005, over 1,000 students, faculty, and investment professionals participated in the fifth annual R.I.S.E. forum representing 133 colleges and universities from 41 states and six countries. We even had a live satellite feed to China.

A veritable Who's Who of the global investment industry has taken time out of their busy schedules to participate as keynote speakers (see Table A4.1).

The great success of this forum stems from two elements: its strategic partners and its format. The strategic partners are the underlying reason for R.I.S.E.'s unparalleled success. R.I.S.E. is jointly sponsored by nine of the most prestigious organizations in the investment industry: CNBC, the New York Stock Exchange, the *Wall Street Journal,* Deutsche Asset Management, the Singapore Stock Exchange, NASDAQ, the Chicago Board of Trade, the Frankfurt Stock Exchange, and the CFA Institute. While the University of Dayton is the glue that keeps the event together, these strategic partners are the reason students initially come to R.I.S.E., and the reason they come back is the format.

The R.I.S.E. global student investment forum has embraced the format of the world's most influential and prestigious forum, the World Economic Forum, held annually in Davos, Switzerland. At the forum in Davos, they bring together political, business, labor, academia, religious, and media leaders. They conduct interview style panel discussions and there are no formal presentations which encourages spontaneous and dynamic exchange among panelists and participants. Likewise, at R.I.S.E. the keynote speakers are not giving speeches. There are no computer-generated presentations or handouts; instead it is a completely interactive environment. Each keynote speaker begins with a five-minute opening remark of what he or she feels is the issue of the day and then we open it up for discussion. Students have an opportunity to interact with the best and brightest the global finance industry has to offer. And to encourage active participation, distinguished

Table A4.1 Keynote Speakers from the Global Investment Industry

Ralph Acampora
Prudential Secuities
Chief Technical Strategist
2002, 2003

Jeff Applegate
Lehman Brothers
Chief Investment Strategist
2003

Maria Bartiromo
CNBC
News Anchor
2002

Joseph Battipaglia
Ryan Beck & Company
Chairman of Investment Policy
2001, 2003, 2004

Richard Berner
Morgan Stanley
Chief U.S. Econmmist
2005

Rich Bernstein
Merrill Lynch
Chief Investment Strategist
2003, 2004

Jack Bogle
Vanguard Group
Founder and Former Chairman
2004

Abby Cohen
Goldman Sachs
Chair, Investment Policy
   Committee
2005

Gerald Cohen
Merrill Lynch
Chief U.S. Economist
2002

Joe Deane
Solomon Smith Barney
Lead Municipal Portfolio Manager
2005

Jeff deGraaf
Lehman Brothers
Chief Technical Strategist
2003

Bob Froehlich
Deutsche Asset Management/
   Scudder Investments
Chairman, Investor Strategy
   Committee
2001, 2002, 2003, 2004, 2005

Tom Gallagher
International Strategy &
   Investments (ISI)
Chief Political Strategist
2004

Chris Garman
Merrill Lynch
Head High Yield Research
2005

Cynthia Glassman
Securities and Exchange
   Commission
Commissioner
2005

(continued)

Table A4.1 *Continued*

Al Goldman AG Edwards Chief Market Strategist 2001, 2005	**Tobias Levkovich** Salomon Smith Barney Chief U.S. Investment Strategist 2002, 2003
Gary Gordon Union Bank of Switzerland (UBS) Chief Investment Strategist 2005	**Jonathan Litt** Salomon Smith Barney Head of Real Estate Research 2005
Lyle Gramley Federal Reserve Board Former Governor 2004, 2005	**Liz MacKay** Bear Sterns & Co. Chief Investment Strategist 2001
Dick Grasso New York Stock Exchange Chairman and CEO 2003	**Tyler Mathisen** CNBC News Anchor 2003
Maury Harris Union Bank of Switzerland (UBS) Chief Economist 2004	**Leah Modigliani** Morgan Stanley Head of Portfolio Strategy 2002
Robert Hormats Goldman Sachs Vice Chairman—International 2004	**Michael Moskow** Federal Reserve Bank of Chicago President and CEO 2004
Hugh Johnson First Albany Chairman and CIO 2003, 2005	**Don Phillips** Morningstar Managing Director 2004
Nancy Lazar International Strategy & Invesment (ISI) Chief U.S. Economist 2005	**Ned Riley** State Street Global Advisors Chief Investment Strategist 2002, 2003

Table A4.1 *Continued*

John Robertson	**Francois Trahan**
Deutsche Bank Real Estate	Bear Stearns
Lead Portfolio Manager	Chief Investment Strategist
2005	2005
Lee Scott	**Sam Zell**
Wal-Mart	Equity Group Investments
Chairman and CEO	Chairman and CEO
2005	2004, 2005
Diane Swonk	
Bank One	
Chief Economist	
2004	

student panelists are selected to join the keynote speakers on stage to ask the first round of questions.

This formula for success has yielded amazing results over the first five years: 257 universities from 47 states and Washington, DC, have traveled to Dayton, Ohio. In addition, 7 other countries have sent students to R.I.S.E. as well, Canada, China, England, Germany, Israel, Mexico, and Russia. These students, who have traveled to the campus of the University of Dayton, are the future leaders of the global investment industry.

Table A4.2 provides a detailed list of the colleges and universities who have participated from around the globe.

The best way to judge an individual's character is to look at who he or she is friends with. It will tell you more about that individual than everything else combined. Maybe the best way to judge a forum is to look at who the partners are. The fact that the University of Dayton's R.I.S.E. forum is jointly sponsored, endorsed, and supported by nine of the most prestigious and influential organizations in the world of global finance today—CNBC, the *Wall Street Journal,* NYSE, the Singapore Stock Exchange, the Chicago Board of Trade, NASDAQ, the Frankfurt Stock Exchange, the CFA Institute, and Deutsche Asset Management—tells you all you need to know. These sponsors are the reason R.I.S.E. has become the largest student investment forum in the world! For additional and up-to-date information, please visit our web site at: rise.udayton.edu.

Table A4.2 Global Participants

United States	Connecticut
	Fairfield University
Alaska	Quinnipiac University
Jacksonville State University	University of Hartford
University of Alaska-Fairbanks	
	Delaware
Alabama	Delaware State University
Jacksonville State University	University of Delaware
Samford University	
University of Alabama-Birmingham	**Florida**
	Florida Gulf Coast University
Arizona	Florida State University
Arizona State University	Rollins College
Northern Arizona University	Stetson University
University of Arizona	University of Central Florida
	University of Florida
Arkansas	University of North Florida
University of Arkansas	University of South Florida
	University of Tampa
California	
California Polytechnic State University	**Georgia**
California State University Northridge	Clark Atlanta University
California State University Fresno	Clayton College
California State University Long Beach	Emory University
Pepperdine University	Georgia Institute of Technology
San Diego State University	Georgia State University
Santa Clara University	University of Georgia
University of California-Berkeley	Valdosta State University
University of California-Irvine	
University of California-Riverside	**Hawaii**
	Chaminade University
Colorado	
Colorado State University	**Idaho**
University of Northern Colorado	Boise State University

Table A4.2 *Continued*

Illinois
Augustana College
Bradley University
DePaul University
Eastern Illinois University
Illinois State University
Northern Illinois University
Southern Illinois University
University of Illinois at
    Urbana-Champaign
Western Illinois University

Indiana
Ball State
Chicago State University
Indiana State University
Indiana University
Indiana University Northwest
Notre Dame
Purdue University
Wabash College

Iowa
Cornell College
Loras College
Simpson
University of Iowa

Kansas
University of Kansas
Washburn University

Kentucky
Eastern Kentucky University
Kentucky University
Northern Kentucky University
University of Kentucky
University of Louisville

Louisiana
Centenary College of Louisiana
Louisiana Tech University
Loyola University New Orleans
Tulane University

Maine
University of Maine

Maryland
Frostburg State University
Loyola College in Maryland

Massachusetts
Babson College
Bentley College
Boston College
Boston University
Clark University

Michigan
Eastern Michigan University
Grand Valley State University
Michigan State University
Michigan Tech University

Minnesota
St. Cloud University
St. John's University
St. Joseph's University
University of Minnesota-Duluth
University of St. Thomas

Mississippi
Millsaps College

Missouri
Central Missouri State
    University
Lincoln University
Southeast Missouri State
    University
University of Missouri Columbia
University of Missouri St. Louis
Washington University St. Louis
Webster University

Nebraska
Creighton University
University of Nebraska-Omaha

(continued)

Table A4.2 *Continued*

Nevada
University of Nevada Reno

New Hampshire
Southern New Hampshire
   University

New Jersey
Ramapo College of New Jersey
Seton Hall University

New Mexico
New Mexico State University

New York
Alfred University
Clarkson University
Cornell University
Iona College
Long Island University
New York University
Pace University
Pace University Monroe
Pace University Westchester
Siena College
Syracuse University
St. Bonaventure University
St. John's University
University of Rochester

North Carolina
Appalachian University
Duke University
Elon University
Wake Forest University

North Dakota
North Dakota State
University of North Dakota

Ohio
Air Force Institute of Technology
Bowling Green State University
Case Western Reserve University

Cedarville University
Cleveland State
John Carroll University
Kent State University
Miami University
Ohio State University
Ohio University
Tiffin University
University of Akron
University of Cincinnati
University of Dayton
University of Toledo
Wright State University

Oklahoma
Southwestern Oklahoma State
University of Tulsa

Oregon
Oregon State University
Portland State University
University of Oregon

Pennsylvania
Carnegie Mellon
Duquesne University
Indiana University of Pennsylvania
King's College
Lehigh University
Moravian College
Shippensburg University
St. Joseph's University
Temple University
University of Pittsburgh
Villanova University

Rhode Island
Bryant University
Roger Williams University
University of Rhode Island

South Carolina
Clemson University
Winthrop University

Table A4.2 *Continued*

South Dakota
University of South Dakota

Tennessee
Middle Tennessee State
   University
Tennessee State University
Tennessee Technological University
University of Tennessee
University of Memphis

Texas
Rice University
St. Mary's University
Southern Methodist University
Southwestern University
Steven Austin State University
Texas A & M University
Texas State University-San Marcos
Texas Tech University
University of Texas El Paso
University of Texas Pan Am

Utah
University of Utah
Weber University

Virginia
James Madison University
Longwood University
Radford University
Virginia State
Virginia Tech

Washington
Seattle University
Washington State University

Washington, DC
American University

West Virginia
Marshall University
West Virginia University

Wisconsin
Marquette University
University of Wisconsin Eau Claire
University of Wisconsin Madison
University of Wisconsin La Crosse
University of Wisconsin Milwaukee
University of Wisconsin Oshkosh

Foreign Participation

Canada
Brock University
Concordia University
McMaster University
St. Mary's University
University of New Brunswick
University of Toronto

China
China Jiliang University
Nanjing Arts Institute
Xi'An University of Architecture
   and Technology

Germany
University of Augsburg

Israel
Hebrew University of Jerusalem

Russia
Moscow Institute of Physics &
   Technology

United Kingdom
Cass Business School (London)

Dr. Bob

ABOUT THE AUTHOR

Dr. Bob Froehlich is the vice chairman of Scudder Investments. Scudder Investments is part of Deutsche Asset Management, which is the global asset management arm of Deutsche Bank. He also serves as chairman of the Investor Strategy Committee. This committee is the first of its kind on Wall Street, providing a link between investment trends, investment strategies, and, ultimately, investment products for the individual investor. He is also a member of Deutsche Bank Americas Tactical Allocation Committee. This committee determines the optimal position allocation between stocks and bonds, large cap and small cap stocks, and growth and value style for the Scudder Total Return Fund, the Scudder Balanced Fund, and the Scudder Pathway Series of funds.

Froehlich is also responsible for providing portfolio managers, research analysts, and product specialists around the globe with timely analysis of global investment trends and developments and what their impact may be on financial markets. Froehlich now serves as the firm's chief investment spokesman. As such, one of his primary responsibilities is to articulate the firm's current investment strategies and market outlook for clients, advisors, media, and the general public.

RENOWNED SPEAKER

Highly regarded by the brokerage community as a dynamic and entertaining lecturer, Froehlich is one of the industry's most sought after speakers, as evidenced by more than 1,000 speaking requests per year. His thought-provoking "Boomernomics" speech gained international acclaim for both his insights and his energetic and engaging delivery. A frequent keynote speaker at events around the globe, Froehlich has the unique distinction of having delivered a speech on investing on all six of the earth's inhabited continents—North America, South America, Europe, Australia, Africa, and Asia. In North America, Froehlich has the additional distinction of having delivered a speech on investing in all 50 states in the United States. In addition, Froehlich serves as one of the select members of the "Distinguished Speakers Series" for Crystal Cruise Line, Inc. Because of his high-profile role, Froehlich has had two national advertising campaigns revolve around him. The first national ad campaign for Kemper Funds—"Dr. Bob Says"—was launched in March 2000. Because of the great success of that campaign, in May 2001, Scudder Investments then launched a second national ad campaign called "Where's Dr. Bob?" Froehlich has the unique distinction of being the only "Wall Street" strategist who has been invited to both open and close the markets for the NASDAQ (April 15, 2002) and the New York Stock Exchange (April 17, 2003).

MEDIA DARLING

As Scudder Investments' leading spokesperson on major investment matters, Froehlich has evolved into the mutual fund industry's most mediagenic investment professional. He appears regularly on a variety of financial television programs on CNBC, CNN, FOX News, and Bloomberg TV as well as other domestic and international financial networks. Froehlich is one of the regular guest co-hosts for CNBC's highest rated program *Squawk Box* and a guest co-host for CNBC Europe's *Squawk Box* based in London and CNBC Asia's *Squawk Box* based in Singapore. He was the first and remains the only person to ever be a *Squawk Box* guest host in all three locations; Asia, Europe, and the United States. In addition, Froehlich has the distinction of having appeared as a guest on every CNBC program.

He was also selected as one of the original regular guest financial commentators when CNN launched its new network, CNNfn in December, 1995. At FOX News, Froehlich has become one of the regular "Special Guests" on its highest rated weekend show, *Bulls and Bears.* Froehlich has been interviewed on some of the industry's most prestigious investment programs, including *Wall Street Week with Louis Rukeyser, Money Line* with Lou Dobbs, *The MacNeil/Lehrer News Hour,* and *World Business* with Alexander Haig. Among the topics on which Froehlich is considered an expert are U.S. and global economics, global currency, and financial markets, and U.S. and global demographic trends. That expertise has led him to author three investment books.

PROLIFIC WRITER

In this, his latest investment book, *Investment Megatrends,* published by John Wiley & Sons, Dr. Bob provides readers with a map on the pitfalls and opportunities of demographic data, what to look for and where. From identifying four prominent global shifts to presenting investment strategies that will benefit from those shifts based in part on his personal experience traveling the world and seeing these shifts for himself. His second investment book, *Where the Money I$,* published by John Wiley & Sons (July 2001), identifies the dominant global investment trends and themes for the decade ahead and explains how his newest investment discovery, which he has dubbed "Sectornomics™," will change investment strategy forever. This book reached #1 best seller on Amazon.com for investment books (August 29, 2001) and has since been translated into both Korean and Chinese. In his first book, *The Three Bears Are Dead!* published by Forbes (April 1998), Froehlich explored the investment impact of low inflation, falling interest rates, and declining government spending around the globe.

The media continually seeks Froehlich's analysis and opinions, and he is widely quoted in the *Wall Street Journal,* the *New York Times* and *Barron's.* His timely and insightful investment commentary interpreting current events driving the markets can be found on

Scudder Investments' web site Scudder.com. This weekly commentary has gained Froehlich acclaim within the brokerage community as one of the most important investment strategists of our day. Financial advisors and investors alike look to Froehlich to be in the forefront, explaining major investment events and issues around the globe as they happen. In addition to his speaking and writing, Froehlich has never lost his passion for research. He has met personally with the CEOs of hundreds of companies around the globe. His perspective regarding what's on the mind of global business leaders today is unparalleled in the industry.

BOTH PUBLIC AND PRIVATE SECTOR EXPERIENCE

Froehlich has the rare distinction of a distinguished professional career combining experience in both the public and private sectors. This background allows him to develop his unique perspective by always seeing issues from both sides. Froehlich began his professional career in the public sector where he served as chief financial officer for a utility and as one of the youngest city managers ever in Ohio. After his tenure in the political arena, which included the role of campaign finance chairman for the lieutenant governor of Ohio, Froehlich was a senior executive with Ernst & Young providing economic, financial, and investment consulting as well as expert testimony for its client base. Before joining Kemper Funds, which became Scudder Investments, he was with Van Kampen American Capital where he served as director of research and was responsible for one of the largest research staffs in the mutual fund industry until his appointment as that firm's first chief investment strategist. While at Van Kampen, Froehlich was elected to three "All-American" Institutional Research Teams sponsored by Global Guarantee, The Bond Buyer and Ratings, Research and Review. He was also appointed to the Board of Directors of McCarthy, Crisanti and McAfee (MCM), one of the world's leading institutional investment and economic research firms. In addition to his professional career, Froehlich's first job was working in the steel mills for U.S. Steel in Pittsburgh, Pennsylvania, in the summers while attending college.

EDUCATIONAL AND ACADEMIC SERVICE

Froehlich received his doctorate in public policy in 1979 from California Western University, a master's in financial management in 1978 from Central Michigan University, a master's in public administration in 1976 and a bachelor's in history in 1975 from the University of Dayton. He has remained actively involved with the University of Dayton, where he currently serves on the Board of Trustees. In addition, he was a long-standing member of the university's Investment Committee, and was appointed the first Executive in Residence for the university's Center for Portfolio Management, which is home to a multimillion-dollar portfolio managed by students at the university. As one of its founders, Froehlich continues to play a key role as the forum moderator and program co-chair in the now annual R.I.S.E. (Redefining Investment Strategy Education) global student investment forum, which has evolved into the world's largest student investment forum by attracting thousands of students from around the world to the campus of the University of Dayton. In 2000, his work with R.I.S.E led the School of Business to bestow on Dr. Froehlich its prestigious Service Leadership Award. And in 2005, he was the first University of Dayton alumnus inducted into the R.I.S.E. "Hall of Fame." Froehlich continues to serve as a special guest lecturer for the School of Business. In addition to the University of Dayton, Froehlich has volunteered his time to speak on numerous college campuses across the United States regarding the future of Wall Street. His educational speaking highlights were when he was asked to speak on the campus of Augustana College (October 2002) while his eldest daughter Marianne was a student there, and the campus of Cornell College (April 2004) while his youngest daughter Stephanie was a student there, and finally when he was chosen to give the keynote commencement speech at his high school alma mater, North Catholic High School in Pittsburgh, Pennsylvania, in May of 2003. Froehlich is married (Cheryl) with two daughters (Marianne and Stephanie) and currently resides in Willowbrook, Illinois.

INDEX

Sub-replacement fertility, 112, 236
Sweden, 76–77, 78

Taco Bell, 181, 182
Taiwan, 134, 161
Technology, 48, 148–151, 165
Telecommunications, 146–150
Ten-bagger, 237
Total return, 237
Toy industry, 38
Toyota Motor Corporation, 178, 179, 185, 187
Travel and entertainment trend, 42–43, 165–166, 174–175
Treasuries, 237
Triple witching, 237

Unemployment rate, 238
United Kingdom, 61–63, 121–122
United Nations, 200
United Parcel Service China survey, 144–145, 183
United States:
  age structure, 45–48, 57, 104, 135–136, 137
  birthrate, 27, 57, 58, 105, 136, 138
  Census Bureau ethnic categories, 26
  death rate, 27, 50, 57, 105, 137, 138
  demographic web sites, 21–22, 193–199
  electricity consumption, 151
  farming, 124
  fertility rate, 112
  infant mortality rate, 27–28, 139
  life expectancy, 14–15, 27, 106, 115, 137, 138
  literacy, 28, 139, 140
  net migration rate, 27, 57, 58, 105, 137, 138
  oil reserves, 148
  old-age dependency ratio, 114
  pension system, 121–122
  per capita income, 116
  population, 25, 135, 136
  population density, 111
  population growth rate, 135
  World Trade Organization agreement with China, 146–147

University of Texas, 200
Urban Institute, 193
U.S. Bureau of Economic Analysis, 201
U.S. Bureau of Labor Statistics, 198–199
U.S. Bureau of the Census:
  American Factfinder, 196
  defined, 238
  as demographic data source, 19–20
  Housing and Household Economics, 196–197
  International Data Base, 200–201
  Population Data, 197–198
  web site, 195
U.S. Centers for Disease Control and Prevention, 192
U.S. Central Intelligence Agency, 202
U.S. Department of Homeland Security, 201–202
U.S. Immigration and Naturalization Service, 20, 238
U.S. Internal Revenue Service, 199
U.S. National Center for Education Statistics, 191
U.S. National Center for Health Statistics, 20, 192–193, 233
U.S. Social Security Administration, 13–15, 190

Volatility, 238

West Germany, 53–54. *See also* Germany
Whites, 26
World's Fair, 159
World Trade Organization, 146–148

Year of the fiery horse, 238–239
Yield, 239
Yippies, 144
Yueguangzu consumers, 154–155. *See also* Chuppies
Yum Brands, Inc., 181–182, 186, 187
Yuppies, 144

Zach's Investment Research, 184–186, 187